Mulligan's Law

Photo by Stuart Smith

MULLIGAN'S LAW

The Wit and Wisdom
of William Hughes Mulligan

edited by

WILLIAM HUGHES MULLIGAN, JR.

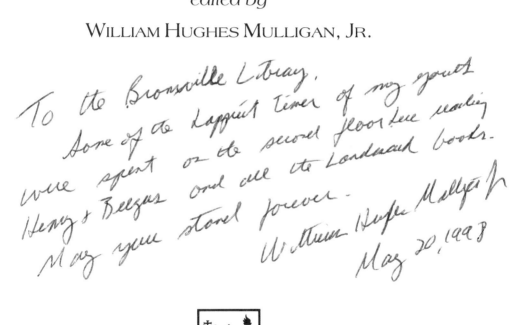

To the Bronxville Library,
Some of the happiest times of my youth
were spent on the second floor here reading
Henry & Beezus and all the Landmark books.
May you stand forever.

William Hughes Mulligan Jr
May 20, 1998

FORDHAM UNIVERSITY PRESS
New York
1997

Library-of Congress Cataloging-in-Publication Data

Mulligan, William Hughes, 1918–1996.
  Mulligan's law : the wit and wisdom of William Hughes Mulligan /
edited by William Hughes Mulligan, Jr.
    p.   cm.
  ISBN 0-8232-1718-3 (alk. paper)
  1. Mulligan, William Hughes, 1918–1996.   2. Judges—New
York (State)—Biography.   I. Mulligan, William Hughes.
II. Title.
KF373.M822A4   1997
340'.092—dc21
  [B]   97-38943
                                                            CIP

Printed in the United States of America

For
Rosebud

Long have I heard of his love for the people, his political sagacity, his towering abilities; long have I sympathized with his complaint that the press fails to do him justice. And now, tonight, thanks to the graciousness of Terence Cardinal Cooke, I have come face to face, at long last with the wit and wisdom of . . . Judge William Hughes Mulligan.

> GOVERNOR RONALD REAGAN
> Alfred E. Smith Memorial Foundation Dinner
> October 16, 1980

Some time ago I was introduced as a man who had, in a short time, won the respect and attention of his fellow judges. I responded that this reminded me of the story of the cross-eyed javelin thrower—although we never won any contests while he was competing, he always won the respect and attention of all the other contestants.

> WILLIAM HUGHES MULLIGAN
> May 9, 1976

CONTENTS

The Lawyer (1981–1989)

INTRODUCTION

My father, William Hughes Mulligan, was born in the Bronx, New York, on March 5, 1918. He was the only son of Stephen Hughes Mulligan and the former Jane Donahue, who was the youngest of twelve children. He loved the Bronx of his youth. He attended a local public school and Our Lady of Refuge parochial school where he was taught by an order of Dominican nuns. He was an altar boy and maintained a love for Latin. He thought he had a vocation and studied briefly for the priesthood. From all accounts he was always at or near the top of the class from grammar school through high school at Cathedral Prep in New York City and later at Fordham College (class of 1939) and Fordham Law School (class of 1942), from the last two of which he graduated *cum laude*. He played sports, which you will read about, and perhaps hear about for the first time, but he was more of a scholar than an athlete. He loved the Yankees and idolized Earle Combs. He attended Fordham in the '30s when the Rams were a national football powerhouse. He was editor-in-chief of the school newspaper and also sang in the glee club. He survived the war, as you will read, and met the love of his life, my mother, Roseanna Connelly, whom he married on October 20, 1945.

He practiced law in New York City but preferred to teach, which he did for some twenty-five years at Fordham Law School, beginning in 1946. He was appointed assistant dean and Ignatius M. Wilkinson Professor of Law in 1954. He became the youngest dean in the School's history in 1956 when he was thirty-eight years old. He is credited with strengthening the Law School's academic programs, developing its physical plant, presiding over the School's move from downtown at 302 Broadway to Lincoln Center in 1961, and beginning the process of changing Fordham Law from an excellent local law school to an excellent national law school. This process has continued under the enlightening and outstanding leadership of his two successors, Joseph M. McLaughlin and John D. Feerick.

He resigned as dean in 1971 and accepted the honor of a presidential appointment by Richard M. Nixon to the bench—

the prestigious United States Court of Appeals for the Second
Circuit. He loved being a judge and enjoyed his position and
colleagues—many of whom you will read about. He reluctantly
resigned from the bench a decade later to return to private practice. He stated that "inflation has rendered continued judicial
service inequitable." His problem was not so much with the salary as with the survivors' benefits then in effect, which, he believed, were "miserable." As to the overall package, he quipped,
"You can live on it but you can't die on it." The New York *Daily
News* editorialized on February 9, 1981:

> We have argued before that federal judges deserve a better
> financial deal than they get now. Judge William Hughes
> Mulligan, one of the most respected members of the fed-
> eral bench in this part of the country, has just strengthened
> our case by resigning from the U.S. Court of Appeals in
> Manhattan for financial reasons.

My father later commented before a conference of federal
judges:

> The reasons for my departure from the bench received
> more publicity than anything I had ever done while I was
> on it. After twenty-five years of full-time teaching and dean-
> ing at a Jesuit law school, my portfolio consisted mainly of
> holy cards, medals, loving cups, honorary degrees and in-
> dulgences. Ever since Martin Luther, the market value of
> indulgences has been severely depressed. In any event,
> since my children were out of school and the mortgage was
> paid, my wife and I thought we could make it. We did not
> anticipate double-digit inflation. In fact, the Congress has
> not yet recognized it so far as the Federal Bench is con-
> cerned.

The New York Times, in an editorial two years later, cited my
father's resignation, his "you can't die on it" quip and later Senate testimony, in urging Congress to legislate a more generous
survivor plan.

His resignation, tendered to President Ronald Reagan, was
effective April 1, 1981, and he returned to private practice as a
member of the law firm of Skadden, Arps, Slate, Meagher &
Flom. He enjoyed his return and the practice. He later said:

> One night in July, as I left the office at a quarter to one in
> the morning in the midst of the Conoco take-over battle, I

wondered why a hopefully successful and certainly happy Circuit Court judge had ever decided to leave the bosom of the bench. I wondered if I could sneak back on the bench some way. But after arguing a couple of motions in the District Court in Washington and then hearing a District Court judge in New York render an oral opinion in our favor and later than evening learning that it had been affirmed by the Second Circuit, my doubts suddenly vanished. I experienced a sense of exhilaration greater than I ever did on the bench, greater than having the Supreme Court reverse when you had written a dissenting opinion. I felt then that the umbilical cord had finally been cut. On reflection, I wonder what my reaction would have been had we lost. I would probably still be in mourning. In any event, there was always time for a new career—ballet dancing, the rodeo or something.

Unfortunately, after several gratifying years at Skadden, Arps, and while on a summer vacation in Bridgehampton, New York, mulling his retirement plans, my father suffered a debilitating stroke in August 1989 and never returned to active practice. He passed away on May 13, 1996, after struggling for the last year with the effects of an even more devastating stroke in July 1995.

My father left a legacy of honor, integrity, scholarship, and unrivaled good humor. Fortunately for all of us, during his years as a young lawyer, dean, professor, judge, and senior partner, my father had discovered, and thousands witnessed, his natural ability to compose and deliver a speech with impeccable timing and delivery, laced with an urbane, sophisticated, timely, and unforgettable wit combined with a sampling of his never heavy-handed wisdom. The combination was perfect. My father was blessed with the gift of communicating, and he did so on every level—as a lawyer, as a teacher, as an administrator, and as a judge. More important, he did so as a husband, father, and grandfather.

I can remember many times when my father would recount a speech he had delivered the night before and the gales of laughter which would erupt from the audience. He would shake his head and complain that no one would remember anything he had taught him or her in law school or anything he had ever written as a federal judge, but everyone would remember something he had said in one of these "damn speeches." Well, Dad, I think you were partly wrong, because I know many, many people who remember your ability and words of guidance as a dean/professor and as a judge, but we are not going to let them forget your speeches because the best are assembled here for posterity.

At my father's funeral Mass on May 17, 1996, in St. Joseph's Church in Bronxville, New York, His Eminence John Cardinal O'Connor preached as follows:

> During the course of the past few days, as happens frequently on the occasion of a death in the family, there was a bit of confusion about who was to be the preacher today. It turns out to be unimportant in terms of who is standing in this pulpit because the *real* preacher today is Judge William Hughes Mulligan. Judge Mulligan's entire life, as many here know, was a dynamic, powerful sermon.
>
> But Bill preached in another way as well, He was well known all over the country, and certainly here in New York, as one of the great after-dinner speakers. He was hilarious in many of his addresses, yet remarkably subtle, never blunt, never offensive, he was always giving a message. Most particularly, he gave a reminder, a call to humility.
>
> I thought that you would perhaps forgive me, therefore, if this morning I called upon the Judge to speak for himself to a significant degree by quoting ever so briefly from two of his more famous address to the Friendly Sons of St. Patrick, where he was always in his glory. I do not do this simply as a tribute to him, or to reminisce, or even merely to lighten the heaviness of heart which some may experience, including myself. I do so because as humorous, as whimsical, as fantastic as some of his addresses were, they reveal that which seems to be his dominant overwhelming characteristic, the one quality that stood out more than any other: his *authenticity*. Bill Mulligan never forgot who he was. This I found to be his important strength. He never seemed to take himself too seriously. He never took too seriously his position or the fame that he accrued. More particularly, he never let Irishmen become pretentious.
>
> His speeches were always an ever-so-subtle psychological, sociological, moral, ethical analysis of the status quo—of who we are and where we are in our lives and more importantly of who we should be, where we should be, and most

importantly who it is that God wants us to be at any given point in our lives.

For those who never heard my father give a public address at a graduation or a communion breakfast, or as an after-dinner speaker before an audience of thousands, you missed something special, and I do not think his delivery can be duplicated. We are, however, fortunate that the copy remains which I hope you will enjoy—in any location.

We have set forth my father's speeches in chronological fashion, giving a biographical touch to the various stages of his life and the subjects which were germane at the time. We have broken them down into three sections, those produced during his years as dean, his years as judge, and his final years as a practicing attorney. There has been minimal editing of the copy, and nothing was or dared to be rewritten. What you read is what the audience got. My father gave so many speeches during his life, it was obvious and necessary that large segments would be repeated to different audiences where there were close time intervals. A bar association in Oregon might well have heard much of what was heard in Brooklyn a few weeks before. Both crowds would be receptive and would not forget the experience. Similarly, my father had many favorite stories and characters. You will come to know Hercules Mulligan. For the sake of the reader, we have slightly edited, by deletion, duplications in the texts of certain speeches. Variations might well remain.

The recurrent themes in my father's speeches are his love for his heritage, his country, his religion, his family, his friends, his schools, and the law. His speeches are legendary in after-dinner circles in New York, often imitated but never duplicated. He is sorely missed, but his memory, his words, and the joy he brought to the world will live forever.

August 1997   WILLIAM HUGHES MULLIGAN, JR.

A PERSONAL REMEMBRANCE OF WILLIAM HUGHES MULLIGAN

John D. Feerick

Bill Mulligan was a presence in my life for more than forty years—a dim presence when, as a teenager, I first heard his name at Fordham College in Dr. William Frasca's government classes; a towering presence after I became a student of his at Fordham Law School; and then an inspiring presence as I made my way as a practicing lawyer and then a successor to the office he graced and distinguished at Fordham Law School. Dean Mulligan was a master builder of Fordham Law School, as everyone knows. But what everyone may not know is the extraordinary influence he had on the students he taught and the thousands of graduates whose diplomas carry his name. He was a lawyer par excellence—perhaps the best there was in bringing joy to others through the medium of humor. I commented elsewhere that he was my hero, representing all that was good and possible as a human being.[1]

Bill is now gone, but he will never be forgotten by those who knew him, and the legacy he left behind will be an enduring and treasured memorial to his greatness as a person, lawyer, teacher, and dean. My own feelings about his impact were expressed in the eulogy I was privileged to deliver at the Mass celebrating his life.[2]

Rosie, Anne, Bill, Steve, Mary Liz, Michael, Jenny, Maura, Billy, Kate, and Rory:

There is so much each of us would like to say to you—so many personal memories of Bill we would like to share with you, as his former students, as faculty members and graduates of Fordham Law School, as colleagues from the Judiciary, as former

---

[1] John D. Feerick, "Remarks Delivered on the Occasion of the Presentation of the Fordham-Stein Award to the Honorable William Hughes Mulligan," 59 FORDHAM LAW REVIEW, 479, 480 (1991).

[2] May 17, 1996, at St. Joseph's Church, Bronxville, New York.

partners and associates, as just friends and admirers. But we know that this is not an occasion for extended remarks. Let me just say that your Bill was our Bill, a towering, gentle, and loving presence in our lives whose great mind was exceeded only by his great heart. It was such a joy to know him and be with him. He drew all of us into his orbit instantaneously.

For Fordham Law School students and graduates, he was our Dean, our hero, our role model, our mentor and guide—our prince among men. He taught us the law in the classroom, pointed the way to how we should conduct ourselves as lawyers, and brought great honor to our School and the legal profession of which we aspired to be a part. He cared deeply for all of us, helping us cope with the cost of a legal education, moving around our résumés, building us up, and, when things became difficult, lightening our burden by sharing his wisdom and the magic of his wit and humor. How can I ever forget the nice things he said about me when I first met my wife at a Moot Court program at Fordham Law School in March of 1960, or the respect I inherited as a Fordham Law graduate because I came from Bill Mulligan's school.

Bill walked on the stage with presidents, governors, cardinals, bishops, and the most famous of Americans, but you would never know that from anything he said in his conversations with you. He treated each of us as an equal, as a next-door neighbor. There was a warmth and basic decency about him—never hurting, condemning, condescending, calling attention to himself, or seeking his own advantage and advancement. There also was a special quality about him—a sparkle in his eye, a turn of phrase or other expression that uplifted every occasion. I remember inquiring of him, when he left the bench and entered law practice, how he wished people to address him—as Dean, Judge, Mr., or just Bill. Without hesitating, he said, "Just call me 'Your Worship.'"

It is a privilege beyond privilege for me to occupy an office that Bill Mulligan graced as Dean of Fordham Law School. It is still Bill Mulligan's office and it always will be.

As I think of Bill Mulligan today, many thoughts rush through my mind—of the great love he had for his beloved Rosie and their family, of the joy he received from them, and of the tremendous admiration, almost adulation, of his students, colleagues, and friends.

The wonderful magic and merriment of the Bill Mulligan we have known will live on in all of our lives—in all of our tellings and stories about him and in our affectionate remembrances of him. Each of us has taken a part of Bill and made it a part of ourselves.

When I last saw Bill at home, we laughed together upon discovering that the one sport we both excelled in, as boys growing up in the Bronx, was stickball. When I visited him last Saturday, all I could think of was how much he gave of himself to us on every occasion and in every possible way, and how much we took and received from him. We could never get enough of him.

Well, Bill, today is your day—a day on which we pray for you, a day we thank God for your presence among us, and a day we let you know how much you have meant to us.

Rosie, I mentioned to you a trip I made to Ireland and a poster my wife and I had purchased because it reminded us of Bill. It contains a poem called *The Fiddler of Dooney* by William Butler Yeats. I would like to give you that poster and read the poem.

> *The Fiddler of Dooney*
> When I play on my fiddle in Dooney,
> Folk dance like a wave of the sea;
> My cousin is priest in Kilvarnet,
> My brother in Mohanabuiee.
>
> I passed my brother and cousin:
> They read in their books of prayer;
> I read in my book of songs
> I bought at the Sligo fair.
>
> When we come at the end of time,
> To Peter sitting in state,
> He will smile on three old spirits,
> But call me first through the gates;
>
> For the good are always the merry
> Saved by an evil chance,
> And the merry love the fiddle.
> And the merry love to dance.
>
> And when the folk there spy me.
> They will all come up to me.
> With "Here is the fiddler of Dooney!"
> And dance like a wave of the sea.

Last night, I asked Rory, the youngest of Bill's six grandchildren, what he remembered most about his grandfather. Rory said, "He made me laugh." He made us all laugh, Rory, and we love him so.

I conclude by sharing with you a verse composed by my wife entitled "Remembering Bill Mulligan."

> When I smile and my eyes start to twinkle
> You know there's a thought in my mind.
> 'Tis a thought that will make you all chuckle
> For it's one of the Mulligan kind.
>
> It's a thought where the parts fit together
> In a sort of preposterous way.
> When I say it aloud it will make you
> Feel jolly and happy and gay.
>
> For life is a mixture of blessings
> With sorrows and joys large and small,
> And when I put on my ROSE glasses
> I just want to laugh at it all.
>
> For when life is a vision of color,
> A garden is made of this earth;
> And when people can laugh at their troubles,
> They find they're united in mirth.
>
> So remember me telling my stories
> That lifted your spirits like leaven.
> And if you can find solace in laughter,
> I'm sure you'll have one foot in Heaven.

Farewell for now, Bill. "May we merrily meet in Heaven."

The Dean
1958–1971

AMERICAN IRISH
HISTORICAL SOCIETY
May 2, 1964

Mr. Toastmaster, reverend clergy, honored guests, ladies and gentlemen:

It is indeed a distinct honor to be invited to address such a distinguished company. My wife and I have had the pleasure of being at this dinner on several occasions as the guests of the late Norman Shaffer and the late David Broderick. They were both devoted members of this society and, like your President General, were devoted alumni of Fordham Law School.

I am delighted to join you in honoring District Attorney Frank O'Connor who throughout his career has brought distinction not only to the profession but to the high office which he holds. I regret that we cannot count him among our alumni but of course find some consolation in the fact that Chief Judge Conway, who presented your medal, is a member of our Class of 1912, which also produced another Chief Judge of New York, John Loughran, and the longtime dean of Fordham Law School, the late Ignatius Wilkinson.

I am also impressed tonight by the fact that at the head table we have three famous Fordham presidents—Father Gannon, Father McGinley, and Father O'Keefe, all of whom of course are of Irish extraction. Father Gannon appointed me to the faculty, Father McGinley appointed me Dean, and the only thing that is left for Father O'Keefe, of course, is to fire me.

For some strange reason Notre Dame is considered to be the American Irish University. This is the school which, you recall, was founded by a Frenchman and has a German president, and which replaced Terry Brennan as head football coach with one Joseph Kuharich. If the term "fighting Irish" has any validity, it is only because the Irish out there are obviously fighting for their lives.

At any gathering of Americans of Irish birth or ancestry it is customary to repeat the usual tributes which we delight in paying to each other—at least in public. It has been said, for example, that when God made the Irish he made us more intelligent and handsome and charming and witty than any other people. Some cynic has observed, "And then God made whiskey and made the Irish even with everyone else." We read how you don't have to be Jewish to enjoy Levy's rye, neither do you have to be a Scotsman to enjoy Scotch whiskey, but stories of Irish enthusiasm for alcoholic refreshment are grossly exaggerated. This is amply demonstrated by the fact that the Irish lead all the nations of the world in the number and fervor of pledges of abstinence. You may have heard of the two men from home on the way to see the pastor to take the pledge. One said "Let's have a last drink before we go in." Having the proper respect for the clergy, the other responded, "No, he might smell it on our breath; let's wait until we get out." Once they were inside, the pastor asked whether they wished to take the pledge for a period of one year or five years, and their response was immediate: "Father, we usually take it for life."

The wit of the Irish is of course spontaneous, unpremeditated, and sometimes quite devastating. On our trip to Ireland last summer I was exposed to quite a bit of it. For example, we attempted to pass a farmer who was comfortably parked on the side of a narrow road in a milk wagon which had a protruding axle. We succeeded only in badly denting in the side of our rented Ford. The comment of the farmer was simply "Mister, that's a wide car you're driving." A thirteen-year-old boy operating a gas pump in Sligo was asked to clean the windshield after he had filled the tank with gas. He responded by dousing it with a pail of water. After I had entered a rather mild complaint he retorted, "Sir, if you're going to be in Ireland much longer, it will get a hell of a lot wetter." Personal pride precludes me from commenting upon the remarks made by a Dublin tailor in the process of measuring me for a suit. I am sure of one thing: the martini is as alien to rural Ireland as Irish coffee is to Moscow. In Adare I made the mistake of ordering before dinner a dry martini with a twist of lemon. I was served with a lemonade. I went back to the bar and watched the barman make the second. After appropriate portions of gin and vermouth he squeezed in the juice of a lemon. Observing me he confided with a wink, "That's the way the Yanks like it." I am still thankful I didn't order a gibson.

Although I am not a member of this society, I do belong to the Friendly Sons of Saint Patrick of New York. This Society was founded in 1784, and one of its charter members was a namesake of mine, one Hercules Mulligan. Despite the epic proportions of his given name, Mulligan was actually a tailor by trade who acted as an intelligence agent for George Washington during the American Revolution. Hercules had a tailor shop on Pearl Street, and when English officers came in for a fitting, Mulligan got not only their measurements but military information as well. Hercules Mulligan is still in New York and is still under cover, reposing in the unconsecrated grounds of Trinity Churchyard. He is one of the very few Irishmen to be in Wall Street ahead of John Coleman.

The society which Hercules "the Apostate" helped to organize has prospered through the years and is the only solvent fraternal organization in which I hold membership. Many of us less affluent members retain membership in the fond expectation that in the event of an eventual dissolution there will be a pro rata distribution of the assets among the members. I was kept on the waiting list of the Friendly Sons for seven years. But I am sure that the waiting period would be at least twice as long were it not for the annual banquets on March 17th. After pre-prandial Manhattans and martinis, the members feast on such traditional Gaelic delicacies as terrapin and sherry, Irish bacon and kale, chicken and champagne, with incidental drafts of scotch and bourbon. As a result of such feasting, the death rate of the membership is much above the national average, and the waiting list is thus kept within manageable limits. Each spring a surprising number of members finally succumb to a variety of gastric disturbances, giving rise to numerous wakes, traditionally the favorite spectator sport of the Irish. The feasts in America have proven almost as devastating as the famines at home.

In view of the dedication of this society to history and my own predilection for law, I thought it might be appropriate to investigate the Irish bench before the establishment of the Irish Free State in 1922. We have all heard of the saints and the scholars, the bards and the missionaries who made Ireland preeminent when the ancestors of some other ethnic groups were still making mud pies. However, one seldom hears of Irish jurists, and my own brief investigation would seem to indicate that perhaps the silence is well deserved. The first recorded judicial history of Ireland commences in 1221 and for my purposes concludes in 1921. For seven hundred years, with a few major exceptions, frankly the history of the Irish bench is one of mediocrity and in some cases mendacity. The reasons for this are not difficult to ascertain. England, of course, controlled the appointments to the bench in Ireland. The vast majority of the appointees were men of English birth or descent. Many English barristers were reluctant to serve and were never fully devoted to the cause of justice. Their attitude was not unlike Jonathan Swift, who, upon his appointment in 1711 to the deanship of St. Patrick's Cathedral in Dublin rather than to the more remunerative English bishopric to which he aspired, confided in a letter "I have been condemned forever to wretched Dublin in miserable Ireland." Two of the sixteenth-century Chancellors of Ireland, Curwen and Weston, were at the same time deans of St. Patrick's Cathedral, both were in poor health, both blamed their illnesses on the Irish climate. Sir William Gerard, who was appointed Chancellor of Ireland in 1576, not only retained his seat in the English Parliament but held on to a judicial office in Wales at the same time. He was also given the deanery of St. Patrick's to augment his salary. He attempted to consolidate the four courts into one and threatened to die if men of English birth were not sent to help him. He finally broke down in health, attributing his ailments, like Curwen and Weston, to the abominable Irish climate. These are typical of many men of English birth appointed to the Irish bench who not only were disinterested but were as a matter of fact disaffected.

Men of English birth dominated the Irish bench not only because of the preference of the reigning monarchs but because until 1760 five years' residence in one of the Inns of Court of London was a prerequisite for membership in the bar in both England and Ireland. Another restriction which obviously limited Irish selection were the laws excluding papists from the learned professions which included the bar. The ability and the agility of the American Irish in obtaining judicial appointments at least until recently is apparently an acquired and not an inherited characteristic.

In the eighteenth century men of Irish birth began to predominate the Irish bench, but again their impact was hardly beneficial for the people of Ireland. A most interesting character was Sir Richard Cox, who was appointed Chancellor of Ireland in 1703. He was born in Cork but was admittedly devoted to England. Although he owned not a foot of land in England, he was as solicitous, he said, for her prosperity as if his whole estate lay within her bounds. Cox was a devotee of music, a gourmet who claimed to serve the best claret in the world and made his own paradise cheese. He had his wigs made in England, dressed in the uniform of a general, and carried a sword. He was a prolific writer of tracts and letters—in one letter written at the age of forty-nine he mentions that his wife has presented him with his twenty-first child, as fine a boy as he ever saw, and he wrote that this was not the last gift of this kind that he expected to receive. Some sixteen years later his bride passed on to her eternal reward, undoubtedly another victim of the Irish climate or possibly the paradise cheese. Cox died at the age of 83 after having been censured by the House of Commons for partiality and corruption in office. In 1791 Robert Boyd of Donegal was appointed to the King's Bench in Ireland. It is reported that he kept an ample supply of brandy beside him on the bench which he kept in an inkstand and that he partook freely of it through a quill, which may have accounted for his premature retirement in 1798.

The Irish bench faced problems not unknown today. Calendar congestion was a continuing harassment, and in 1721 an Irish Chancery decree was reversed in a matter which had been pending for fifty-one years. There are constant references to the physical dilapidation of the Irish courthouses—for example, in 1721 a chimney in the Dublin Court house caught fire with a resulting panic that killed twenty and injured one hundred; in 1719 the Roscommon Court House collapsed and several were killed and an abundance injured. Rather sadly it is reported "neither judges, counsel nor any of the attorneys got hurt." During the reign of Victoria not only did the Irish predominate on the bench but Roman Catholics also began to show strength. As Ball, the historian, points out, however, with one or two exceptions they had all passed through the same mill—the University of Dublin—they had all represented big business and the wealthy interests and, whether Protestant or Catholic, did little to respond to the real interests and yearnings of the Irish people. I do not purport that this survey is in any sense an exhaustive study of seven centuries of the Irish judiciary—but my own reading satisfied me at least that before the independence of Ireland, the Irish bench was distinguished much more for its defendants than for its judges. The members of the bench generally deserved the well-known oblivion of time while the memories of Arthur O'Connor, Padraic Pearse, Robert Emmet, Michael O'Brien, Richard Burke, and Timothy Featherstone remain fresh and green. I should like to close this evening with an excerpt from a speech of Sir Roger Casement to the jury which convicted him of high treason for his part in the organization of

the Irish in 1914. It is much more memorable to me than anything ever written in an Irish judicial opinion:

> Gentlemen of the jury, Ireland has outlived the failure of
> all her hopes—and yet she still hopes. Ireland has seen her
> sons—aye, and her daughters, too—suffer from generation
> to generation always for the same cause, meeting always
> the same fate, and always at the hands of the same power;
> and yet always a fresh generation has passed on to with-
> stand the same oppression. For if English authority be om-
> nipotent—a power, as Mr. Gladstone phrased it, that
> reaches to the very ends of the earth—Irish hope exceeds
> the dimensions of that power, excels its authority, and re-
> news with each generation the claims of the last. The cause
> that begets this indomitable persistency, the faculty of pre-
> serving through centuries of misery the remembrance of
> lost liberty, this surely is the noblest cause men ever strove
> for, ever lived for, ever died for. If this be the cause I stand
> here today indicted for, and convicted of sustaining, then I
> stand in a goodly company and a right noble succession.

INSURANCE LAW SEMINAR, AMERICAN BAR ASSOCIATION
August 10, 1964

Gentlemen:

I am sure you will be relieved to know that I have no intention of fitting my remarks this morning into the advertised title. After I had been invited to speak, Mr. Stichter telephoned me to advise that it was most difficult to get anyone up to attend a breakfast meeting at 8:00 A.M. especially to hear a law school dean. He therefore suggested that I select a very catchy title which, for some reason, might capture the imagination of the members of this section. I submitted several bits of trivia to him including "Up from the Serbonian Bog" and "Sex and the Single Premium." After consultation with several of his associates, members of the section, and other equally busy legal minds, he suggested the present combination "Up from the Serbonian Bog, or, Sex and the Single Premium" which presumably is twice as intriguing as either title alone. Even *The New York Times* was intrigued. Although I was prepared to take on either subject singly, I confess that the combination is so overwhelming that I am forced to retreat. The "Serbonian Bog" allusion of course is taken from the late, great Mr. Justice Cardozo in his famous dissenting opinion in *Landress v. Phoenix Mut. Life Ins. Co.* 291 U. S. 491 (1934) in which he stated that "any attempted distinction between accidental results and accidental means would plunge this branch of the law into a Serbonian Bog." Several years later the Supreme Court of Colorado in *Equitable Life v. Hemenover* 100 Colo. 231 stated "Whatever kind of a bog that is, we concur." The courts have gradually eroded the distinction and hence the title "Up from the Serbonian Bog." "Sex and the Single Premium," I confess, is not as easily handled—aside from the innate delicacy of the subject especially in view of my being the Dean of a church-related school, I find surprisingly very little discussion of the matter in legal literature. Although there are numerous references to sex and premiums, no one except a sick law school dean has ever apparently combined the two. All that I can say is that the payment of a single premium saves both the carrier and the insured valuable time, postage, and correspondence and therefore I suspect that in this affluent society we are just as much in favor of the single premium as we are in favor of sex. Gentlemen, your chairman has requested that I be both brief and light. This advice has been made necessary ever since that old law school dean Senator Wayne Morse became a United States senator. *The New York Times* profile on Saturday indicated that as a speaker the Senator combines a remarkable lack of terminal facilities with a remarkable lack of humor. I cannot promise humor at this ungodly hour but I can promise brevity.

For the past eighteen years I have been engaged in the rather suspect occupation of teaching law to law students; more accurately, I suppose, I should say that at the beginning I taught and now, having acquired age and wisdom, simply conduct classes. Whether this makes me an expert on insurance law or the teaching of insurance law is a distinction I hesitate to press. Insurance law is the one law school subject I have stayed with for the entire eighteen years, and the reason, of course, is that for some strange reason I am fond of it. The affection is largely unrequited. Some of my colleagues have ascribed a base motivation for this attraction—one suggested that the only law involved in the course is the maxim "Stick the insurance company." This of course is an oversimplification—the insurance company is stuck only if the language of the policy is ambiguous, so that the first law is find or, if necessary, create an ambiguity, and the second and great rule follows as the night the day, then stick the insurance company. Of course the insurance companies have, as you well know, developed a complete defense to these rules, taking the position that they are invulnerable, because if they are stuck too badly or too often, they will have no alternative but to raise premium rates, so that all the juries and judges are accomplishing is a depletion of their own personal assets. Thus, sticking the insurance company is not the justifiable homicide which normal red-blooded American judges and juries delight in, but rather a form of financial suicide completely at odds with the natural law and our American heritage. Actually, of course, law school classes do not speculate about this subterranean clash of conflicting propaganda—the psychological warfare engaged in by insured and insurer—we speculate about such intriguing subjects as binding receipts (when is a binding receipt binding), friendly fires (these are fires which are hostile to the insured but friendly to the insurance company), waiver and estoppel (including the waiver of a non-waiver clause), warranties (what is a warranty in New York, by the way?), and the intricacies of double recovery and subrogation.

Insurance at Fordham is an elective course, as it is to the best of my knowledge in most American law schools. One would suspect that after two years of study in law school, a bright young senior would conclude that from the exposure he has had to cases and statutes, there would be much sense in learning something about insurance law.

After all, he realizes that he will be dealing with adjustors, brokers, and insurance company lawyers all of his professional career. Insurance is the greatest risk-shifting device ever invented by man—all of his clients will carry insurance and in most cases the perils which they face in this vale of tears will probably be covered by an insurance contract. Hence it would be sensible, I suppose, for the law student to learn something about it in the comparative calm of law school before being evicted and discharged into the harsh reality of law practice.

Actually, however, one finds that in practice this ideal method of selection seldom materializes. The decision to select Insurance as opposed to such courses as Labor Law or Federal Practice, or even such esoteric favorites as the legal aspects of finger painting or a survey course on the tribal laws of the Congo, is based on supposedly more practical considerations.

On what day or at what time of day will Insurance be given? If a law student can so arrange his schedule that Friday afternoons or Monday mornings are free, you can be sure that if Insurance is given at either time, he will show a remarkable lack of interest in the subject. This is one advantage in being Dean—he makes up the schedule. Theoretically, of course, if he schedules Insurance on Friday afternoon or Monday morning, he will attract the better student, the man who really wants to take it, he will have a smaller, more teachable group, and let's face it, he will have fewer blue books to struggle with at the end of the term. On the other hand, of course, even deans were former law students. If he schedules Insurance at either end of a weekend, he ruins his own opportunity to personally engage in the uninterrupted library study during the weekend which is the regular pursuit of all law school deans, or so I am advised. At Fordham since schedule making is a very complicated pursuit, almost as difficult as legislative apportionment, I have never found it possible, I regret to say, to find a place for Insurance on Monday morning or Friday afternoon.

A second criterion for the law student, of course, is the marking habits of the faculty. Law students become very expert in gauging and calculating the marking range of faculty members and of course preferring those who are the most liberal mathematically; those who adhere to the belief that just as there is no such thing as a bad boy there is no such thing as a bad law student. Some of the older students who have been with us for four years in a three-year course can even differentiate between the same man's marks in each course he teaches. Each teacher has a batting average for marks as carefully computed and studied by law students as the batting average and fielding records of ball players are studied by the manager. Sometimes these elders call emergency sessions when the marks reveal a sudden decline or increase in the blue-book value of the teacher. For example, in this last year, I failed three seniors in Trade Regulation in January and gave another dozen D's. The effect was immediate: I had the smallest class in Insurance this spring in my eighteen-year history, even though Insurance was scheduled on a Wednesday afternoon. Since all of the heroic or uninformed fourteen passed Insurance in June, I look forward to a reasonable popularity this fall in another elective, Trade Regulation.

Other teacher habits are also of interest to law students. Just as lawyers are always commenting on judicial demeanor and attitude toward counsel, so, of course, do law students observe and rate teachers. Is he reasonably friendly? Does he ask embarrassing questions such as "Have you read the next case, Mr. Jones?" How does he react to the law students' historical Fifth Amendment plea of "Unprepared"?—all of these are carefully weighed in making the selection of an elective. It may account for a boy who intends to join his father's one-man firm in Tupper Lake or Poughkeepsie electing International Law instead of Partnership.

There are other real factors at play in this game of selecting electives. We have the car-pool syndrome in the urban school—if members of the car pool get out of class at different times, this can be discouraging to rapid and efficient transportation aimed at avoiding the metropolitan traffic snarls. The members of the pool will therefore elect in common giving major consideration to traffic conditions on the West Side Highway and scratching off those subjects which might impair a speedy departure. We also have the rich kid, usually the son of a doctor who drives some of his less affluent classmates, usually the sons of lawyers, to law school. In this case of course the elective for the driver and all passengers is selected by the driver, who, after all, has title to the vehicle and possession of the keys. For this reason the whole group will usually elect Estate Planning.

One type which often elects Insurance Law no matter how ugly the teacher, how inconvenient the time, or the place, is the law student who has worked or is working for an insurance company. He elects the course generally because he believes it will be easy since he has absorbed so much in his six months as an adjustor—in some cases he elects it to help out the teacher and his fellow classmates. He is easily discernible after the first few weeks in class because of his eagerness to answer questions during the classroom discussion. He is detected immediately because in answer to a question of coverage, he will automatically respond, "How much is the claim?" If you suggest that this is not pertinent, he will look at you with mixed feelings of pity and regret and respond that if the damages are small his company will pay to avoid the nuisance; if they are middling, the answer will be negative; if it will cost more for the plaintiff to get expert evidence to prove his case than the damage is worth and if the claim is heavy, there is no coverage but the claim might be set-tled. These answers considerably rattle a young teacher and bring blushes to the cheeks of the classmates of the old pro. After a semblance of order is restored, the teacher will announce the law supported by Appellate decisions, law review articles, all edi-tions Vance and Patterson. Rather than be vanquished by such an array, the student now in a defiant mood will often retort— "Well, I don't know about that; all I know is my company wouldn't pay."

Gentlemen, at this point one might wish that the law student while on his way to the life insurance office to pay an overdue premium before getting married and going on his honeymoon would fall into a sea of quicksand—hence my title "Up from the Serbonian Bog, or, Sex and the Single Premium."

Actually, of course, I have painted an exaggerated picture. The average law student is sincere, earnest, intelligent and has gone to school at least sixteen years before coming to law school. He has been tested, vaccinated, may even have been under anal-ysis. He is even at times able to read and write English with some degree of efficiency. Spelling, of course, is a lost art, and his handwriting resembles some of the less decipherable inscrip-tions on Mesopotamian artifacts. Any experienced law school teacher who has read blue books for any considerable period of time, I am sure, would have no difficulty with the Dead Sea Scrolls. The theory seems to be that stenographers can be retained who are able to spell and to type, so reading and writing abilities are becoming atrophied. With the advent of electronic computers, I am sure that artithmetic will soon join readin' and writin' as lost arts. In any event, law students are wonderful people and much nicer than clients, whether or not they have elected Insurance; they will make wonderful additions to your offices. I recommend them to you without reservation and with complete confidence that they will be resourceful, energetic, and enterprising.

I have taken enough of your time, gentlemen, and as the sun rises in the East we bid a fond adieu to Serbonia.

BROOKLYN BAR ASSOCIATION
December 1, 1965

Gentlemen:

It is an honor to be invited to speak to this distinguished bar association. Although I am a native of The Bronx now living in Westchester and working in Manhattan, I want you to know that I do have ties to Brooklyn. In 1942 I was shipped out of Fort Dix as an Army private and arrived by train at an Army Pier on 58th Street, in Brooklyn. I had had a total of six days of army service, and the rest of my colleagues were equally untrained and unskilled. After lining up on the pier with our barracks bags we were given the command "Prepare for embarkation." This was a rather unnerving experience. We were loaded on a seagoing tug which we thought would take us out to a troop transport but instead took us to Fort Hamilton. I took basic training at Fort Hamilton and the Brooklyn Army Base and became a military policeman patrolling the taverns on 58th Street armed with a nightstick and a Colt 45. The perfect assignment for an Irishman with a law degree. After several months in the Peace Corps in Brooklyn, I was shipped overseas—to Staten Island. I look back fondly on my Brooklyn experiences and I am pleased to see so many familiar faces here which I recognize from my wartime career.

My initial impulse was to take this opportunity to discuss the problem of conglomerate mergers under Section 7 of the Clayton Act. But that, of course, has been done before, so I thought it might be edifying instead to discuss a subject with which presumably I would be more familiar—the business of law deaning. The subject of discourse is, therefore, "The Care and Feeding of Law Students," which, no matter how inelegantly phrased, is really the job of a law school dean. At one point or another, either before or after admission to the bar, willingly or perforce, we have all been students of the law, so, hopefully, my comments may be of some interest to you.

I must emphasize, gentlemen, at the outset that times have

dramatically changed since you and I were law students. In those days we looked upon all members of the legal profession with great respect. Each was assumed to have all of Corpus Juris, Primum et Secundum, at his fingertips. Law teachers were viewed with tremendous awe since presumably they knew everything ever enacted or decided since the law of the Medes and the Persians. We lived in a comparatively uncomplicated world and also in a depression. In those days the ability, real or apparent, to pay a modest tuition, was a principal qualification for admission to a law school. Registrars had many of the instincts of credit investigators—they observed applicants warily to detect telltale signs of insolvency such as shirts worn for three days instead of the customary two, or feet shod with sneakers instead of the usual half-soles. In those days "white shoe" meant Keds. Some admissions officers were surprisingly considerate; I knew of one who even lent money to law students—he eventually died of malnutrition and was deeply mourned by his creditors. The possession of a bachelor's degree not only was presumptive evidence of course of the ability to study law but also gave rise to the inference of tuition-paying ability. In many cases two years of college were sufficient, and in earlier days a high school diploma was enough for admission. One such high school graduate, John T. Loughran of the Kingston Academy, even had the temerity to graduate from Fordham *summa cum laude*—within one year he was a member of the faculty, perhaps the best it ever had. Eventually, of course, he became Chief Judge of the Court of Appeals.

Gentlemen, those days are gone forever. Today we are living in the affluent—soon to be great—society. Solvency is no longer a requirement for admission to law school, and humility is a lost virtue. Today, rather, the applicant is interested in determining how solvent the law school is. Can it provide him with a grant, a full-tuition scholarship, room and board, or at least a long-term loan without interest in return for the enhancement of the reputation of the school which results from his enrollment? Although we are living in comparative affluence, he is the beneficiary of state grants, guaranteed loans, and assistance from universities. In our day scholarships were normally reserved for football players, and scholars, historically poor, were expected to earn their daily bread. Today not only is the full-time law student not expected to earn his way, he is precluded from gainful employment while attending law school since it may interfere with his studies.

In our times almost everyone goes to college so that college-degree credentials are about as commonplace as birth certificates. Today we are concerned about the reputation of the college attended, the subjects studied, extra-curricular activities, postgraduate work, and the Law School Admission Test score. If John T. Loughran applied for admission today, he wouldn't even be given an application blank.

The beneficiaries of the affluent society are the so-called "New Breed"—the postwar disenchanted generation which believes that it is the victim of some gigantic conspiracy perpetrated by its elders, with nothing in prospect but the dropping of the bomb which will wipe all of them out. Their inner turmoil is evidenced by their addiction to beards, Beatle haircuts, pointed shoes, and tight pants. The shoes and the pants are uncomfortable and add, of course, to their suffering. Their unhappiness is nurtured by guitar-playing folk singers who are uniformly unkempt and equally lugubrious despite incomes which rival those of the medical profession. Much of the largesse is due to royalties from records which the parents of the new breed not only finance but are forced to listen to. With the increased birth rate, for which I suppose we must accept some responsibility, they are swamping not only the colleges but the law schools as well. At Fordham our applications doubled between 1961 and 1964, and in 1965 some 1,410 of those applied for admission for some 300 vacancies. Our experience is not atypical. One wonders honestly whether the quality of the profession will be so much improved in the days ahead. How valid in fact are the testing devices? How substantial are the college degrees?

At the risk of injecting a serious note momentarily, I will only make this observation: we are in a period of mass education with large universities becoming mammoth and with large classes commonplace even in many small colleges which have had to expand to keep up with the demand. One concomitant is that many examinations are machine graded—the student has to learn to make an X or a check mark in an appropriate box with an indelible pencil or a ballpoint pen to create a proper electrical impulse for the machine. Even the so-called "writing exam" on the Law School Admission Test is machine graded—the student is not expected to write or compose but rather to select preferences in sample compositions by making an X. The student may select the right box but he may not be able to construct a paragraph or a sentence in logical, intelligible English. Grammar and spelling have become lost arts. One law school in New York has even found it necessary to give a course in English to its students, all of whom are college graduates. Numerous colleges give their freshmen remedial reading and English courses appropriately called "Bonehead English." One wonders whether the opinions of the courts in another generation will be as lucid and logical as those we studied in law school. The ability to read and write quickly, skillfully, and analytically is a principal qualification for success not only in law school but also in the profession. Let us admit frankly that while law school admission standards have been raised to new heights, it does not follow that the Golden Age of the super lawyers is at hand.

While the dean of the law school may surround himself with such natural obstacles as admission officers or admission committees, much of the burden of selecting the entering class, of picking and choosing the elect of the New Breed, will fall upon him. It is at this point that he discovers that all of the candidates whom the admissions office considers unqualified are the intimate friends of judges, barristers, legislators, and clergymen each of whom think that Johnny Jones would be a great asset to the law school. A typical letter would indicate that the author has known Johnny's family for generations, that he had a B average at an outstanding college, despite a tendency to become ill or highly nervous before exams so that his transcript does not fully indicate his potential. Johnny is described as high-spirited, a talented musician, active in extracurricular activities with a lifelong ambition to become an attorney. Johnny sometimes forwards supplementary letters from his psychiatrist, parole officer, or the leader of the college marching band.

On investigation of the facts one discovers that Johnny's scholastic record indicates that he would have difficulty in parting his hair. He has matriculated at an obscure institution awarding an unaccredited degree in home economics and his only B was in finger painting. Johnny's high spirits are evidenced by his transcript, which indicates that he has been suspended for assaulting the professor of driver education. His principal extracurricular activity has been that of a tort feasor. He did make the college band, and while he did not learn to play the drum he at least carried it at the football games. He has lost three during the college season for which he is being dunned by the school. He has also had some difficulty in spelling "Rah, rah" in band formations but is otherwise considered qualified. His lifelong ambition to become a lawyer has become evident only since the prospect of immediate military service became apparent.

Johnny's rejection is, of course, simple, but there are thousands of other Johnnies who are being rejected for law school admission who are close to the mark. These applications are rejected with sincere regret because we always have the lingering thought maybe Johnny would be a good lawyer after all. Maybe the *summa cum laude* Eagle Scout whose aptitude is near genius will never want to represent clients who are in trouble and need help. College transcripts cannot always indicate motivation or inspiration; testing procedures cannot measure the qualities of heart and spirit essential to the lawyer.

The business of deaning is not always as pleasant as speaking in New York in the springtime. To the practitioner of law annoyed by the importuning of clients and the intransigence of judges, the prospect of devoting one's life to a professorship at a law school is quite appealing. Universities are not noted for exorbitant salaries; there are no profit-sharing schemes or stock option plans, but they do meet payrolls; and with the high birth rate, business prospects are excellent. The law professor does not have any overhead; he does not have to worry about collecting fees from impecunious clients. There is the strange academic phenomenon of "tenure" which assures him of permanent retention, a device unknown in the relationship of lawyer and client. Judicial decisions are impersonal and can be criticized with the same impunity enjoyed by the student editors of law reviews. In the classroom he has innumerable opportunities to feed his ego which was never a victim of malnutrition in any event. In the classroom he can pontificate and determine complicated questions of law without fear of reversal and with no fear of encountering a cantankerous adversary or unsympathetic judge. The vacation is long and the hours are comfortable. There are occasional wise guys in law school who actually read the footnote cases, but the experienced teacher has little difficulty in smothering them with a variety of techniques which law students become familiar with only shortly after graduation, if ever. One of these is to rephrase the student's question until it becomes one you can answer. Another is to suggest the question really involves another subject taught by another expert. Another is to overwhelm him with the polysyllabic, enigmatic vocabulary which our profession possesses in such rich abundance. For example, in Antitrust Law we have such gems as horizontal integration, conscious parallelism, oligopolistic and duopsony.

In moments of extreme desperation we resort to the ploy of the physician—*caput lupinum*, for example, is sure fire.

Life for the law professor is idyllic until a vacancy occurs in the office of dean through his death, disablement, judicial appointment, or the designation of a lunacy commission. Not only is the unsuspecting law teacher who finds himself elevated now fully occupied with the care and feeding of law students but he is also charged with a task of keeping amused a variety of groups with inherently conflicting interests—the alumni, the faculty, the students, the accrediting associations, the bar associations, the university administration, the Association of American University Professors, and the Student Bar Association.

Law professors would naturally like more money; they would like students to work harder so that the teachers could work less. The student would like to pay less tuition, have the teachers work more so that they could work less. The university would like everyone including the dean to work harder. The law teacher would like to teach Comparative Oriental Law with a sabbatical in Honolulu. The bar associations would like the law school to teach the law students how to try a case or at least how to settle one. The alumni would like the law school to take all its friends and relatives, while the accrediting associations would like admission standards so high that ideally all applicants would be denied and the faculty would be fully free for research.

The dean's job is to keep all elements reasonably happy while at the same time advancing the character and reputation of the school before he himself becomes a victim of ulcers, barbiturates, or neuroses. An excellent counter irritant that I have discovered is a large amount of gin mixed with a small amount of vermouth.

In 1962 a study of male adults in Manhattan purported to establish that three out of ten adults have serious mental disturbances. A study reported in *The New York Times* recently would indicate that the 1962 study was rather conservative. This is indeed frightening to the dean. In a faculty of thirty men does he have nine who are fully sick or, hopefully, only eighteen who are half gone. He wonders indeed about himself. Perhaps the fact that he accepted the deanship is in itself some evidence of mental instability. There has been a decided increase in the rate of resignation of law school deans comparable to that of university presidents. One happy solution adopted by at least two deans in this state has been to resign and return to full-time teaching at the law school. This is ideal if one is able while he is dean to raise full-time faculty salaries to such a high point that he can still afford the imported gin to which he has become accustomed.

Gentlemen, as you hopefully understand, I have indulged in hyperbole this evening. In all honesty and candor the care and feeding of law students is a most rewarding and satisfying experience. The New Breed does begin to act and to think and to talk like lawyers. The haircuts and guitars and tight pants disappear, to be replaced by the gray flannel suit and the attache case. The New Breed is insecure, but they are essentially conscientious, ambitious, and highly intelligent—at times they can even be inspiring. After all why not—they are our own sons and daughters. Their care and feeding is a thrilling challenge. I wouldn't trade it for anything—then again I may be one of the three out of ten.

JOINT MEETING OF THE JEWISH, PROTESTANT, AND CATHOLIC LAWYERS GUILDS
February 26, 1969

Mr. Chairman, reverend clergy, fellow members of the bar, and friends:

I am delighted to have this opportunity to give you some thoughts I have on the subject of "Religion and Rebellion." I have no really valid credentials in either subject, but if the topic had been broadened to include Rum as well as Romanism and Rebellion, I could probably speak with greater authority and certainly with deeper experience. I speak only for myself, not for the Guild or the Law School, and certainly not for my three children, who are all of college age.

It is quite evident that we are in the midst of a worldwide frenetic rebellion by youth, particularly those in the colleges and universities. It is not unique to America and the democratic West; it exists in Japan, in Czechoslovakia, and probably would in Russia were it permissible; some glimmerings have been apparent in Spain and even in Ireland, as I can attest from first-hand experience. I believe it is spontaneous and not artificially provoked, at least not by Russian Communists and, I doubt, even by Chinese Communists, although they are obviously pleased by our discomfiture. Here it is basically a rebellion against authority—parental, religious, educational, and governmental. It questions, in essence, the norms, the values, and the pretensions, if you will, of the "power structure," "the establishment"—which, as far as I can determine, is anyone over 30 who is neither in jail nor in an asylum. In general, they consider us at best insensitive to social inequity, to human suffering, to racial prejudice. We are in their eyes a mink-and-martini, hypocritical, hedonistic society totally dedicated to the perpetuation of our comfort, the growth of our portfolios, and the middle-class mediocrity of color television. They are the first generation to have discovered disease, deprivation, and discrimination and are at the very least embarrassed by our apparent toleration of and even enjoyment of the affluent society *of* which, incidentally, they happen to be the principal beneficiaries.

I applaud in general their concern and their interest. It is not a put-on; it is real. We have noticed for the past several years an increasing number of law students who are concerned with the problems of the poor and the culturally disadvantaged. This concern is healthy, in my opinion, and those college youths who are involved are articulate, dedicated, and well motivated. I cannot avoid saying parenthetically that they also, on the whole, lack both humor and humility; their judgment is untested and their ardor will predictably and unfortunately diminish when they face the harsh economic realities that marriage and children will eventually bring. There is among them a hard-core group of militants, however, typified by the S.D.S.—Students for a Democratic Society. This is the group which finds the establishment not only selfish but corrupt. The common adjectives are "racist," "imperialist," "war-mongering" America. Their solution is simply this: smash the establishment. Gentlemen, they mean it! They are not wild-eyed idealists; they are pragmatic, hardheaded anarchists. They really do mean to smash you; they do not hesitate to burn, to bomb, and to vandalize. The right of their fellow students to study, to learn, is callously disregarded. They do not tolerate any dissent from their dissent.

Let me quote you the concluding paragraph of an article in the latest issue of the Fordham University S.D.S. magazine which purports to be an answer to Sidney Hooks's recent article on freedom of speech:

> In conclusion, students in S.D.S. must not be swayed by liberals and others who wish to turn us from our true goal. Progressive students wish, not to debate the ruling class, nor to do "free and untrammelled" research on it, but to smash it. In order to do this, they must firmly understand the true meaning of class democracy and freedom. None of the bourgeois "freedoms" are in the long run significant for exploited people; the only one that counts is the freedom [to] overthrow the exploiters.

This organization can hardly be described as representative of either students or freedom. I think it is about time that we took them seriously before they do burn us down.

It is not simply their truculence which concerns me; it is their ability to influence not only the starry-eyed sophomore but the starry-eyed professor and even the university administrator who really should know better but actually has led a very sheltered life with only vicarious, textbook confrontations. The recent comment of the president of a major university in the press is typically pathetic: "I've never been through this before, I don't know what to do." The ability to confuse the right of dissent with disruption, the failure to distinguish between the right to stay out of class and the obligation to respect the right of a fellow student to attend class, is particularly shocking to me as a lawyer. Jollification, mollification, and even amnesty are purportedly justified by the end of avoiding violence. Given the goals of the S.D.S. militant, this approach can only be reminiscent of Neville Chamberlain's naïve negotiations with Adolf Hitler. I applaud the return to sanity exemplified by Father Hesburgh's statement of February 24th, which has been endorsed by President Nixon, *The New York Times*, and apparently overwhelmingly by the Notre Dame community. There is no other solution if we are to continue a viable university community.

I think further that our generation, while admittedly complacent in its affluence, can hardly be charged with insensitivity to the needs and aspirations of the underprivileged either here or abroad. Our generation did after all fight a depression and a war and managed at the same time to feed and educate ourselves and our progeny. We did build the bomb and we did drop it, but we were battling a tyranny which, had it triumphed, would be totally repugnant to the youth who now are so disaffected. As Louis Nizer pointed out in a recent address to the Fordham Law Alumni, what country, what generation has done more to succor the world than our own; who has done more to fight racial discrimination, to combat poverty and injustice? No human institution is perfect, but our governmental establishment is unsurpassed by any in history, so let's stop being apologetic. Unfortunately, pride in country—patriotism, if you will—adherence to the rule of law, have become equated in some psuedo-sophisticated circles with Birchism, McCarthyism, or even police brutality. I think we have been at fault in not praising and publicizing our own virtues and our own accomplishments. We have to stop beating our breasts and begin beating the drums.

The role of religion in the rebellion is most difficult for me to assess as a layman. Even if I had the time I could give you only some rudimentary personal observations. To a great number of our disquieted and disquieting youth, the organized religions, the major faiths represented here this evening, have become in reality an integral part of the comfortable middle-class establishment and hence are suspect. The efforts of my own church since John XXIII to open the windows, not only to reach our so-called separated brethren but also to make our faith more meaningful and relevant to all in the church, are well known to all of you. I think it is too early to gauge the success of the effort. Certainly the concern of the well-motivated youth we mentioned earlier, for their fellow man, their announced dedication to the virtue of "love," is completely compatible with religious affiliation. Without it, all is meaningless, as St. Paul's Epistle to the Corinthians read on Quinquagesima Sunday so beautifully points out. It is the fact that regular attendance at church services is hardly characteristic of college youth who sometimes are placed in the uncomfortable dilemma of listening to liberal theologians in Catholic college classes during the week and then on Sunday listening to middle-aged parish priests give comfortable sermons to middle-aged establishment Catholics. I think that here is the heavy burden of the church today in seeking renewal—the clash which occurs when we attempt to attract the youth without alienating the old. I think the vehicle most likely to bring both together in my own church is the Parish Council now being created in this Archdiocese, which will bring clergy and laymen together in close association to direct the parish community. I can only stress that youth must be an integral part of that association. I do not believe for a minute that there is any long-term or even short-term solution provided by the priest who takes off his collar, takes on a bride, and serves chianti and pretzels in his living room to others who equally lack humility and patience with a church which has moved so rapidly in such a short time that it is a wonder to all of those outside the fold. I believe that they can be somehow equated with that small core of militant activists who see the only solution in smashing the establishment and proceeding with the infallibility they pretend to despise. Religion to the hard-core youth is the one opiate that cannot be tolerated. Their sexual habits, their language and general behavior are expressions of contempt for all the mores of organized religion. But even here I am not totally pessimistic—I recall the young Augustine's prayer: "Oh God give me chastity, but not too soon." In conclusion, gentlemen, I thank you for your patience, your benignity, and your charity.

NEW YORK CITY
POLICE DEPARTMENT
HOLY NAME SOCIETY
COMMUNION BREAKFAST
March 23, 1969

Mr. Toastmaster, Your Honor the Mayor, Commissioner Leary, reverend clergy:

I am very pleased to be here this morning, gentlemen, but, frankly, one hardly ever declines an invitation from the police, even at 8 o'clock on a Sunday morning. My relationship with police departments has, on the whole, been reasonably amicable. This is not only because I have the inherent Irish sympathy for law enforcers but also due to the fact that I don't have a driver's license and don't drive a car. This not only renders me some sort of curiosity, but also has substantially reduced the risk of any confrontation with the police. My most recent invitation to the Bronxville Police Station was when my teenage son was apprehended with a bazooka. While this sounds a little hairy, the bazooka was unarmed and was only intended to be pointed at the Xavier cadets as a friendly gesture on the part of the Fordham Prep football team on the occasion of their annual bloodletting.

My relationship with the police goes back to law school when I was a part-time employee of a police civil service school operated by Messrs. Casey and Caddell and known to the public as "The Columbian Institute"—much to the annoyance of Columbia University, a somewhat more respected institution of learning, at least at that time. I was the registrar of the school until the athletic director absconded with all our towels, soap, and secondhand sneakers. I then succeeded him, inheriting a 10'-by-12' gymnasium on 12th Street and several broken-down strength machines which had been rejected at Coney Island. I held this august position, checking on applicants for appointment or promotion in the Police Department, until I was called to the colors and was of course assigned to the Military Police. I graduated from the army's criminal investigation school, where, among other things, I took a course entitled Methods of Entry, which was really basic lock-picking. I got my highest marks in this field and have kept it up as a hobby, which, in my present occupation as Dean, I find to be a very helpful skill.

I was initially assigned to the Brooklyn Army Base, where I patrolled the piers and the bars armed with a nightstick and great fear that someone would take it away and beat me on the head with it. I also served in the same capacity overseas—in Staten Island; but after six months I was transferred to the Counter-Intelligence Corps and spent the next three years in civilian clothes chasing spies. We never found any, and I never knew whether there were never any around or whether we were just too dumb to find them. I give you these facts, gentlemen, not to impress you with my undistinguished war record but to indicate my empathy with the police.

In my present extra-hazardous occupation as dean, I never know when I may need you in an awful hurry. Last year we did have a bomb scare at the law school and I did call the police, who responded with alacrity and in numbers. I was asked if I wanted to evacuate the building at the time the anonymous caller said the bomb would go off. I refused and, on the contrary, indicated that I was thinking of calling a faculty meeting for the same time.

Gentlemen, I appear today with the permission of the student body, which let me out for the occasion and asked me to keep my remarks brief and to report back immediately after the last speech. If this is like some of the Communion breakfasts I have attended, I will return to Fordham on Tuesday.

Seriously, I should like to make some random observations which are not only your business but that of all the citizens in the community. I am of course an advocate of the rule of law: that I should even have to say that is perhaps some indication of the confusing times in which we live. The only alternative to the rule of law is the rule of force or of anarchy, and any mature, or even immature, observer who believes otherwise is a potential inmate of a jail, an insane asylum, or a concentration camp. Who disagrees with this proposition? Certainly not organized crime. Their difference with our society is not philosophic or logical but solely for profit-making purposes, and I leave their evil and odious activities to your tender ministrations. The ghetto rioter and the drug addict are compelled and driven to crime and, while I do not condone and I do condemn, I can understand their desperation. My concern, frankly, is the campus criminal who is not motivated by profit, who is not usually an addict and certainly not a victim of poverty or ignorance but who is a conscious, persistent, articulate opponent of the rule of law. Despite his freedom from disabilities, he seems to think that his status as a student exculpates him from criminal guilt and that, as a member of the academic community, he should be immune from arrest. Let me be perfectly clear: I come in daily contact with students, and all those at my law school and the vast majority of college students throughout the land are perceptive, sensitive, and dedicated people—far more so than my generation. They are a little more arrogant and humorless than I would like but, after years of observation, I can tell you that I admire them immensely and that if I didn't say that, they wouldn't let me back in my office on Tuesday.

My serious concern is the minute but malignant growth in the academic community—Students for a Democratic Society. Many of them are not students, and none of them believe in either democracy or society. They boldly announce their objective, which is to smash our society. They are not simple dissenters but violent disrupters who do not hesitate to assault, to commit arson, to terrorize. Their present target is the university community, and their next can only be the state. I have read their literature and they do disdain what they term the bourgeois freedom of speech, press, and assembly. They are the greatest opponents of academic freedom abroad. I am concerned that their philosophy and motivation are not grasped by many academicians and academic administrators who somehow feel that the campus is a sanctuary even for the criminal. I applaud and commend the approach of Presidents Hesburgh and Hayakawa, whose credentials for liberalism are unimpeachable. We often read about the apathy and stupidity of the German public which permitted Hitler's hoodlums to terrorize the German populace, but we have the beginning of it here if we do not insist on the maintenance of law and order.

Now, who are those who disagree with these views? There are some who say that rebellion and violence are part of our American heritage and that therefore presumably their continuation is almost patriotic. This, frankly, in my view, is hogwash. There is no analogy at all between the circumstances which gave rise to the Boston Tea Party and the American Revolution, and campus violence. We now have a constitutional republic, we have elected representatives, we have ample opportunity and indeed an obligation to cure injustice by legislation. Moreover, the argument proves too much. Our history of violence also included the burning of crosses, the lynching of Negroes, the slaughter of Indians. Would anyone seriously argue that these ugly episodes become modern practice?

There are also those who say that there is no obligation to obey an unjust law and, in fact, a positive obligation to break it. Gentlemen, we cannot live in an organized society and pick and choose the laws we wish to obey on the basis of a private concept of justice. This can only lead to the chaos of the jungle. Once again, those who oppose a law must participate as citizens in the community. Let them protest, let them vote, let them organize opposition by ballot, but let them unilaterally determine when the law is not binding and we are back to the jungle.

The function of police in all of this is, of course, clear to you. Force and violence cannot be quelled by conversation, and this is precisely the reason police are armed. There are some journalists who equate the use of force by police to quell violence with the term police brutality. This is unfair and unrealistic. One cannot reason with the looter, preach to the rapist, or cajole the burglar. Our persons and our property must be secure, and if discussion were enough to avert violence we could disband our armed services overnight. Since peace officers are subject to the same frailties as the rest of mankind, it is expected that on occasion there will be so-called overreactions, but this is certainly not the policy of any police organization; nor is it ever condoned. I am a little sick of reading the comments of some psychologists that police reaction is because of their middle-class Irish or Italian ancestry and background which is particularly offended by the sexual license, promiscuity, perversion, obscenity, and drug addiction of the S.D.S. and the hippie. Some of those quoted seem to feel that this reaction is unique and unrepresentative. I can only say that the values of the police are my values and the values of the vast majority of civilized Americans, irrespective of social, racial, or religious background. I believe that in this community there is a growing support and understanding of the police and I do agree that there is no real alternative to the slogan "Support Your Local Police." This is not difficult in this city because we do have the finest. May I express the gratitude of your fellow citizens for your continuing excellence in the performance of an increasingly difficult job.

ANNUAL DINNER
OF THE VINSON CLUB
November 19, 1970

Mr. Chief Justice, distinguished members of the bench and bar:

I am very pleased and honored to have this opportunity to address The Vinson Club. I understand that this organization has no rules, no officers, and no dues—this is precisely how most American students would like our universities to operate. If it could be done this successfully, they may have something I never noticed before. I wrote for some information about this group and its dinner and was sent a menu of a past dinner. The contents were extremely informative and persuasive and left no doubt in my mind that I should be here with you tonight instead of appearing before The Association of the Bar of the City of New York as a panelist and instead of taking my usual two hours of Antitrust Law. The students accepted my decision not only with aplomb but also with applause. The Bar Association was much less understanding, and I may need a certificate of attendance from the Chief Justice.

Gentlemen, it could not have escaped your notice that the casualty rate of law deans has risen astonishingly during the past two or three years. The only parallel I can think of is the growth of the venereal disease rate in this country during the same period. I am certainly not suggesting any relationship between these phenomena but, by the same token, candor compels me to admit that no definitive study has been made on the subject. In view of the decanal necrology I have entitled my talk "The Decline and Fall of Law School Deans," as a fitting sequel to my other speech "The Care and Feeding of Law School Students" which, with pocket parts, has served me fairly well for some fifteen years.

I started in the law school deaning business some fourteen years ago when New York had ten law schools with ten deans. Out of that original number only two are still around, although wounded, and at the end of the next scholastic year, there will be no little Indians surviving. The New York experience is not unique. Throughout the country law school deans are falling like flies; some of course have expired of natural causes, but others have been zapped or have deliberately opted for a genteel retirement to the faculty. While I do not propose this evening any formal autopsy, I thought you might be interested in why law school deans, like other academic administrators throughout the United States, are suddenly deciding to spend the rest of their lives in research, study, and teaching.

Most of you attended law school in what I call the Golden Age of the Divine Right of Deans where the dean was supposed to last for life and acted accordingly. He was feared as well as respected and sometimes even looked upon with affection. He was a combination of Mr. Chips with occasional overtones of Captain Bligh. This Golden Age came to an abrupt halt shortly after World War II, coinciding with the demise of Hitler, Mussolini, and the Emperor of Japan. During the '50s and '60s the dean's mantle of infallibility had to be shared with the faculty, and he became more and more of a constitutional monarch. The Association of the American Law Schools became more and more an association of law professors fixing working conditions, wages, hours, and courses. Although the dean could keep his large office and private john, his powers were limited pretty much to signing diplomas, travel vouchers for the faculty, and service contracts for the secretaries' typewriters. Moreover, he still had to bear the slings and arrows of the students, the faculty, the alumni, the accrediting association, the university administration, and all of their respective wives. The newest group of course are the wives of the Jesuits.

The '70s have brought the third, and hopefully the last, stage of decanal decline. The governance of the law school is now to be shared by the faculty and the students. The reason for the student participation and authority is, of course, that they are young and therefore vibrant, intelligent, committed, and imaginative, and if the establishment fails to recognize these obvious virtues, they will strike, commit trespass or arson, or give other tangible evidence of their superior moral claims. The law students are admittedly somewhat younger and even less experienced in the profession than the youngest faculty member whose own experience with the practice of law, the church suffering, has been growing more and more vicarious. The rush for the exits really commenced with this phase although the public announcements of the retirements would hardly convey this fact. They are resigning before becoming committed or being assaulted or even more addicted to hard liquor or hard drugs than they are currently. As an indication of the extent of decanal panic I need only cite the case of one of my colleagues who ran for Congress this year and was surprisingly elected.

The law school dean, despite his diminished authority, is still deemed by the alumni, the bench, the bar, and the public generally as the person to call when Junior seeks admission to law school. Junior is usually described as a paragon of virtue, highly motivated, articulate, with superior intellectual abilities. He is described as a combination of Pericles, Cicero, Vinson, and Burger which Junior thinks is a rock quartet. Junior's application is also supported by letters from his psychiatrist, his probation officer, and the members of the desert commune in which he spends his summer contemplating his own and whatever other navels are available. A reference to Junior's application reveals that he has been on academic probation for the past five years in a four-year unaccredited college where he was majoring in driver education with a minor in remedial reading. His marks would indicate that he would have difficulty in parting his hair, and a look at his picture confirms the observation. His principal extracurricular activity has been trespass *quare clausum fregit*. The yearbook indicates his activities—Demonstrations 1, 2, 3 and 4. A letter from the McGuffey professor of remedial reading indicates that Junior's reading level has now reached that of the average eighth-grade Bulgarian. English is his second language; he has no first. The Hertz professor of driver education thinks that Junior should be permitted either to drive or to chase an ambulance. Rejecting Junior while maintaining the support of the university president who has been offered a bombproof shelter on campus by Junior's father is an occupational hazard of deaning.

Junior's application, like almost all the others, indicates that he wishes to attend the law school because he has lost faith in the imperialistic establishment which has created and fostered poverty, racism, and pollution. Junior has selected this particular law school because of its great reputation, its outstanding faculty, and its rich curriculum. It's amazing that within a few weeks after his admission Junior has acquired a more comprehensive knowledge of the curriculum and the intricacies of the legal profession than any of the faculty or the dean. He therefore, with equally skilled and experienced other Juniors, demands a complete overhaul of the antiquated curriculum and the decapitation of the even more antiquated faculty. Although he is ardently in favor of increasing the services and facilities of the law school, Junior is always prepared to strike in the event the law school raises tuition. This is somewhat surprising since Junior wasn't paying tuition in most cases. Either he is on a scholarship or his father is paying for it. His father is also paying for his apartment near the law school since Junior does not have the time to commute. The old man, of course, is also paying for Junior's sports car, which is adding more to the pollution of the city than the local gas company.

Junior objects, of course, to grades since they lead to competition which is, of course, an evil in itself. The theory is that one should develop one's own natural capacity—to do one's own thing, untrammeled by class assignments, recitations, or examinations which are artificially imposed obstacles to the real search for truth and beauty. Some of the briefs of the future may well be directed to problems not faced by clients but which are intriguing to Junior. Instead of examinations he proposes research papers which are, of course, always in depth and always prepared by a group called a task force. Instead of grades he wants pass/fail, although some conservatives would prefer a high pass/pass/fail. None would strenuously object to the elimination of the fail option. A recent article in a law school newspaper pointed out the following weaknesses in the examination system: (1) the student may not have felt well on the day of the exam; (2) he may not have understood the question; (3) he may have forgotten the answer; (4) his answer may be different from the professor's. Finally, the article pointed out that in an effort to pass the exams Junior may be forced to permanently borrow books from the library. Therefore, it was seriously urged that the elimination of examinations would cut down on book thefts in the library and hence save money for the university.

Of course, law students do not object to grading teachers. The law school newspaper of one law school in New York carries the grades of professors out to four decimal places, together with brief descriptions of his more repulsive habits. While law students find that receiving their own grades may irretrievably injure their egos, they find nothing incongruous in publicly plastering Professor Smith whose psyche has been subjected to a continuing assault for the past several years and, in any event, was flabby to start with.

There are other educational advances being proposed by students, most of which, frankly, have one common basis—less work for Junior. They have been and will continue to insist on having more time off for political activity, which apparently can take place only during the school year and never during vacations, which are used apparently to regain energy for the fall term demonstrations.

It is interesting to note too that at least one law school has advised the profession that it is inappropriate to ask a student for his grades or class standing—this is on the assumption that some schools are still determining class standing. It is of course dirty pool to ask if they are boys or girls which is not as easily detected today as it once was. While the employer is not permitted to pry into the student's accomplishments, many law firms have received a questionnaire from a law school placement office which embraces a multitude of questions which one would think are highly personal: How much does the firm contribute to law schools? How much free work do you do? Do you take a case because of an opportunity to develop an interesting branch of the law or simply to get a verdict for your client? My impression was that the only law firms which would get an A+ or even a high pass on a questionnaire like this would never be able to afford the $16,000 which Junior is claiming—not for compensation, but as a good faith token of the firm's interest in elimination of poverty.

Ladies and gentlemen, as you can understand, I have been dealing to some extent this evening in hyperbole—but I do believe in today's youth—for one practical reason: we have no alternative. Like all generations, they have their virtues and their vices. They are not quite as dedicated as some of you may think; nor are they quite as degenerate as some others of you may think. Their virtue is their true concern for their fellow man, their awareness of the cruel injustice which has damned some of our fellows simply because of the color of their skin or their lack of material resources. They are fully concerned with the absolute necessity for banning war and conquering poverty and pollution.

I look upon them with mitigated enthusiasm not because of their views or even their clothes or their hair, but rather because of their arrogant, humorless, monotonous group psychosis that theirs is the only approach, the only solution to all of the ills of mankind, their acceptance of all the material benefits of our generation and their failure to comprehend our own history of conquest over depression and oppression. We certainly have a long way to go but our experience and good will should not be rejected too cavalierly.

I conclude by saying that I have three of them—I love them, and my principal cause for optimism is that someday soon they, like yours, will be paying the tuition, looking for the report cards, and defending themselves from the antics of our grand-children.

The Judge
1971–1981

NEW YORK COUNTY
LAWYERS ASSOCIATION
December 9, 1971

It is indeed a great honor to be invited to be your speaker this evening. I have been a member of the New York County Lawyers Association for many years, but my first contact with the Association was made more than thirty years ago and the relationship was employer-employee or, perhaps more accurately, master-servant. While a student at Fordham Law School I was indentured to the Association as a book-boy at Vesey Street charged with the responsibility of shelving the books in the south reading room. I was paid the princely sum of $8.00 a week less deductions, plus the free use of a gray linen jacket to distinguish me from the members—most of whom wore suspenders and smoked cigars. Except for books, the room's major decoration was the brass cuspidors. I managed to read a few cases but spent most of my time shelving books, an occupation which required only a knowledge of the alphabet for the textbooks and numbers for the Reporters. The dense smoke of the room of course made the task more difficult. Now all libraries use the Dewey decimal system for cataloging just as doctors use Latin for prescriptions. The result is that today you have to have a Master's Degree in Library Science to become what was once a book-boy and now is probably a legal research technician. In any event, the end result is the same—the volume you want is lost, missing, or out at the bindery, but at all times of course properly marked with Dewey's decimals.

The little free time I had I spent at the window looking down at St. Paul's Cemetery, which is, as you know, just across the street from the library, serving counsel as a constant reminder that we not only have been admitted to the bar but someday will be crossing it. It was really a most dismal outlook, gazing through the smoke at the decaying headstones and mausoleums, one of which incidentally was the final resting place of Hercules Mulligan, a tailor who had a shop on Pearl Street which was really a front for his major hobby—spying for General

George Washington. He is known to us more familiarly as Hercules the Heretic, since he still lies under the unconsecrated grounds of St. Paul's. Seeking to escape the smoke and the view, I managed to flee in the fall of 1941 to a law firm on Nassau Street. The senior partner of the two-man firm, after learning that I had a straight-A average, was an editor of the *Law Review* (only one class after Mario Procaccino) and a bibliophile, offered to equal the $8.00 I was paid by your generous association. I insisted that I wanted to better my station in life and argued that the County Lawyers had given me in addition the free use of a jacket. We settled at $9.00 a week, but I was placed on probation—I didn't mention of course that the new view of the windows here was far superior. On a clear day, if the windows had been washed, one could see a small part of City Hall Park which had not yet been dedicated for the purpose of demonstrations. Incidentally, the firm dissolved at the outbreak of the war. The senior partner is now a successful psychiatrist in The Bronx and tells me that he found his vocation once I became his law clerk. I stayed on, still on probation, until the President of the United States invited me to join the United States Army at a salary of $50 a month plus the use not only of a jacket but also of four full uniforms. I was one of the few professional or even semi-professional men to enter the U.S. Army as a private at a wage far in excess of my civilian income. Frankly, this was the only time in my life that I took a new job which paid more that the one I had had before.

Enough of my career. I imagine that I was invited here not only because I was a former employee but also because of my abrupt elevation to the Court of Appeals for the Second Circuit—a court known, at least up until this time, for the wisdom, scholarship, probity, and dignity of its membership. My initial encounter with the Chief Judge was rather awkward. The Congressional Record and the press generally accurately reported that President Nixon had nominated me to succeed Judge Edward Lumbard. The Senate confirmed. Since I was to succeed Judge Lumbard and since he was a Chief Judge, it seemed crystal clear to me that I become the new Chief Judge. My mother who didn't even have the benefit of a legal education had the same understanding. Chief Judge Henry J. Friendly, who, up to this point, I had thought, was a distinguished scholar, disagreed rather violently. He did, however, offer to submit the matter to arbitration, suggesting as sole arbiter Judge Irving Kaufman whose judgment he said, especially in a matter such as this, was

impeccable. I decided not to press the point. This was not the
first time that the President's wishes have been frustrated by a
small group of willful men.

I am afraid, however, that the damage was done. When I in-
quired as to the location of my chambers I was told that the last
one in the building had just been rented and, in any event, he
didn't think I would like the neighborhood. He suggested several alternatives such as Niagara Falls, Attica, and Central Islip.
I have been sent to places on three-judge courts where no circuit
judge has ever been standing, much less sitting. I even had to
remind the Chief Judge that Belfast was not in the Northern
District but in Northern Ireland. The Chief Judge kept repeat-
ing that my chambers did not have to be in the courthouse. The
rule is clear he said—separate but equal—*Plessy v. Ferguson*, 163
U.S. 537 at 551–52 (1896). This is the way the Chief Judge cus-
tomarily speaks. I never bothered to Shepardize the case, and
for all I know it may not even be the law any more.

Actually, I am adequately housed in chambers at the Palazzo
Rao, sometimes known as the Customs Court, which is not only
separate but more equal. I have demanded busing to the courthouse, and I am quite confident that it will be forthcoming.

I am, of course, delighted to renew my contacts with the practicing profession after spending so many years with academicians and law students. Exactly half the lawyers who have
appeared before me since I ascended the bench have been
pleased with my appointment. Lawyers generally are misunderstood by all other segments of society—even people as gentle as
poets for some reason become infuriated by our profession. I
think it was Carl Sandburg who authored the lines: "Why is
there always a secret singing when a lawyer cashes in? Why does
the hearse horse snicker carting the lawyer away?" Apparently
mounting a counter offensive, the American Bar Association
Journal recently published an article pointing out that at least
two dozen lawyers have been canonized. A careful reading of
the list, however, reveals that no member of this Association and,
in fact, no American lawyer has been made a saint. The reason,
I understand, is that none were found qualified by the American
Bar Association Committee on the Judiciary—insufficient trial
experience. The Association of The Bar of the City of New York
refused to endorse any since none had agreed to appear before
their committee. The Queens County Bar Association approved
all last week *nunc pro tunc*.

I am honored to be a member of this court, which is the most efficient circuit in the country. It decides more cases per judge and in a shorter time than any other in the United States. Since I have so recently joined the court, I think I can also appropriately say that its quality is excellent. This is a little surprising since only two of us have ever had any actual experiences as professors of law. The rest, for the most part, were district court judges whose errors of course we are now charged to find. I can tell you in confidence that one of the time-saving devices employed is that all correspondence is addressed to your initials rather than your full name. When you join this court, for intramural purposes you give up your name, rank, and serial number and become a set of initials. HJF, PRH, IRK, WF, WRM, WHM, JLO, and WHT—and always of course in that order. My suggestion that seniority be based on weight rather than the accident of the date of appointment was summarily dismissed. Thus William Hughes Mulligan, Dean and Wilkinson Professor of Law, was suddenly reduced to WHM. This saves a great deal of time supposedly, but it also takes a great deal of time to associate the initials with the name. For example, I sent a message of congratulations to HRM for an opinion written by WRM. For weeks I thought I was getting memos from Dwight Eisenhower only to find out that the author was David Edelstein. It is truly difficult to tell the trees from the forest, or, as we say on our court, to tell the Oakes from the Timbers.

The system would be completely destroyed of course if we had two judges with the same initials. It was a close thing when I went on the bench at about the same time as Walter R. Mansfield and William H. Timbers. We all had the same first initial, two of us had the same middle initial, and two of us had the same last initial. If we had all come out with the same initials, neither of them would have made the bench. One of the first questions that the F.B.I. asks is what is your middle name and was it ever changed? When Judge Wilfred Feinberg was discovered to have no middle name at all, his confirmation was held up for months. My own view is that this system should be dropped and that social security numbers should be employed to replace the initials. In fact, I think they should be tattooed on the forehead of the judge so that at first glance you would know whom you were addressing.

Now that I have revealed these secrets of the bench, I suppose that you are naturally interested in my judicial philosophy. I assure you that I have not found it possible as yet to formulate a total philosophical schema, writing so many bank robbery and drug opinions. However, you may see some initial postulates in my more important decisions. For example, (1) it is no defense in a Christmas Eve bank robbery case in Vermont that one of the defendants was a member of the Christmas Club; (2) a lodger in Connecticut whose personal effects had been seized by an unfriendly and unpaid landlord is the victim of a tort and had not been denied freedom of speech even though his dentures were confiscated; (3) a fire on a luxury liner which ruins the stoves so that the passengers could eat only cold-cuts for the rest of the cruise constitutes a "shipwreck" despite the defense of the ship owner that the bar remained undamaged. In a dictum we indicated that had the bar been destroyed but the stoves remained undamaged, a much stronger case for abandonment of the cruise and even the vessel would have been made out. There are a few other leading decisions which I could call to your attention, but I commend them to your leisure reading at home or, if business is slack, even at the office.

Ladies and gentlemen, every speaker I suppose—particularly a judge of the Circuit Court—is expected to have a serious message. In my view, attendance at dinners in New York and elsewhere has dwindled not because of crime on the streets in Fun City, not because of rubber chicken or irascible waiters, but because we have had too many speakers with serious messages. All serious messages should be reduced to writing and given to the guests as they depart, to be read at one's leisure rather than being absorbed at a table after a dinner such as this. The serious messages which all of my colleagues and I have, are being collected by the West Publishing Company and can be found in the Second Series of the Federal Reporter. In conclusion, I want to thank all of you for your forbearance and your friendship over the years. I cannot claim that the Association was generous in its treatment of me in the earlier days but at least it was fair. I am honored to be here, I am flattered that some of my colleagues took the time to be present, and I sincerely hope to prove worthy of this bench which is distinguished, of course, not only by its members but by the counsel who appear before it.

LAWYERS DIVISION, UNITED JEWISH APPEAL
March 1, 1972

In retrospect I find that the advantages of law teaching over judging are indeed many. In the first place the hours are much better—if a law teacher has a teaching schedule of more than six hours a week, he is ready to file a lawsuit for invasion of his civil liberties. Moreover, his calendar is more liberal than any state or federal court I know, with the possible exception of the northern district of North Dakota. He sits from the middle of September till about the middle of December, recesses until February, and quits in early May. This permits vacations of a month in the winter and almost four months in the summer. I have been sitting regularly since August and will get my winter vacation in May. The law teacher, moreover, specializes in only two courses at the most and has to keep abreast in only those fields. When I taught insurance law I found that my original notes in 1946 were practically the law in 1971. In that field there hasn't been a major decision since the days of Lord Mansfield. I will admit that antitrust law was a different question—but still I could focus on one subject. In my present job I have had to decide what the law of suretyship was in New Jersey; the law of remittitur in Connecticut as well as federal labor law, admiralty, patents, tax, constitutional law, criminal law, administrative law—just to mention a few. The law teacher moreover does have a captive audience—if he has to answer a pertinent question but does not know the answer he has several alternatives:

(1) Rephrase the question
(2) Indicate that the question is silly or impertinent
(3) Answer it with another question
(4) Suggest that we will come to that problem next week
(5) Suggest that the question involves another subject, hopefully one they won't get to in another year.

None of these is available to a trial judge and not even to an appellate judge, although I confess that I am new to the job.

The law teacher doesn't have to worry about a reviewing court or the publication of his classroom views. He can dissect and bisect opinions of all courts with complete aplomb and without fear of reversal. He does have to write law review articles but apparently the only ones who read them are other law professors. While his basic salary is less than that of the trial or appellate judge, he is not precluded but in fact encouraged to supplement it. Foundation grants, opinion letters, state assignments, arbitrations, and even an occasional retention by a law firm are not unknown to the law teacher. I will admit that he does have a problem which judges have not yet encountered: he has to deal with law students. Law students are no longer of the breed of my generation. We worked hard to get a legal education and were there to learn—we were therefore docile, which is a bad word today; however, a certain amount of docility, in my view, is necessary if the education venture is to be successful. Today one wonders if law students come to get an education or to start an argument. After one week in a law school, students become experts on the law school curriculum, the library, the faculty, grades, and the general administration of the school. Some of them at least seem to have the impression that law schools are part of an establishment plot to preclude them from the active representation of clients. While law schools, like the administration of justice, can be improved, one wonders what the credentials of the adolescent law student are to create the change. One theory advanced, of course, is that they are equal members of the community of scholars and in fact the only paying members and hence their views are entitled not only to be aired but to be heeded. Hence we have so-called non-negotiable demands. Thus far I have not seen any brief in which counsel, experienced or not, has argued that the court must accept the proposition, no matter how well settled counsel thinks it is. I think that after the initial retreats on a large scale by educational administrators the pendulum may be swinging back somewhat. Students should be seen and heard, but the faculty of the school and its dean, who are responsible to the trustees, must in the long run accept the responsibility for mature decision. I should also add that the vociferous are as usual a minority, but the volume of sound they generate sometimes makes this difficult to determine. I am, of course, sanguine; this generation—and I have three members in it—has to be good in view of the fine stock which generated it.

Despite all the pleasant aspects of law teaching, I am completely happy that the President with the consent of the Senate saw fit to appoint me to the Second Circuit. It is a court of great ability and character and reputation. It is deserved. The amount of work involved is heavy by any standards. I have done more legal research and written more legal material than I had in years of teaching. While this may be a reflection on me, I can only compare it with my first two or three years of teaching. Since our curriculum constantly changes I am told by older members of the bench that it never gets any easier—in fact the more you know the more difficult it becomes. When I say difficult, I do not mean onerous—I happen to love it and so do my colleagues; if you did not, it would be absolute torture.

I do feel that experience on the trial bench is most helpful to an appellate judge; however, I obviously do not believe it is a sine qua non. An appellate court of nine former trial judges, in my view, would be just as odious as a panel of nine former law teachers. The outstanding jurist on my bench, in my view, is Henry J. Friendly, who was neither. He just happens to know all the law and can write it with clarity and grace. Law teaching gives one an overview of some subjects which is unique and most helpful in deciding specific problems which can be seen in total perspective. I only wish now that I had taught more subjects than Criminal Law, Equity, Corporations, Damages, Insurance, and Antitrust Law.

I can assure you that in this court not only are your briefs read in advance of the argument but preliminary research is done and each judge submits independently after argument a voting memorandum stating his views. That is followed by a conference where if differences are not ironed out, a dissent will follow. I am honored to be on this court but I do not think any new judge will make a particularly major contribution until he has had his judicial feet dampened by a couple of years of experience. His major accomplishment is to avoid serious error. I can say that no decision of mine has yet been reversed or even modified—the fact that none has yet reached the Supreme Court is really not relevant. I have one case in which both sides have sought reargument which is a good indication of even-handed justice.

Lawyers, gentlemen, have always been subject to criticism—early in my speechmaking career I decided to go through anthologies, thesauri, and other sources to discover something flattering to say about them. I find that in every culture, in every language, the references are uniformally critical and at times almost blasphemous. I am delighted to find therefore that a group of lawyers is engaged in a charitable and philanthropic enterprise. This is no news to me, but apparently the public feels that lawyers are concerned only with their private aggrandizement. The organized bar has done little to correct the image. Although I have never done anything for the U.J.A., or even the I.R.A., I have worked for Catholic Charities and the Fordham Law School. While I know people consider it offensive to say that some of my best friends are Jewish, may I be so brash as to say that some of my best donors were Jewish.

I thank you for inviting me. No Irishman can ever turn down an invitation to cocktails, and the fact that lawyers are sponsoring it for a good cause made the offer irrevocable and non-negotiable.

ANNUAL DINNER
OF THE SOCIETY OF
THE FRIENDLY SONS
OF SAINT PATRICK
IN THE CITY OF NEW YORK
March 17, 1972

May it please Your Eminence Cardinal Cooke, and Your Excellencies the Bishops, President Morgan, Your Excellencies Vice President Agnew and Governor Rockefeller, Senator Buckley, Lieutenant Governor Wilson, distinguished guests, clerical and lay, fellow Friendly Sons of Saint Patrick, and friends of the Friendly Sons:

I am honored indeed to be in such distinguished company and to be invited to respond to the toast "The Day We Celebrate." Toasting reminds me of an Irish friend who, when asked that most welcome question "Will you have another drink?" responded, "I answered that question in the negative only once—and that time I misunderstood the question." I thought it might be appropriate, on this evening particularly, to comment on some Irish achievements and characteristics not generally appreciated or in fact even known.

A few years ago I when I was in Ireland, I visited the ancient port city of Galway where I was assured by a local that Christopher Columbus had stopped there to bring on board an Irish navigator who actually guided him to the New World. A few months ago I was in the company of the Chief Judge of the Supreme Court of Ireland, a typically urbane, scholarly, and intellectual Irishman not given to the easy acceptance of leprechauns or unfounded legends. I asked him about the story of the Irish navigator and I was frankly surprised when instead of debunking it, he responded, "Oh yes, the story is well authenticated. The man's name was Lynch." With all due respect, I could not accept the story; there was no record that Columbus ever made any such diversion to Galway, pleasant though it might be. It seemed more logical to me that Lynch, great sailor that he must have been, had sailed from Ireland to Portugal and was the navigator from the start. Becoming more interested, I studied the celebrated work on the subject, Samuel Eliot Morison's *Admiral of the Ocean Sea*, and I discovered to my dismay that Lynch's name does not appear on the list of the crew of any of the three vessels. This in turn led me to a somewhat spectacular discovery which I must share with you tonight in the privacy of this room. Morison's book gives a physical description of Columbus which was provided by his own contemporaries; I quote pages 40–41: "He was more than middling tall, aquiline nose, blue eyes, complexion light and tending to bright red, beard and hair red. When he was angry he would exclaim 'May God take you'. In matter of religion he was so strict that for fasting and saying all the canonical offices he might have been taken for a member of a religious order." Gentlemen, in all honesty and frankness, how many religious, blue-eyed, red-faced, red-haired Italians have you met in your life? Friendly Sons and friends, not only am I am suggesting but I think the facts clearly establish that in reality Columbus was Lynch, or Lynch was Columbus, whichever way you want it. There is even further evidence: Morison, who claims that Columbus was born in Genoa, admits that Columbus could not read or write Italian; neither could Lynch. Morison—and we, of course, could expect no help from Samuel Eliot Morison—further states that Columbus spoke Spanish with a Portuguese accent. Actually, of course, it was Irish he spoke, and isn't it a mark of Lynch's great leadership and seamanship that he could make that Mediterranean crew understand his orders even though they were given in Gaelic. Gentlemen, we have convicted men of serious crimes in the federal court on less evidence than we have here and my court has affirmed them. Lest our Italian friends take offense, I assure them that I intend no disrespect at all and on October 12th I will attend the annual Lynch Day Parade, at Lynch Circle, and watch with pride as the Knights of Lynch pass by.

I should further point out as proof of my devotion to Italy that I studied Italian in high school and actually won the first prize for the highest mark in the subject for two years. In fact, I elected to take Italian—that is, in the form that the elective systems operated at Cathedral College forty years ago. The administration of that minor seminary made the election for the students, thus eliminating any decision-making trauma on their part and at the same time ensuring that the French, German, and Italian classes were all the same size. A classmate of mine in Italian class at Cathedral was another Bronx Irishman, Joe Cooke, who kept bragging about his younger brother Terry, who was two years behind us. I was introduced to him one day on the playing field of our campus, the sidewalk on Madison Avenue and 52nd Street. It was freely predicted then that Terence Cooke would go far, but he really didn't—after forty years he's still where I met him, on Madison Avenue, one block south. Since the administration of Cathedral had assigned me to study Italian, my mother thought that this was a "sure" sign that I would be assigned to Rome. Apprehensive at the prospect of becoming the first American pope, I left Cathedral and headed for Fordham, which, at the time, was a Roman Catholic College in The Bronx, a few blocks east of Loew's Paradise. I was very disappointed to find that Fordham did not teach Italian although we were only a tomato's throw away from Arthur Avenue, which then had a larger Italian population than the city of Pisa. Neither did it teach Irish—only 98 percent of the student body at the time was Irish and Italian, and I guess the Jesuits were afraid of offending minority groups. I should point out, however, that this was the year 1 B.G. (before Gannon). Since Fordham could not provide my beloved Italian, I elected instead two more years of Greek on top of the three years I already had at Cathedral. In fact, I had so much Greek that I spoke Italian with a Greek accent—however, unlike Lynch, I could never make the Italians understand me. I must observe that many Irish American boys of my generation were required to take Greek in Catholic high school, but I never heard of a Greek-American youth who was ever forced, or who even elected, to study Gaelic. This is a rather harsh comment, I admit, especially if by some remote chance there are any Greek Americans within the sound of my voice, but I think, in fairness, it must be made.

Another indication of my love of Italy is the fact that my son Steve is now studying at Loyola University in Rome. Steve left the warmth of his coed dorm at Georgetown to take his junior year abroad. There is a precedent for the grand tour in my family. In my junior year at Fordham my father sent me to Palisades Park one Saturday afternoon. At my request, Steve is searching in Italy for a tall, blue-eyed, redhead who can't read or write Italian, and he has found one—the Rev. Vincent O'Keefe of Jersey City, former President of Fordham and now the Deputy

Black Pope. Steve told me that it was important for him to go to Rome since he wanted to study Chaucer. I did not immediately get the connection; Shelley, Keats, or Byron I could understand, but Chaucer—no. However, when I got a letter from Steve telling me that he was celebrating Mardi Gras at Monaco and Nice, I realized that he was undoubtedly much brighter than I had thought. My only foreign travel since ascending the bench has been an occasional walk through Chinatown.

Of course, Mr. Vice President, it is only logical and reasonable for us to assume that the great Irish seaman who visited Italy, and for all I know may have discovered it, undoubtedly took the Greek Island tour. We now know that it was their custom to adopt the names of the natives. My only regret is that my work on the court has precluded me from establishing the true identity of Plato, Socrates, and Aristotle. It is interesting to note, however, that Socrates died after drinking too much hemlock, which affords us some small indication that his origins were in some colder clime.

One need not go further than the annals of this Association to discover that one of our founding members in 1784 bore the name Hercules Mulligan, an unsung American hero and George Washington's personal spy. Mulligan had a tailoring establishment on Pearl Street catering to British officers during the Revolution. He not only measured the British but extracted secret information from them. When this got out later, it, of course, ruined the tailoring business for the Irish here, and to this day you won't find an Irish tailor in New York. Two or three nights a week Hercules would row across the Hudson and give a personal report to George Washington. Despite all his travel back and forth across the Hudson, when they finally built a bridge across the river, wasn't it ironical that it was named after George Washington instead of Mulligan who had really earned it? Incidentally, Mulligan, or whatever is left of him, is now reposing in the unconsecrated ground of St. Paul's Churchyard; hence he is known to us as Hercules the Heretic. While it is too late now, I suppose, to rename the Washington Bridge, or even one level thereof, there are other bigger and newer bridges around. I intend to take the time to investigate the true identity of one Mr. Giovanni Verrazano. In any event, my new book, *The Real Verrazano, or, It's a Long Way from Tipperary*, will appear this summer, published of course by McGraw-Hill. The research is being done by Chief Red Fox.

Gentlemen, very few of us here tonight were born in Ireland. As a matter of fact, the only one I know is Jack Mulcahy who was born there and came here, he says, with a patch on his pants— which he can now afford to have rewoven. Actually, most of us Friendly Sons are the sons and grandsons and the great-grandsons of Irish immigrants. Despite all the claims of royal Irish antecedents and the proud display of coats of arms, they came here as the impoverished victims of oppression or hunger. Whatever thirst they had, we have inherited with a vengeance. My friend O'Dalaigh, the Chief Judge of Ireland, blames the thirst on the cold climate of Ireland. It must have been awfully cold in those days—the chill lingers on through generations of Irish Americans in Florida, California, and the great Southwest. Whatever virtues we have we owe to our Irish forebears. I don't know much about my paternal antecedents except that my grandfather, Michael Mulligan, was the son of Catherine Hughes, a first cousin of John Hughes, our first archbishop. I do have a family Bible which relates that her brother, who was bashful and shy, left the farm and set forth on his own for America. His handwritten message in the Hughes Bible reads: "Good Bye, sister Kate, I am sick of farming, and being mechanically inclined, I am taking the toolkit and heading for Texas. Affectionately, your brother Howard." This message has been authenticated by a handwriting expert who says that it unquestionably is authentic—if not, he says, it is an exquisite forgery.

On my mother's side, my grandmother, Anne Scriven, and her husband, John Donahue, left the hills of Macroom in the County of Cork and settled down on a farm, of all places, in Ulster County, New York. My grandmother came with little more than a shawl and a Sacred Heart badge. You can still buy shawls. She did give birth to twelve children, but the strain of bearing the dozen took its toll and my grandfather died when my mother was only eight years old, the youngest of the twelve. If the Irish had known about birth control, it would have been most difficult for me to make this appearance this evening. My mother, at 82, is the sole survivor of that family and would have liked to be here tonight except that she had to go to confession.

Gentlemen, although few of us were born in Ireland, most of us were all reared in a distinctly Irish tradition—it was marked by a fierce devotion to our faith. It was a demanding faith of fast and sacrifice and self-discipline. The tougher it was to follow, the easier it was for the Irish to pass it down to their children. Now that its strictures have been somewhat relaxed, it will be so much more difficult to give and bequeath or even to inherit. But we will meet the challenge. We also inherited from our Irish forebears a fierce love of country—in peace or in war; particularly perhaps in war, we contributed much more than our share. But why shouldn't we love America—after all, we discovered it! God bless!

LADIES OF CHARITY
September 30, 1972

Madame Chairlady, Your Excellency Bishop Hurd, Madame President, reverend clergy, Sisters, Ladies of Charity, and your guests, fellow members of the Friendly Sons—

I am pleased and flattered to be invited to speak on the occasion of the Annual Communion Breakfast of the Ladies of Charity. This is the first communion breakfast I have addressed in at least ten years. As a young law professor I was on the communion breakfast circuit with a vengeance. I have spent more time in school cellars on parish basketball courts speaking to Holy Name Societies than most basketball players. In the course of this activity, I have been fed as much powdered eggs, stale rolls, and cold coffee as a lifer in a State prison. I finally gave up after one experience which convinced me that my true role was after-dinner and not after-breakfast speaking. I was invited to speak at a communion breakfast in The Bronx. I had told the president of that Holy Name Society that I lived in Westchester, did not drive, and would need transportation to the church. Promptly at 7:30 on that Sunday morning my transportation arrived—it was the pick-up truck of the parish undertaker, a mini hearse, which conveyed me to Mass. Thankfully I was permitted to sit in front with the driver. I had been advised that I was to be the principal speaker. So apparently were two other fellows including a high school baseball coach who spoke for one hour on the subject of amateur baseball—a subject in which he was apparently well versed but which had a singular lack of appeal for me and the audience. The second speaker was a local politician whose oratory was so flamboyant that I vowed to send his opponent a contribution. At about 1 P.M., I was finally presented to an audience that not only was exhausted but was anxious to escape to a local pub to watch a pro football game with which I was now unsuccessfully competing. At about 2:00 in the afternoon, I was returned to my home still in the front seat in the same vehicle which was parked outside while the chauffeur, who, of course, was dressed in a black suit and a black tie, had a scotch and watched the remainder of the game with me in the den. Although I live on a quiet street where neighbors normally mind their own business, the presence of such a vehicle was bound to cause comment. My wife was later reduced to telling the neighbors that although I had been picked up in the morning the undertaker concluded that I was not yet ready and therefore I was rejected and returned. God knows what they really believed. A sobering reflection is that the next time I make use of such a conveyance I will not be in the front seat and in no position to make complaints.

From that point on I accepted only evening engagements which I found to be much more attractive. The food was better and the audience much more receptive. After pre-prandial cocktails and scotch with the steak, I found that mildly humorous comments which never titillated the Catholic War Veterans at nine o'clock in the morning were greeted with thunderous applause and gales of laughter in the evening. In such fashion I gained a small reputation as a humorist. I even found that I could persuade reasonable men that Columbus was really an Irishman named Lynch. Hence, I gave up matinees and concentrated on evening performances.

This breakfast is the only exception I've made and, of course, I could not resist it. For one thing, I could expect a decent meal without cigar smoke. Another factor is that this is one of the few times I have been asked to address an audience composed primarily of newly liberated women. A third reason is that it provides an opportunity to really hear the Friendly Sons Glee Club. While they don't sing any louder in the morning, at the annual banquet they have to face the competition of my fellow Friendly Sons which brings to the fore for some reason the strident musical and oratorical talents of the erstwhile mute and inglorious members and guests. Finally, of course, the cause of Catholic Charities of this Archdiocese has always been close to my heart—now more than ever since right after my daughter's wedding next month, I intend to apply for admission to the Mary Manning Walsh Home. Law professors and judges are not able to contribute to charity with any great degree of monetary munificence but they can afford service. About the only thing I have been able to acquire since going on the bench has been this mustache which has had mixed reviews except for my bride, who doesn't approve. I thank the committee for inviting her this morning but she is attending a competing event—a shower for my daughter. The audience there will not be as large as here but I hope they are at least as charitable. I never realized the pageantry which now accompanies the pre-nuptial festivities. My own suggestions have not been well received. For example. although the wedding is in October, I thought the reception should be held on Election Day. Although the club might not be permitted to serve booze, people would certainly be free to bring their own.

I normally like to avoid serious messages, either after brunch or after dinner. In my view, it is not crime in the streets, rubber chicken, or unfriendly waiters which have killed or seriously injured the banquet business in New York, but rather after-dinner speakers with serious messages which could more effectively have been printed and distributed to the audience to be read under more salubrious conditions. My serious messages are found in my judicial opinions and, frankly, there has been no great demand for reprints.

There is another problem which federal judges have as speakers—their choice of topics is severely circumscribed by the Canon of Ethics. Therefore, although this is an election year, whatever interesting views I might have on national or even local issues are out of bounds. Under the Canon of Ethics, I cannot take any position with respect to an issue which is likely to come before the federal courts.

In my brief judicial career, I have found that federal judges are called upon to judge a wide variety of topics that I hadn't even thought were justiciable. In one recent case, a plaintiff sued the Secretary of Defense, Melvin Laird, plus the United States Army and Air Force because he claimed they had damaged his teeth and his jaw. The injury was accomplished, according to the complaint, when Laird inserted the plaintiff's head into Laird's mouth. While we have all heard of people in public life putting their foot in their mouth, we had no precedent for their putting other people's heads in their mouth. Despite this lack of precedent, we dismissed the appeal, and the plaintiff has now joined me and two colleagues as defendants in his appeal to the Supreme Court. Most of today's controversial issues are therefore off limits for me. It was therefore with some trepidation that I learned that your committee had not only selected me as your speaker but had also selected the topic—"Our Christian Responsibilities." My first reaction to this was to simply say to you this morning—"Dear Ladies, your Christian responsibilities are indeed heavy, but I am sure that with the help of God you will be able to discharge them with your customary charm and grace." While this might take care of your responsibilities, it cannot dispose of mine. Actually, it is refreshing and intriguing that somebody today is speaking about responsibility. Our entire framework of law, of course, depends upon the recognition that every right denotes a corresponding duty to respect the rights of our fellows. However, most people, not only in litigation, but in ordinary social intercourse, think only of their rights and tend to slough off their obligations.

Any federal judge at the trial or appellate level cannot help but be utterly shocked at the volume, the breadth, and the depth of the narcotics epidemic which is scourging the area in which we live and work. Drug addiction, which is practically incurable, is spreading like a cancer. Not only does it destroy the intellect and the will of the addict, it spawns the maimings and the murders of the innocent who are assaulted for money to support the appetite of the addict which constantly becomes more voracious. It drives women to the streets, and venereal disease is at an all-time peak. Profits from drug traffic are so enormous that the corruption of law enforcement agents has become a public scandal. It is the most hideous and alarming phenomenon of our time and, as a judge who has experienced at least some of its effects firsthand, I must share with you very briefly some observations which relate to the question of responsibility.

Today, more than ever, large segments of our population are properly concerned with prejudice, pollution, prison conditions, and consumer protection. Law students and others, including women's groups, are deeply concerned with the pollution of our rivers and streams which is killing the fish and destroying marine vegetation. They are properly concerned about the quality of the air and the mercury in the tuna. Yet those who are most concerned about the noise and the fumes seem to me to display an appalling apathy to the popping of pills and the injection of drugs which have such an immediate impact on the person and the social environment. People march and picket over impurities in the air and the water but show an astonishing indifference to the deliberate infusion of poison into the human bloodstream. So-called soft drugs and pills are an acceptable life pattern, not only for students on college campuses and in high schools, but tragically for many whom we have entrusted with their education. While most pot smokers may not go on to heroin, it is also true that most heroin addicts started with pot. Those few who have conquered their addiction and those who deal immediately with the problem will attest that the whole drug scene typically compels association with heroin users who urge experimentation either to support their own habit or simply to have company. There is a physical and psychological attraction so that the risk of the ultimate drug and the fatal dosage is real and fraught with such peril that I cannot understand any attitude of toleration or acceptance of the prelude. The position that people have a right to indulge their own appetites not only is pathetically fallacious, but totally overlooks the potential and actual menace to the innocent citizen who is murdered for his wallet. The claim that our generation uses alcohol as a lubricant or soporific and therefore this new generation is entitled to drugs is equally illogical. No one condones alcoholism or drunken driving for one thing, but, as bad as the abuse might be, it cannot be equated with the evil of drugs. No one, at least to my knowledge, has ever killed or assaulted to support a martini habit.

Another unfortunate attitude on the part of many in our society is a total distrust of law enforcement agencies and agents. The police are vilified, and law and order are looked upon by some as a conspiracy of the establishment to suppress individual liberties. We learned a long time ago to distinguish between liberty and license and this is what we are talking about. While Nader and others are properly attracting those who wish to war on corporate malefactors who befoul the environment and cheat the public, I only wish they would show the same enthusiasm in cooperating with those who are fighting the traffic in drugs. This attitude is particularly disturbing when we realize that the principal victims of addiction, over-dosage, and concomitant crime are not the establishment but the disadvantaged ghetto inhabitants already victimized by other social blights. Until we can mount total public support and understanding, including the private agencies, the battle will continue to be lost. This, I feel, is a responsibility for all of us as citizens and as Christians.

Our responsibility as Christians and American citizens to our neighbor is not simply to respect his rights but to administer to his needs when he is deprived. For the Christian, love of God is expressed in part by love for His creatures, our fellow man. I do not have to tell this audience what Catholic Charities means to those who are sick or disabled, afflicted and addicted, old and unwanted. I cannot think of any worthier cause than Catholic Charities; nor can I think of any more meaningful title than Lady of Charity—and that is really why I ventured to come here today to salute you ladies of charity.

Thank you.

FEDERATION OF JEWISH PHILANTHROPIES
December 11, 1972

Mr. Chairman, members of the Federation and your guests, and my brothers Gurfein and Pollack:

I imagine Murray Gurfein's and Milton Pollack's mothers would be surprised to learn that they have a brother named Mulligan. Another brother of mine, Irving Kaufman, made the comment the other day that he found it quite amusing that a Mulligan should be addressing the Federation of Jewish Philanthropies. I don't think it is quite as interesting as the fact that not only are the soon-to-be Chief Judge Kaufman, and the Chief Judge of the Southern District, David Edelstein, both graduates of Fordham Law School but both received all their undergraduate education at Fordham College, a Jesuit institution. Jesuit education has, of course, changed considerably. My son, Steve, who is currently a senior at Georgetown, did not have a single Jesuit teacher in the first three years. He did have a course on religion which was taught by a rabbi. Although the rabbi gave Steve a C, he made up for it by throwing a St. Patrick's Day party for the class.

Actually, the Irish and the Jews have much in common—both have been the victims of oppression and bigotry. The only difference is that when the Irish run out of oppressors, they turn upon each other.

Another thing we share is a sense of humor. I saw a good example of this before I went on the bench. At that time I was acting as an arbiter in an international dispute, and one of the parties was represented by an attorney named Max Abrahamsen. Max is a Dublin lawyer who was born and raised in Ireland and is a graduate of Trinity College. He has a delightful brogue, and the only character defect he has that I am aware of is a disinclination to drink hard liquor. After some meetings abroad we met in New York to conduct the hearings. I asked Max if his wife was with him—"No," he answered. "She has a deathly fear of flying." He said, "You know, I have a brother, a psychiatrist in Dublin, and I asked him to talk to her to see if he could do any good." "Did it work?" said I. "No" said he—"In fact, when I talked to my brother about it, he said 'You know, Max, I will have to give it a lot of thought before I go up in one of those damned things again.'"

Actually, of course, I feel perfectly at home with this audience. After all, I was born and raised in The Bronx and, while I did not live on the Grand Concourse, I was only a few blocks east. I seldom ventured on the Grand Concourse, but there were rumors in my neighborhood that some of the apartment buildings actually had elevators. Nobody really believed that, but it was an interesting possibility to speculate on. After all, I knew kids who used to ride on the dumbwaiter so it was not unimaginable that buildings had more reasonable means of vertical ascent, as some of my brothers would characterize the conveyance. In The Bronx in the twenties and thirties, we had a mixed cultural environment—one was either Irish or Jewish. Although Edgar Allan Poe allegedly lived there at one time, he apparently moved out when the Jerome Avenue subway was built and the neighborhood began to change. I never met a live admitted Protestant in The Bronx until I was 15. In those days the gathering place of my gang was, of course, the corner candy store, which was invariably operated by a Jewish family. I grew up not on chicken soup but on a combination of malted milks and orange ice. At an early age I learned the distinction between a candy store and an ice cream parlor. Ice cream parlors never sold newspapers and were always run by Germans. Italians operated barber shops and shoe repair stores. The Irish were either cops or clerks in the A&P, and the Jews, in addition to candy stores, operated apparel stores. In those days, The Bronx had an ordered and structured society that rivaled the medieval guilds. Social intercourse among ethnic groups was never of major proportions, but it was rarely antagonistic and, for the most part, warm and cordial. My mother did chase the neighborhood bully, Booby Schwartz, for several blocks one day, but not because he was Jewish but only because he had transplanted his bubble gum from his mouth to my then golden hair. I never went to schul, of course, but I did attend a reasonable facsimile thereof, P.S. 46. Incidentally, I resent, very frankly, the generally accepted belief that stickball was played only by Jewish boys. They apparently all became novelists and grew lyrical about the game in middle age. I not only played stickball and lied to the police about the location of sawed-off broomsticks, I also played chinese handball, punch ball, box ball, and points. If these need translation, I doubt that you grew up in New York.

Having, hopefully, established my credentials, I imagine that I was invited here because of our mutual interest in the law and my rather recent and abrupt elevation to the Circuit Court from the comparative obscurity, if not the safety, of a law school deanship at Fordham. If you want to know about the reactions of a new judge to life on the Second Circuit Court of Appeals, I commend to you reading Chief Judge Friendly's article on the subject in 71 Yale L.J. 218 (1961).

Actually, it has been my experience that judging is not at all that difficult; what takes the time and effort is writing the opinions. As lawyers, of course, we make it particularly difficult for ourselves by the custom of documenting by footnote almost everything we say—something which never bothers newspaper columnists or even historians. We have made it a fetish. In my maiden year on the bench, I was assigned quite a few bank robbery cases—so many, in fact, that I got to know quite a bit about the business and think it would be an interesting hobby on retirement. In most cases the facts are not complicated and neither is the law, and my colleagues figured, I guess, that I could handle both without too much difficulty. However, they did take a long time to write because of the footnotes. I might start out by saying—"On December 24th, 1970, four men entered the Chase Manhattan Bank on Madison Avenue and 56th Street at three P.M. armed with shotguns." This would require at least two footnotes—to wit: The Chase Manhattan Bank was organized under the Banking Law of New York in 1870, see McKinney's Pocket Parts 1871. Second: Madison Avenue runs north and south in the Borough of Manhattan, County of New York, City and State of New York, between Fifth and Park, and so on.

After Shepherdizing all the cases, plus McKinney's and the City Atlas, the next step is to circulate your proposed opinion to the other two members of the panel. This is not as much fun as you might think. You are liable to get from some brother the following suggestions: "I concur in your opinion with the following comments. After 'three P.M.,' insert 'Eastern Standard Time.' In your footnote on Madison Avenue, insert 'except south of 42nd Street where it lies between Vanderbilt and Fifth Avenue.' Change four men to three men and a juvenile delinquent," and so on.

Another possibility is the simple "I concur in the result."

Freely translated, this means "You reached the right result but it must have been by accident." Another rather disastrous eventuality is that one of your brothers will dissent, saying something like this: "I dissent from the learned opinion of my distinguished colleague who has here exhibited a total disregard of the Constitution of the United States which presumably he has heard of but which obviously he has never read. In my view, the defendant was denied the effective aid of counsel since the record does not at all indicate that his assigned attorney attended Harvard or even the Yale Law School."

The worst disaster, of course, is that the opinion you have been assigned to write is so unpersuasive that it becomes itself a dissenting opinion. This has not happened to me yet, but I have reason to believe that this week may see the end of the streak.

Submitting my first opinion to Chief Judge Henry Friendly was of course a particularly frightening experience for me as a new judge. Even though I had taught law for twenty-five years, nothing I ever taught seemed to arise in the cases. I felt like a high school student submitting a math paper to Einstein. Actually, of course, I found that he was most gracious and patient and even encouraging, so much so that I was bold enough to direct my first dissent in part to one of his masterful opinions. I think I was partially motivated by a spirit of bravado. Although everyone knows that Chief Judge Friendly is an outstanding scholar and writer, few people realize that he is also an excellent administrator. For example, he has not assigned me to sit on a panel with him during the entire '72 term. Although I realize there are other possible inferences, it is quite obvious to me that he desires to spread the strength of the bench rather than concentrate it in such a devastating fashion in one panel. At least that's the way I look at it.

I have often been asked why I don't try to inject a little more humor into my opinions. There are several reasons. In the first place, my colleagues would have to approve not only my law but my jokes. In the second place, my law clerks are seriously afraid that it might bring discredit to me as well as disrepute to the old Law School. Some may think that scholarship and humor are incompatible, but I do not think lawyers are that pompous or unsophisticated. Actually, last year I did have a bank robbery which occurred on December 24th. The first draft of my opinion started this way: "'Twas the night before Christmas when a man in a ski mask and a bag entered the Burlington Bank. He was not Santa Claus and was not even a member of the Christmas

Club. In fact, he came not to make a deposit but a withdrawal. Since he maintained no account at the bank, this led to his eventual indictment and conviction." My law clerks disapproved this just as they had one of my dissents: "I dissent for the reasons given by the majority": and my other: "I concur with great hesitation." A third reason, of course, is that the losing attorney who is usually the only one who ever reads the opinion, and who is annoyed enough by an adverse verdict, becomes quite incensed if you show any levity.

For example, last year I had an admiralty case and the last paragraph of the opinion read: "Matters involving impossibility or impracticability of performance of contract are concededly vexing and difficult. One is even urged on the allocation of such risks to pray for the 'wisdom of Solomon' citing Corbin on Contracts." I then said "On the basis of all of the facts, the pertinent authority, and a further belief in the efficacy of prayer, we affirm." The following week I received a letter, signed by one Solomon King, which said "If you really believed in and had prayed, you would have reversed." (You may be pleased to know that the Solomon King routine did not fool me, at least not after my law clerks had checked Martindale–Hubbell.) I dictated a reply which was never mailed. It simply said "Your letter was much better written than your brief."

After all the stress and strain of writing the opinion and obtaining the concurrence of your colleagues, the new judge is somewhat shocked to find that his magnum opus is greeted by a thunderous silence. The only one who reads it is the attorney who lost on appeal and very often, instead of accepting defeat in a gentlemanly fashion, he has the audacity to ask for reargument or to petition for a writ of certiorari. This product of all of your energy and ability which has caused sleepless nights and long days of labor is interned in the graveyard of the West Publishing Company with suitable headnotes on the headstone. It is disinterred only when some law student or some lawyer wants a second viewing—half of those who look proclaim, "he knew not whereof he spoke" or "what the poor fool was trying in his inarticulate way to say, was . . ." The best that can happen is that you will be cited with approval in another opinion by another judge and will be re-interred in another plot in a new section of the cemetery—possibly, Fed Third.

Of course, the final reason, particularly in a criminal case, is that a defendant, whose conviction and sentence for five to ten years is being affirmed, will hardly appreciate the humor.

Actually, I find the work in the court constantly challenging and always fascinating. If one did not, it would be a most painful method of earning a living. All that I have acquired since coming on the bench are humility, a mustache, and aggravated insomnia. While I can shave off the mustache, the humility and the insomnia linger on.

I want to thank you for giving me the opportunity to speak to you this evening. I congratulate you not only on your devotion to our profession, but particularly your devotion to private charity. All of the government subsidy in the world cannot eliminate the misery, pain, and suffering of many of our fellow human beings. Not only do we need the private charity, but it is really more blessed to give than to receive.

I thank you.

PATENT LAW ASSOCIATION DINNER
March 30, 1973

It is indeed an honor to be invited to speak to this distinguished association. I am particularly gratified that after my mere year and a half on the bench the leaders of the Patent Bar have so quickly recognized my interest in and true affection for this esoteric branch of the law. I am not ashamed to confess that had I not embarked on the study of law I was seriously considering a career as an inventor. This came about after I had received my first erector set from Santa Claus. After several months of hard work, the use of diagrams plus assistance from my father, I was able to make a box. Several years and several sets later, I was able to put wheels under the box and make a wagon. In fact, it was a five-wheel wagon which was the result of a flash of genius plus the presence of five wheels that came with the set.

In view of this experience, Mr. Justice Frankfurter's comment in *Marconi v. United States*, 320 U.S. 60, that the training of Anglo-American judges ill fits them to discharge the duties cast upon them by patent legislation has proven to be unsound.

At the same comparative age as I was playing with my erector set, Chief Judge Friendly was translating Kent's *Commentaries* into Latin and my brother Timbers was preparing the first draft of his opinion in *Bangor Punta* which was filed last week and can be simply cited as 473 F.2d and 474 F.2d.

Not finding a market for my five-wheel wagon, which for some reason was found to suffer the fatal defect of obviousness, I decided upon a career in the law, which is why I am here with you this evening instead of working in my laboratory

In view of the presence here of women, as well as some of my fellow judges who are not so well versed as you and I in the intricacies of patent law, I thought it might be more suitable to discuss a more general topic, to wit, the writing of judicial opinions. I grant that I do suffer the disability of having read more opinions than I have written and I am advised by experienced lawyers that the longer I am on the bench this will balance out and eventually I will be fully qualified, having written more opinions than I have read.

The writing of judicial opinions necessarily begins with legal research and normally a good place to start is with the examination of the briefs which have been filed by counsel—hopefully, some reasonable time before the argument. Unfortunately, this cannot be the end of the search—sometimes advocacy overcomes scholarship and we do find that in many cases both sides use the same authority to reach opposite conclusions, and sometimes a close reading of the case will support even a third interpretation which coincides with your own concept of what the law should be. Sometimes, indeed, also there is no authority at all and one must resort to reason, a somewhat risky and dangerous alternative. For example, I recently was faced with an intriguing and novel fact pattern arising in the sophisticated and busy Second Circuit. The plaintiff *pro se* alleged that one Melvin Laird, then the Secretary of Defense, had in some way unknown to the plaintiff succeeded in putting his (Laird's) head into the plaintiff's mouth causing severe injury to plaintiff's teeth and gums. Although the Nixon Cabinet has since been accused of many trespasses, this was the first occasion as far as my law clerks could discover that any cabinet member had been accused of putting his head into the mouth of any ordinary citizen. The pleadings did not indicate whether the plaintiff was a Democrat or a Republican, which might have been helpful if intent were to be an element of this tort. We had all heard of unofficial reports of cabinet members of various administrations putting their foot in their mouths, but, after a conference, we found the cases quite distinguishable. We also found cases of animal trainers or visitors to the zoo who had playfully put their heads into the mouths of lions and tigers but, oddly enough, no case of a suit brought by a lion or even his guardian for injury to the molars. On the other hand, we did find suits brought by lion-tamers or, more properly, next-of-kin seeking damages against negligent or deliberate lion tort feasors. I only cite this as typical of the perplexing questions of first impression brought into our court. We affirmed the dismissal of the complaint here without an opinion. I wanted to write on this subject, but my colleagues persuaded me not to lest we encourage this disgusting practice which might spread even to lesser federal or even state officials.

After one researches the law, one begins the lonesome and laborious task of writing the opinion. The first problem, of course, is that after you finish your draft, you must first circulate it among the panel members who sit with you. My colleagues on the bench have been unusually kind and forbearing to the neophyte. I must admit, however, that I was particularly apprehensive in surrendering my first draft opinion to the scrutiny of Chief Judge Henry Friendly. He will be retiring shortly and all that I am permitted to say on that subject is that I have been assured that the next Chief Judge of the Court of Appeals for the Second Circuit will be a graduate of Fordham Law School. Since there are only two Fordham alumni on this bench—Judge Irving Kaufman and myself—I consider that my chances are roughly 50-50.

I understand that members of the bar are now being sent a questionnaire requesting their reactions as to whether or not judges are writing opinions which are too long or are writing opinions which should never be published. There is some belief that lawyers are being forced to read too many opinions or, more accurately, perhaps they are running out of shelving space for the Reporters. The suggestion that it is a hardship for lawyers to read cases does not strike me as a cause for real concern. That is our business and it can be performed on the back porch, in the bathtub, or on a commuter train. Having spent the major portion of my adult life as a law teacher and therefore forced not only to read cases but hopefully to understand the message, I am somewhat annoyed by the coincidence that The Bar Association of the City of New York should become concerned with opinion writing only upon my entry into the profession. As litigation and appellate practice have grown, so too must opinion writing. Litigation is more complicated, just as life is, and opinions on trover for a horse no longer command attention. I have no sympathy at all for the position that lawyers have to spend too much time reading opinions—I think it is a bogus and a sham. We have become a profession of specialists, whether we like it or not. Anyone who reads the Keynote Digest in the advance sheets can easily reduce or eliminate the reading of opinions in which he has no interest. Moreover, as we all know, there are more and more services providing bulletins and law letters for specialists calling attention to and digesting cases which can be read at one's leisure. With respect to the problem of shelving space, I think law firms have become aware of the fact that the first series of the Federal Reporter, as well as the first series of the New York Supplement, can be easily removed from an office and obtained in a law school or Bar Association library. I should also point out that gifts to the law school libraries not only are an exercise of charity but also result in tax deductions.

I do not however suggest anything as drastic as that practice of the great Trinity College in Dublin which I visited several times. The dean of the law school at Trinity advised me that the annual reports consist of one volume per year. He told me in 1966 that he visited the library to read an opinion in the 1964 Irish Reporter only to be told by the librarian that they had received the 1965 Reports and naturally discarded the 1964 volume it replaced. Someone entrusted with the custody of the Book of Kells is hardly concerned with the transitory advice of mortal men on or off the bench.

I object most vigorously to the suggestion, apparently seriously made, that an appellate court such as the Second Circuit, prepare a private opinion to be circulated only among the parties, never to be published and with the parties and the bar admonished that it shall not even be cited. If it is necessary to write an opinion at all in an appellate court, it must in my view be published for the scrutiny of the bar as well as that of the parties. When the Law Revision Commission of the State of New York was conducting hearings throughout the State on the subject of a proposed Administrative Procedure Act, as a member I was particularly impressed with the vehemence of lawyers throughout the State directed at those agencies which made unpublished rulings known ultimately only to the agency or a small coterie of practitioner specialists. The concept of an appellate court directing counsel never to cite a decision ultimately resolving a justiciable controversy not only is repulsive to me but in fact would be unenforceable. In short, I am of the opinion that the fear here is spurious.

While I have no idea what the poll will indicate, I am always interested in knowing what percentage of those circulated bothered to answer. If there is a significant degree of abstention, I would conclude that the question has not reached a point of major concern to the bar generally.

I am delighted again to be with you and to have this opportunity to speak. I find it much more enjoyable than writing opinions which are ultimately destined for that large but well-tended graveyard maintained by the West Publishing Company with suitable keynotes marking the place of interment.

This is, of course, a much longer subject than I have had time to develop tonight, but it has occurred to me that perhaps on occasions such as this some serious note should be injected to spoil an otherwise pleasant evening. In any event, all the views expressed here tonight, none of which are earthshaking, of course, express only my opinion and should not in any event be attributed to the Second Circuit Court where I am so proud and happy to be serving. I conclude by thanking you for your friendship and hospitality, so abundant that I shall regretfully have to disqualify myself in all future patent appeals.

GOVERNOR ALFRED E. SMITH
MEMORIAL FOUNDATION DINNER
October 18, 1973

Your Eminence Cardinal Cooke, Mr. Chairman Silver, Your Ex-cellencies Vice President-Designate Ford, Governor Rockefeller, Mrs. Cox, Ambassador Lodge, Governor Harriman, Senator Javits, Senator Buckley, Lieutenant Governor Wilson, Your Honors Mayor Lindsay, Chief Judge Kaufman, Generals Farley, Abrams, and Lefkowitz, distinguished guests on the dais, distinguished guests all, family and friends of Al Smith:

It is a great honor and privilege to be invited to address this distinguished audience at the wonderful dinner which has become so well known in New York. Since this year marks the centennial of his birth, I thought it would be appropriate that my subject tonight be Alfred Emanuel Smith.

Al Smith, as everyone knows, was born on the Lower East Side, which, at that time, was populated predominantly by the Irish and their progeny. His maternal grandparents were the Mulvehills from West Meath, Ireland. What is not generally known is that the Happy Warrior—always considered to be an Irish American folk hero—might well have been, in part at least, an Italian American. A biography published in 1969 makes the astonishing claim that his paternal grandfather, Emanuel Smith, was actually born in Italy. If Mario Procaccino had known this, he might have been mayor of New York today.

In my view, the case for Smith's Italian origins is somewhat thin. It rests in part upon the contention that Emanuel is an Italian name. If Congressman Celler had known this, perhaps Congressperson Holtzman might still be practicing law full-time in Brooklyn. First names are hardly persuasive of ethnic origin. For example, Abraham Lincoln was born in Kentucky, and Abraham Beame in London. Every schoolboy knows that Hercules Mulligan, George Washington's favorite spy, was Irish and not Greek. Smith, in any event, is hardly a Mediterranean name, but the biographer seeks to avoid this fact by claiming that the immigration inspector could not spell his long Italian name and simply wrote "Smith" instead.

The 1855 census of the City of New York did contain this listing: Emanuel Smith—Oliver Street; Born Genoa; Italy, Occupation Mariner. However, by a curious coincidence, it has now been established that not all alleged Genoese mariners are necessarily Italian. We know that Christopher Columbus, also thought to be an Italian mariner born in Genoa, was in reality an Irish navigator from Galway named Lynch. At least an impartial audience of scholars at the Friendly Sons of Saint Patrick annual banquet in New York in 1972 was so persuaded. This part of my talk that evening was reprinted in the Congressional Record by Senator Buckley without objection by Senator Pastore, so I suppose it is now an accepted historical fact. I suggest therefore that Al Smith was a direct descendant of Lynch and 100 percent Hibernian. If you have any doubt, go up to Lynch Circle and look at the statue of the man they call Columbus. The resemblance to Al Smith is striking—particularly at dusk.

Mistakes by immigration officials of course do happen. My research disclosed that when Charles McGillicudy left Cork for Ellis Island, the last name was so difficult to transcribe that the officer simply wrote down "Silver." Somewhere in America tonight there is a Charlie Silver who is really a McGillicuddy.

Al Smith's only formal education was at St. James parochial school on the Lower East Side where he was an altar boy and excelled in amateur theatrics. He left in the eighth grade, just before graduation, in order to support his mother and sister. His education at St. James was left in the tender hands of the Christian Brothers, and he learned not only the catechism but also how to duck a left hook. Apparently neither subject is taught anymore. His rise from the Fulton Fish Market to the leadership of the Assembly was meteoric. He was a brilliant student of state government and he worked hard and long hours to master its intricacies. In the State Constitutional Convention of 1915 Smith was recognized widely even by the Citizens Union as the ablest and most knowledgeable man in the legislature. His four unprecedented terms as governor followed.

In his rise to the leadership of the State, Smith was aided immeasurably by a then unbeatable combination in this State—Irish politicians and Jewish intellectuals. The Irish politicians had wonderful nicknames—my favorite is "Blue-Eyed" Billy Sheehan, which is much more lyrical and memorable than "Four Eyes" which was the usual fate of myopic urchins like myself. Some of the nicknames were rather cruel like "Snow Shoes" Shanahan—so called, of course, because of his flat feet. The Irish, having to some extent become affluent, have deserted politics and taken up golf instead—a sport in which they have demonstrated a pronounced and almost spectacular degree of failure. I always thought that it was not any native lack of ability to hold a club which held us back but rather the unnatural underhand swing as well as the small, inanimate, and stationary target.

By 1928 Smith had reached sufficient stature to be nominated for the Presidency of the United States by the Democratic party gathered in convention in Houston. Rumblings that his Roman Catholicism would prevent his election had hopefully to some extent been stilled by his response to an open letter which was published in the *Atlantic Monthly* in May 1927. The reply was prepared with the assistance of Judge Joseph Proskauer and Father Francis Duffy, a legal and theological combination which was a typical Smith improvisation. The response was a classic and the precursor of John F. Kennedy's address to the Greater Ministerial Association in Houston, Texas, some thirty-three years later. My favorite speech of that genre however is quite obscure and, in fact, was not even made in America. In 1906 Hilaire Belloc was running for the House of Commons and was advised that his religion should be soft-pedaled because he was running in a district which had very few Catholic residents. In his very first campaign speech the irrepressible Belloc announced, "Gentlemen, I am a Catholic. As far as possible I go to Mass everyday . . . as far as possible I kneel down and tell these beads everyday. If you reject me on account of my religion, I shall thank God that he has spared me the indignity of being your representative." He was elected by a large plurality, a great tribute to the English, and I admit that adulation of the Sassenach does not come readily to the lips.

As Frances Perkins later reported, "We who campaigned for Smith in 1928, and also the candidate himself, were not prepared to deal with the degree of prejudice we encountered." *The New York Times* reported editorially that the attacks on Smith were ferocious and senseless and were provoked primarily by his religion. For example, Smith was greeted by burning crosses when his party visited Oklahoma City. They were clearly visible from the windows of the campaign train. Smith, gazing out at them made a typical comment to Judge Proskauer, "Well, Joe, how did they ever know that you were on the train?"

I remember the campaign of 1928 rather well—the Ku Klux Klan even burned crosses in New York State. In the summer of 1928 I was visiting my relatives in Gardiner, New York, a small hamlet in Ulster County. One of my numerous uncles, Jim Donahue, operated a meat market, and one night, which I recall vividly, a large cross was whitewashed on his store window and another on the stone walk in front. He was forced to close down the store a few months later. I freely admit that it was not because of the Klan but because he was a terrible butcher. He knew nothing about meat and seldom even ate it. He later opened a saloon and enjoyed a modest success.

I distinctly remember being ejected from a Fordham Road movie house that fall for noisily booing a newsreel of Herbert Hoover. The usher was decorated for bravery in action and years later retired as full Colonel from the Loew's Paradise Usher Corps.

The rumors of Smith's staunch Catholicism and fanatic loyalty to the pope were legion. One popular tale was that he planned to build a tunnel from New Jersey to Rome so the pope could secretly come to America. I checked this story with Bob Moses, a Smith adviser, and he said there was absolutely no truth to it at all. It was a bridge we planned, said Moses! Bob explained that no Church/State problem existed—the upper level was for the pope and Catholics in general, the lower span for the rest. Separate but equal or almost equal. The only problem was the projected expense of completing the lower level—there was not enough money to close a substantial gap over the middle of the ocean. Smith figured, however, that a strong swimmer who survived the dive—and had enough strength to jump back up—might have a good chance of getting here.

In the fall of 1928 I was in the fifth grade at Our Lady of Refuge grammar school in The Bronx. Were it not for my unorthodox approach to long division it might have been the sixth grade. Some critics have made the claim that Catholic education is "divisive." Nothing could be further from the truth. In 1928 every single student and nun in my school was *solidly* behind Al Smith. I well remember the funereal atmosphere of our classroom the day after Smith's crushing defeat when he was rejected by the Democrats of the solid South as well as the people of his own State who strangely now, for the first time, found Smith wanting, although they elected a Democratic governor. Smith was a clear victim of bigotry, a wicked sport which never lacks for new players since the victims are always changing. I remember our good Dominican nun telling the class with tears in her eyes that America would be punished for rejecting Al Smith. Nobody in my class was a bit surprised therefore by the stock market crash of 1929 and the great depression that followed. To be perfectly frank, most of us didn't know there was a depression anyway. Things were mostly the same before and after. Nobody jumped out of any buildings in The Bronx.

After considerable research into the career of Al Smith, I think that one would have to conclude that he was a uniquely gifted man. My childhood enthusiasm for him was not misplaced. He was a liberal in the true sense, and decades ahead of his time in proposing social legislation. His empathy for ethnic and economic minorities was real and not feigned. When the Jones Beach development was projected, some of the landed gentry protested that those sacred precincts would be invaded by the rabble. Smith thundered back, "*I* am the rabble." He never forgot his humble origins and his days in the Fulton Fish Market. In the Assembly the competence of this man from the city to discuss fishing and game laws was questioned by an upstate legislator. His response recorded:

> Mr. Speaker, if all the fish I handled in Fulton Fish Market were put into the Capitol Building, they would pry the roof off, bulge out the windows, cover the lawn and cascade down the hill to the Hudson River in a stream fifteen feet deep. I am the only member of the Assembly who can talk the fish language.

The criticisms of Smith were indeed petty and mean—for example, it was said that he spoke with a decided New York accent. Since he was born in New York, I cannot imagine what other kind of accent he could properly have. To those of us born and bred in The Bronx, Smith's radio speeches were perfectly understandable—as far as I am concerned it is the people who *don't* come from New York City who have the accents—not us. I was married several years before I understood Roseanna.

Another criticism of Smith was that he did not have the benefit of higher education. Like Abraham Lincoln, therefore, Smith was forced to get along with the natural equipment of a first-rate mind, a great intellectual curiosity and energy, and an innate humanity which was never maudlin and always tempered by a sense of humor. Smith established his credentials by his performance, and all of us here are the richer for it. His virtues were homely—he loved his God and his country and his wife and his family. This makes him, I suppose, in today's parlance, a square. On behalf of all those similarly situated I say, long live the squares and our memories of Alfred Emanuel Smith.

COMMENCEMENT ADDRESS,
FORDHAM UNIVERSITY
June 6, 1975

I am, of course, honored and flattered to receive this degree from Fordham University. It is my sixth honorary degree, but, naturally, it is the one I most cherish. Not only is Fordham my alma mater but I have spent the largest part of my life at Fordham as a student, as a member of the faculty, and as a law school dean. For this recognition today, I sincerely thank the Trustees on behalf of my family and myself.

Graduation ceremonies I thought for a time were on the decline. In an iconoclastic world, particularly in academe, custom and ritual and the traditional trappings of yesteryear were and are going by the boards. Student dress habits have obviously changed, class attendance is not treated with the concern it once was, and punitive authority once vested in academic officials gradually became the responsibility of the faculty and ultimately the student body.

In an era which supposedly scorns tradition and defies convention, the strange survivor is the graduation ceremony. Not only are such ceremonies alive but they are more numerous and more gaudy than ever before. When I graduated in 1939 from Fordham, the faculty appeared at graduation in black gowns, often moth-eaten, and in hoods of fading tints and modest proportions. Today's faculty appears in garish garb. Robes are more colorful than rainbow hues, and academic caps are often bizarre. I have seen grown men with eton collars and bow ties, cerise robes, velvet hoods, and academic hats which defy description. Professors normally known for unpolished shoes and wrinkled suits appear on commencement day in an extravagance of costume which makes them almost unrecognizable to their students. The academic procession is fast approaching the splendor of a Philadelphia Mummers Parade. While the Catholic Church is gradually repressing pomp and pageantry, the campus seems to be moving in the other direction—at least on commencement day. When Fordham was at the peak of its period of modernism in the '60s, the University still saw fit to acquire an immense, bejeweled mace for use in academic processions. Incense and floats may yet appear.

When I was Dean of the Law School, the law degree became a doctorate, and the students demanded and received the right to wear newly designed maroon robes. The fact that students were willing to pay higher rental fees for more elaborate gowns was particularly meaningful to me. Not only that, but a separate graduation ceremony was provided, a custom which is becoming fashionable throughout the nation. At Villanova last year the graduation ceremonies took three days, with a separate speaker each day. This was indeed cruel and unusual punishment for academic officials especially since I was the speaker on the third day.

The concomitant phenomenon, of course, is the survival of the graduation speaker as a necessary element or evil of the ceremony. Despite the traditional caustic comments which equate Fourth of July oratory with commencement speaking, the speaker is not an endangered species like the American buffalo; on the contrary its tribe increaseth.

While there is an obvious reason for the presence of students, faculty, administration, and all of your friends and relatives here today, there is no satisfactory explanation known to me at any rate to justify a speech at this time. Commencement addresses are as much subject to ridicule as political orations. They are traditionally platitudinous and pedestrian, and I assure you that I have great respect for tradition.

One of the brighter aspects of all this is that even if you are listening, you won't remember what is said. I have forgotten not only what was said here in 1939 but also who said it. Parenthetically, a glance at my 1939 yearbook reveals two advertisements which you may find interesting—at that time on Fordham Road you could buy a five-course meal for 35¢ and a three-piece suit for $22.50. We have certainly progressed since then.

In any event, my brief homily today does concern graduation speakers and the United States Constitution. This year two outstanding attorneys—one a member of the federal bench and the other a distinguished professor of law with a nationwide reputation—were invited to speak at commencement exercises. Chief Judge Irving Kaufman of the Second Circuit Court of Appeals and a Fordham alumnus, both earned and honorary, was invited to speak at Pomona College in California, and Professor Charles Wright of the University of Texas Law School was invited to speak at the Wesleyan University commencement in Connecticut. Both men accepted the invitations; both were later advised by University officials that splinter student groups had threatened to disrupt the ceremonies if they did appear to speak. Not wishing to cause a scene on a day which means so much to graduates and their families, both men withdrew.

The reason for the student opposition to Judge Kaufman was the fact that some twenty-five years ago he had presided at the trial of the Rosenbergs, who were found guilty of treason by a jury and whose convictions were upheld after numerous appeals to the Second Circuit and the Supreme Court. Professor Wright's crime against the state was his agreement to act as counsel to President Nixon during the dying stages of Watergate.

The conduct of the student groups responsible is indeed shocking in a country which has taken justifiable pride in its constitutional recognition of freedom of speech. No judge is infallible, but there are in the federal system several layers of appellate review. We have, further, cherished our system of justice which presumes innocence, not guilt, and which provides every man the right to his day in court—which might well be meaningless if he did not have the right to counsel—no matter how egregious his crime, no matter how horrible his conduct. No sane person would attribute a social disease to a doctor because he treats a syphilitic, and no reasonable man should attribute to an attorney the misdeeds of his clients or condemn a judge for imposing the penalty provided by statute. The ministry of justice does not operate in a vacuum. Its very nature requires that it be manned by professional independent men of law, both on the bench and at the side of the accused. Aside from the basic misunderstanding or ignorance of the American system of jurisprudence which these two incidents reveal, there is a more fundamental assault here upon the First Amendment guarantee of freedom of speech. This amendment applies not simply to lawyers and patriots but to the dissident and the disenchanted as well. It even applies to graduation speakers, not to the extent that they say what you would like to hear but essentially because they may say what you may *not* wish to hear.

In these cases those in protest did not even know what was about to be said but rather invaded not only the right of the speaker to be *heard* but the right of the university community, including the vast majority of their classmates, to *hear*. What is particularly abhorrent is that the scene of the assault on constitutional liberties is the academic community which, presumably, is the marketplace for the exchange of ideas, no matter how unpopular. This is not the mindless mob which hates people because of the color of their skin, their ethnic origin, or their religious affiliation but rather young Americans receiving a higher education in respected institutions.

If assaults on constitutional rights to free speech and assembly are permitted on any large scale, the students here involved who undoubtedly consider themselves "liberals" should consider the alternatives to the political society which we now enjoy. They are anarchy or the fully regulated zoo, whether the management be of the left or right. We believe that God created man with certain inalienable rights and that our government is not the source of these rights but the guardian. In the zoo, man is at once the creature and the victim of the state; his rights, if any, are submerged to the omnipotent state. American visitors to such states often enough return and remark that the poor animals seem to be happy, well fed, and do not bite. They apparently forget that freedom of speech, of conscience, of assembly are unknown and that freedom to travel abroad is not tolerated. I think that on the eve of our Bicentennial we should all re-examine the premises of our governmental structure and not only recognize its virtues and blessings but our own responsibility to be alert to the challenges made to the liberties we cherish.

I conclude by congratulating all of you for your academic achievement, your parents and family who paid the tuition, and the University which received it and which made it possible for you and me to enter and participate in a society which provides us all with an opportunity for service.

JUDGE TIMOTHY J. SULLIVAN TESTIMONIAL DINNER, POLICE EMERALD SOCIETY OF WESTCHESTER
March 6, 1976

Mr. Chairman, Judge Sullivan, members, guests, and friends all of the Emerald Society:

It is an honor and distinction to be invited to speak briefly this evening as part of your tribute to Judge Timothy J. Sullivan. I have known him for more than forty years—I first recall him as a basketball player for Regis High School. I was a student at Cathedral at the time, studying for the priesthood, and Tim was at Regis preparing for sainthood. Regis defeated Cathedral that day by one point as I recall, but Tim missed twelve foul shots, creating a record which, I believe, still stands.

We became classmates at Fordham in 1936 along with Bill Bave. Joe Crowley joined us in our senior year, having been invited to leave the seminary when he admitted having impure thoughts. I saw Tim almost daily at the college. His favorite haunts, of course, were the library and laboratory where he could further research problems generally beyond the scope of the classroom. He was so anxious to stay close to his beloved college that one night he even slept in the baseball dugout so that he would be first in class the next morning.

In World War II Tim had an enviable record as a combat infantryman seeing more action and surviving more battles than anyone I know. My only overseas service was as military police-man in Staten Island—I saw plenty of action breaking up fights in waterfront bars but was never given any battle stars.

After the War, I started to teach law, and among my first students were Timothy Sullivan and Joe Crowley. Bill Bave was rejected at Fordham and had to go to Columbia, which surprisingly does have both a law school and a football team. Sullivan was a brilliant student, particularly in my classes, where he sat with his eyes closed most of the time. He told me this eliminated distraction and permitted him to soak in and analyze the meat of the lectures. Occasionally he emitted what sounded like snoring noises but again he explained it was really like a baby's cooing—a sign of deep satisfaction with the scholarly lecture. I knew then that Sullivan would go far in our profession, and my predictions have borne fruit.

The Irish have a great tradition on the bench. One noted Irish jurist always presided with a quill pen in his mouth. At the other end, however, was not an inkwell but a jug of whiskey carefully camouflaged lest he create any scandal in the courtroom. He was said to grow more eloquent as the day wore on. One of his famous opinions involved a defendant, Murphy, accused of stealing a sheep. Murphy presented in his defense seven neighbors, all of whom testified that Murphy was a man of unquestioned character with a reputation for honesty unsurpassed in the vicinage. The judge, hearing the case without a jury, gave his opinion from the bench. He said, "These are my findings: first, Murphy is a man of unexcelled reputation for honesty and probity in his community. Second, beyond any reasonable doubt he stole the sheep."

Seriously, ladies and gentlemen, I must say that your selection of Timothy J. Sullivan as Irishman of the Year is one which we can all approve and applaud. Tim possesses all of the principal virtues of the Irish. What vices they or he possess are unknown to mortal man, at least those who are proud of their Irish heritage. His parental home which I often visited had the warmth, affection, and generous hospitality that mark the Gael and which he has inherited. It was a home of faith and reverence, and that faith has maintained him in time peril and stress. He is highly articulate and courageous, and his probity is unquestioned. He has never stolen a sheep in his life—the only bad thing I know about him is that he once borrowed a bottle of whiskey from a bar in Pittsburgh, but I am sure he will return it if he ever gets back there. The most intelligent thing he ever did, of course, was to woo and win the sister of one of our classmates—Henrietta Hasey. They have raised a wonderful family in the best traditions of our race and faith. On behalf of all of you, I wish Tim and all the Sullivans, and all Sullivans to be, the peace, prosperity, and happiness they so richly deserve.

ANNUAL DINNER OF THE SOCIETY OF THE FRIENDLY SONS OF SAINT PATRICK OF WESTCHESTER COUNTY

March 12, 1976

Mr. President, Your Eminence Cardinal Cooke, Your Excellency Governor Wilson, reverend clergy, honored guests and friends:

It is indeed an honor and privilege to be once again invited to address the Society of the Friendly Sons of Saint Patrick in Westchester on the day we celebrate. My last appearance here was seven years ago when in my preamble I referred to His Eminence as "Your Grace, Archbishop-Designate Cooke." The other speaker that evening was Senator John Hughes, who has since passed on. Four years later I addressed the New York branch of your Society and my co-speaker was the late Vice President of the United States, Spiro Agnew. There is apparently some sort of jinx or curse attached to those who speak with me on March 17th at St. Patrick's Day banquets, and in recognition of this your committee wisely decided this evening not only to advance the dinner by five days but also not to invite another layman to speak. A year ago, I should advise you, I spoke on March 17th at the annual dinner of the Hibernian Society in Savannah, Georgia. My co-speaker was Senator "Scoop" Jackson, and I mentioned the jinx in my remarks that evening. He responded that it was all right with him since I had spoken that morning at the annual breakfast of the Sinn Fein Society in Savannah with Jimmy Carter.

When I ascended the bench, this Society very generously provided me with the judicial robes which I am now wearing on the Second Circuit Court. If Congress does not give us a raise soon, I will still be wearing them when I leave the bench. By that time they will be green, but perhaps that is perfectly appropriate. Your Society formally presented the robes to me at a lovely dinner party some short time after I had been sitting. In order to make the formal presentation I brought the robes up to the dinner in a somewhat battered suitcase which I placed under the head table. The presentation was made by the late Judge Landy, who delivered a gracious introduction, and when it came time to present your gift, he turned to the late Senator Condon, who pointed under the table. Grasping the old suitcase, with perfect aplomb Judge Landy announced "and now on behalf of the Society, Judge Mulligan, as a token of our esteem, I present you with this attractive piece of luggage." After Ned Sullivan recovered from the shock, the old satchel was finally opened and the resplendent robes were duly presented by a somewhat befuddled but nonetheless gracious Judge Landy.

I have given so many St. Patrick's Day speeches that I have to check to be sure I am not repetitive. When I discussed this with Professor Crowley he told me not to worry since nobody remembered what I had said here before anyway. I did say then, however, that when God made the Irish he made us more intelligent, more witty, and more charming than anyone else. But a cynic added "but then he made whiskey and made us even with everyone else." Since then I have ascertained that the fondness of the Gael for spirits is not limited to mortals. There is a story, although obviously not capable of authentication, that several years ago St. Patrick himself expressed a great desire to revisit Ireland in human form on St. Patrick's Day to witness the nation pay tribute to him in the annual parade in Dublin. The request was unprecedented and opposed by St. Peter, the keeper of the gates of heaven. However, in view of the tremendous contributions made by the Irish to the true faith throughout the entire English-speaking world, the request was ultimately granted by higher authority. However, there was one condition—that Patrick return at midnight, like Cinderella and equally sober. Patrick left with glee but, as we say, fell into evil companionship: he ran into some of the boyos at a clandestine pub. At three in the morning he returned to heaven, singing the newly learned *Soldier's Song* and *Kevin Barry*, much to the dismay of the Seraphim and Cherubim. An alert and angry St. Peter was watching at the gate. Observing Patrick, who obviously had more than one pint of Stout, St. Peter announced in stern tones, "Patrick, the Gates of Heaven are closed against you; you have betrayed your trust and you shall not enter." With typical Irish wit and presence, St. Patrick whispered in St. Peter's ear, and the gates were immediately opened. What he said to Peter was simply "Cock-a-doodle-doo." I now understand that the trip back is an annual event, and, for all I know, if he can take a long weekend, St. Patrick may be here tonight.

At our last gathering and on similar occasions I have referred to Hercules Mulligan, the New York tailor, who was George Washington's secret agent in New York during the Revolution. My attention has been called to an article in the most recent issue of the official Irish Tourist Board publication *Ireland of the Welcomes*. The article by Maurice Hennessy describes the exploits of the Irish in the Revolution and highlights the gallant Hercules Mulligan. Hennessy reports that Hercules has become the center of considerable controversy in the United States, which I am sure will come as a great surprise to American historians. He also reports that Mulligan's family later became very involved as legal experts in drawing up the Declaration of Independence. This again is somewhat surprising—Hercules was a tailor, his father was a wig maker, and while his son John was a lawyer, he was only two years old in 1776.

The Hennessy article concludes "One of Hercules' descendants is currently a well-known judge in New York." This indeed came as quite a shock to me as well as my friends and relatives. My daughter Anne immediately made application for membership in the Daughters of the American Revolution.

I thought I had better investigate. Mulligan was born in Mayo according to Hennessy, but in Antrim according to his official and sympathetic biographer Michael O'Brien. No matter where he was born, he certainly died in New York on March 4, 1825, surrounded by his sons and grandsons. He was buried in Trinity Churchyard, and his vault is directly under the chancel of the present church. Since my Irish-born great-grandfather Patrick Mulligan arrived in the United States in 1844, shortly ahead of the famine, it is indeed difficult to imagine how he could have been a descendant of Hercules's. In fact Hercules was declared insolvent in 1785, and he could hardly afford carfare home to sire Pat Mulligan.

In my research on Hercules, I discovered that his mother, also born in Ireland, was Sarah Cooke and that he had a brother Cooke Mulligan who was named after her family. I plan to write to Hennessy in Ireland and advise him that it may well be that he missed the really big story of the Bicentennial—that Hercules's New York descendant is not the judge but His Eminence the Cardinal Archbishop. While Hercules died outside the faith, I am sure it was only to protect his cover and gain the confidence of the British. While it is probably too late for the last rites, I think it would be a wonderful ecumenical gesture, Your Eminence, in this Bicentennial year if you visited Trinity Church and said a few prayers for our brave ancestor Hercules.

The Irish gift for slight exaggeration which I find both in Hennessy's article and O'Brien's biography is well known. As one native cynic commented, "If all the Irishmen who claimed they were in the General Post Office during the Easter bank holiday weekend in 1916 had been actually there, we would have outnumbered all the British forces by 20 to 1." There is also the story of the *Skibereen Eagle*, a weekly newspaper which had a circulation of 200 in 1914. When the Great War broke out, a special edition was published with a banner headline which announced "The Skibereen Eagle Is Keeping Its Eye on the Kaiser."

Gentlemen, on occasions like this, orators become highly emotional and nostalgic about the old sod. Joe Crowley, born in Yonkers of Yonkers natives, makes annual trips to Ireland and always announces the he is going "home." Billy Bave, who is half English, gets misty-eyed when he sees the rocks of Connemora. Judge Gagliardi, who is Irish by marriage, cries at the sight of Kilkenny. There is great loyalty to the Counties Mayo and Cork, Kerry and Clare. Although I am obviously proud of my pure Irish ancestry, the county of my birth was and remains "The Bronx." When I was a boy there were more Irishmen in The Bronx than there were in all the counties of Ireland I have mentioned. My boyhood heroes were not Daniel O'Connell or Patrick Pearse, or even Eamon De Valera. Instead, they were Ed Flynn, Charley Buckley, and Senator Dunnigan. My Robert Emmet was Borough President James Lyons, who, while certainly not as articulate or as eloquent as Emmet, was at least garrulous. It was Lyons who named The Bronx the Borough of Universities—in fact we had two. It was Lyons in person, accompanied by a photographer from *The Bronx Home News*, who intrepidly crossed the Spuyten Duyvil and, armed only with a borough flag, attempted to annex the tip of Manhattan to the Bronx.

The only national hero we ever recognized was Al Smith, and when he was defeated, the good nun who was teaching our class led us all in tears and prayers the next day for the conversion of the South. Although we had no River Shannon, we did have the majestic Bronx River, which, oddly enough, to the best of my knowledge, has never been the subject of song or poetry.

We had no *Irish Times* or *Independent*, but we did have *The*

Bronx Home News, then owned and operated by an Irishman. That paper even had a foreign correspondent who was stationed at the Manhattan office of the Associated Press where he borrowed or stole foreign dispatches which were printed daily without attribution in our local paper.

We were closely identified with our local parishes then, much as our ancestors had been with theirs. If you ask Joe Hopkins today where he lived in The Bronx, his answer will be Tolentine. I say OLR, others say OLM, St. Brendan's, St. Augustine's, St. Benedict's, and so on through the litany. The only gang I ever joined was the Altar Boys.

Our games were not Gaelic football or hurling but principally stickball. Since it was played with a sort of club, the Irish Americans were quite adept. We also played games called "Salugi" and "Ringalevio." I do not know their origin or even how to spell them—however, I seriously doubt that they were Gaelic in origin. Those were the times not of The Troubles but only of the Depression, but we didn't know it; we thought it was ever thus. We lived in a highly structured society in The Bronx. The Germans had the butcher shops and the delicatessens; the Italians, the shoe repair and barber shops; the Jews, the candy and clothing stores; the Irish, the fire and police departments or, at best, Con Ed and the telephone company. Of course, all of that has changed. The Bronx Irish have emigrated to Westchester, living now in genteel poverty. Gentlemen, you can take an Irishman out of The Bronx, but you can't take The Bronx out of an Irishman. Instead of stickball they now play golf, which they will never master. Give an Irishman a club, and he naturally swings down hoping to hit someone on the head. To learn to swing up and underhanded is unnatural. There are very few, if any, Irish American golf champions.

A recent poll indicated that the Irish Catholics are the most affluent religious ethnic group in America. This increased my distrust of all polls—I figure that the only man interviewed was Jack Mulcahy. If they had interviewed instead Bob Abplanalp, I am sure the Swiss Catholics would have won the nod.

Gentlemen, a year ago I was amazed at the celebration of St. Patrick's Day in Savannah, Georgia. It is the biggest event in the state, and all participate irrespective of race, color, or religious persuasion. The celebration started with a High Mass celebrated by the bishop in the cathedral. Most memorable to me was the sermon of a young Irish priest who concluded with an Irish blessing which he later gave me and which I share in part with you this evening.

    May the blessing of light be on you, light without and light within.

    May the blessed sunlight shine on you and warm your heart till it glows like a great peat fire, so that the stranger may come and warm himself at it, and also a friend.

    And may the light shine out of the two eyes of you, like a candle set in two windows of a house, bidding the wanderer to come in out of the storm.

    And may the blessing of the Earth be on you—the great round earth; may you ever have a kindly greeting for them you pass as you're going along the roads.

    May the earth be soft under you when you rest upon it, tired at the end of the day, and may it rest easy over you when, at the last, you lay out under it; may it rest so lightly over you, that your soul may be out from under it quickly, and up, and off, and on its way to God.

God bless!

THE DEFENSE ASSOCIATION OF NEW YORK, PRESENTATION OF CHARLES C. PINCKNEY AWARD TO JOSEPH M. McLAUGHLIN

June 16, 1976

Mr. Toastmaster, distinguished members of the bar and bench, ladies and gentlemen:

It is indeed an honor and privilege to be here with you this evening to join in your tribute to Dean Joseph M. McLaughlin, the first recipient of the Charles C. Pinckney Award. I have known Joe for many years—first as a student at Fordham Law School, later as a faculty colleague, and finally as Dean of the Law School. I must admit that I know considerably more about Joseph McLaughlin than I do about Charles Cotesworth Pinckney. I am indebted to Dick O'Keefe for having forwarded to me a brief biography of Pinckney to further enlighten me on the subject. Frankly, I was intrigued as to why the Defense Association of New York would name an award after a South Carolinian patriot-soldier-statesman-lawyer. I believe that the explanation lies in his service in Paris as an emissary of President Adams in 1797 for the purpose of negotiating a settlement of the XYZ affair with the French government. The French suggested a monetary payment and Pinckney responded: "My answer—'No, no, not a sixpence.'" How many plaintiff's attorneys have had a comparable response from insurance company representatives—"No, no, we won't pay a nickle." I suggest all future awards be inscribed simply "No, no, not a sixpence."

My next inquiry was to ascertain, if possible, any relationship between Pinckney and McLaughlin which might explain the latter's selection by your association for this honor. I discovered that Pinckney learned his law at Oxford where he attended the lectures of Sir William Blackstone. McLaughlin learned his law at Fordham where he attended the lectures of Sir William Mulligan. I concluded that each had received an equivalent legal education, although my lectures were probably, although not necessarily, more up-to-date than Blackstone's.

Pinckney had a distinguished military career reaching the rank of brigadier general. He was later invited by the President to become Secretary of War. McLaughlin left the law school after one year when we became involved in the Korean conflict—he too was invited to join by the President. The letter was captioned "Greetings from your President." While Pinckney refused to accept the offer to become Secretary of War, McLaughlin did not refuse to accept the order of induction. The argument might therefore be made that McLaughlin was even more patriotic than Pinckney. This is an achievement. When Pinckney was a prisoner of the British, he wrote "If I had a vein that did not beat with the love of my country, I myself would open it. If I had a drop of blood that could flow dishonorably, I myself would let it out." I have not read Joe McLaughlin's letters but I assume that equal protestations of loyalty could be found.

There are other striking analogies. The *Dictionary of American Biography* describes Pinckney, and I quote, "He was not a brilliant lawyer but he was possessed of sane common sense and he had an immense practice." This is as accurate a description of McLaughlin as I can imagine.

I therefore congratulate the Society for naming Joseph McLaughlin as the first Pinckney Award recipient, and his choice as well assures future committees of your Association that there will be no problem in discovering other awardees of comparable qualifications who will fully live up to the tradition established here this evening.

Gentlemen, as you can well understand, I can speak so freely about my distinguished successor not only because I know him so well and respect him so highly but because no words of mine can detract a jot or a tittle from his accomplishments or his stature at the bar. He was and is a dedicated scholar of the law. He was generally recognized even as a young man as the outstanding authority on New York Practice and his commentaries on the CPLR are cited as Bible by not only the courts of the state but the federal courts as well. There was not much he could do to enhance or enrich the Law School I bequeathed him but in all honesty I must say that he has preserved it in practically as good condition as it was when he inherited it. He is a gentleman as well as a scholar, and his career is just beginning to blossom. I wish him and his family all of God's blessings *ad multos annos*.

VERMONT BAR ASSOCIATION, MONTREAL, CANADA
October 1, 1976

It is indeed an honor to be invited to address the Vermont Bar
Association, particularly in these magnificent surroundings. I
should confess to you that I had also received, at the same time,
a conflicting invitation to be the dinner speaker at the Third
Circuit Judicial Conference which was scheduled a few days ago.
I rejected that offer for two reasons. First, I was initially approached to speak here by Judge Sterry Waterman, and it requires courage—more than I possess—for a comparative
neophyte on the bench such as I am to reject an offer made by
such a distinguished jurist. Secondly, and in all candor, the
Third Circuit meeting was at a Philadelphia hotel which itself
constitutes a health hazard which was not particularly appealing. After watching the Montreal Olympics Games on television
I am not sure whether this talk should be given in English or
in French, or both. Since my command of English is superior,
although only slightly to my fluency in French, I will proceed in
that language together with whatever strange accent a boyhood
in The Bronx has bequeathed me and forever separated me
from your native New England patois.

I should like today to dwell briefly on my experience of five
years sitting on the Second Circuit court. In the first place, I
should frankly advise you that I came onto the bench under a
misapprehension, fully contemplating that I was to become
Chief Judge of that court. My appointment by the President
clearly provided that I was to succeed J. Edward Lumbard and
he was then the Chief Judge. It appeared quite evident to me
that the presidential intent was that I succeed not only to the
bench but also as Chief Judge. My mother, who isn't even a lawyer, had the same understanding. After all, I had been the Dean
of a law school and had the administrative experience. However,
Henry J. Friendly, who has some small reputation as a legal
scholar, discovered an obscure statute under which he, as the
senior active judge, was entitled to become Chief Judge. Since

he obviously had his heart set on the job, I made no issue of it at the time. I mention it now since a friend of mine who is a New York State Court judge visited Ireland this summer and had an audience with the President of that country, Cearbal O'Dalaigh, who was formerly the Chief Justice of Ireland. O'Dalaigh asked my friend if he knew the Chief Judge of the Second Circuit— yes, replied my friend, I do know the Chief—Judge Irving R. Kaufman. The President responded—Oh no, the Chief Judge is Bill Mulligan. Although I have had dinner with Judge O'Dalaigh in New York and he visited my chambers, I am sure that the opinion of this eminent scholar was not influenced by those meetings or even my Irish ancestry but rather in fact that his own scholarly research had confirmed my own claim that I was truly entitled to the position. I assume that at least in Ireland and, for all I know, perhaps even in Canada I am recognized as the Chief Judge of the Second Circuit.

Actually, I have not raised the issue with Chief Judge Kaufman because after five years of experience I have learned that he gets the same salary, has many more headaches, and is subject to much more abuse than a humble member of the court.

The main responsibility of the appellate judge is of course to adjudicate and to write opinions which hopefully elucidate his reasoning. In my maiden year on the bench I was assigned several bank robbery cases—the fact patterns are not particularly difficult and there have been no major changes in the law since Blackstone's *Commentaries*. It was an area in which my brothers apparently concluded that I could not create too much controversy or commit too many errors. I learned enough about the bank-robbing business to think seriously of it as a hobby. However, since we federal judges have to report all sources of outside income, there wouldn't be much sense in it.

One of my earliest opinions involved the robbery of the Merchants National Bank of South Burlington, Vermont, which did occur on Christmas Eve, 1969, and I must say it was rather clumsily managed. The defendants, who were locals, drove around the block where the bank was located three times before mustering enough courage to enter. Their car was hand-painted—light blue—and every time a fellow townsman recognized them they ducked down in the car. After completing the job (they left with about $20,000), they repaired to the local tavern, "The Roostertail," only three-quarters of a mile away, leaving their ski masks and money wrappers outside in a snow bank where they were eventually recovered. They became filled with scotch, good cheer, and good will to all men. Although previously penurious, they had spent all of their ill-gotten loot locally and lavishly within a few weeks, drinking scotch instead of beer and tipping barmaids extravagantly; one even had the driveway to his trailer home snow-plowed, which I need not tell you is a rather conspicuous event in January in Vermont. They were convicted without any difficulty but of course appealed. The first draft of my opinion started this way "'Twas the night before Christmas and three men in ski masks and carrying bags entered the Burlington Bank. They did not come down the chimney and, in fact, it was not Santa Claus and his helpers. The evidence was overwhelming that they came not to make a deposit but a withdrawal. Since they maintained no account at the bank and were not even members of the Christmas Club, their conviction is hereby affirmed." My law clerks rejected that opinion and a more prosaic rendering is found in 449 F.2d 649 (1971).

The most difficult job of the appellate judge in my view is to write his opinion. The task is made more difficult because you realize that your prose will be preserved for posterity as well as for profit by the West Publishing Company. Not only your contemporaries but future generations of lawyers and legal scholars will have the opportunity to admire or to abhor your decision, depending upon what side of the case they have or what academic biases they bring to the issue. This used to bother me until I began to realize how few people read my opinions. I still teach a course in Antitrust Law at Fordham and even after assigning some of my own opinions I am amazed how few read them. The lawyer who loses the appeal, of course, reads every word, and you know that his view of your wisdom and scholarship will be dim indeed. The lawyer who wins looks only at the tag line—judgment affirmed or reversed and he doesn't care what you said, assuming that the best part of it, in any event, was lifted from his brief. Similarly, the district court judge who is affirmed doesn't bother reading it wondering only why you didn't simply say—judgment affirmed on the well-reasoned, scholarly, brilliant opinion below. The judge who is reversed, of course, has the same view of you that losing counsel has. I conclude therefore those who really study your opinion are naturally inclined to be hostile.

Some district court judges claim that they pay no attention to reversals. The most recent issue of the *St. John's Law Review* contains an article by Judge Jack Weinstein with a rather blunt statement of this view—I quote: "The Judges read the law reviews and profit from them; a bad review of an opinion may be more important than a reversal, for appellate judges are generally no wiser than their *nisi prius* brethren, but student-run law reviews contain certain articles and notes by those learned in the law who may influence future developments."

At least this is a point of view, but I should point out that casenotes are invariably written by law students, and having been a professor of law for thirty years, and even the moderator of a law review for several years, I would much rather be roasted by a law review than reversed by the Supreme Court. *De gustibus!* I had also believed that appellate opinions have a much greater effect on the future development of the law than law review articles.

The primary purpose of the opinion is to give the parties the basis for our reasoning and the authority, if any, upon which it rests. The parties, I suppose, are at least entitled to this, unlike the Irishman who one Saturday night was thrown into the slammer without explanation. On Sunday morning, the jailer asked him, "Pat, do you know why you're here?" "No," said Pat. "You're here for drinking" said the jailer. "Fine," said Pat. "When do we start?" The second purpose of the written opinion is to further develop the law, hopefully providing the profession with some guidance in advising clients in future transactions. In any event, I believe the opinion should be as succinct as possible. Some jurists assume that all statements must be supported by hundreds of citations and law review articles, most of which cite each other; others insist in deciding not only the case before them but all peripheral issues under the mistaken view that their magnum opus will somehow set the law straight for the next century. Just as John W. Davis and Rufus Choate commanded the appellate advocate to go for the jugular, the appellate judge should go to the heart of the matter and do it as quickly and as briefly as possible. We tend too much, in my view, to spend page after page in needless detail. In the New Testament we are told, "A man went down from Jerusalem to Jericho and fell among thieves. They robbed him and beat him and left him half dead by the roadside." If those thieves were tried and convicted today and then appealed, and an opinion had to be written, those two sentences would become at least two pages. We would be told how the man was dressed, what kind of car and model he was driving to Jericho, where he stopped for lunch and what he ordered. The height and weight of the thieves, plus a footnote setting forth the altitude and population of Jerusalem, would all appear before we got to the legal defenses, which undoubtedly would include insanity, entrapment, a failure to read the Miranda warnings slowly and sonorously, as well as the absence of an environmental-impact statement when the Jerusalem to Jericho highway was constructed. The late Judge Dore, a great scholar and appellate judge in New York, urged judges and lawyers to read the Bible not only for its spiritual values but because the authors had the greatest power of utterance in the history of our race. "What they said they said so well, both in substance and in form, that the human race has refused to let it die, and it has lived on." While I don't pretend that our language should be, or is, inspired (except perhaps that of the Chief Judge), it at least should be understandable, brief, and to the point.

There is much more I could say about the problems of appellate judging—primarily that we need more judges. We have the same number of authorized judges now as we had fifteen years ago with a calendar which has trebled in volume. We also need a pay raise or else we will never be able to attract any new talent to the bench unless they come directly upon graduation from law school. In any event, despite all the problems, I assure you that the Second Circuit Court is doing its job and that I, for one, am honored and proud to be a part of it.

ANNUAL DINNER
OF THE SOCIETY OF
THE FRIENDLY SONS OF
SAINT PATRICK
IN THE CITY OF NEW YORK
March 16, 1979

Your Eminence Cardinal Cooke, Your Excellency Archbishop Maguire, Governor Wilson, Brother Driscoll, reverend clergy, distinguished guests, Fellow Friendly Sons, and friends all:

It is indeed an honor to respond to the toast to the United States. I bring to you all the felicitations and best wishes of the United States Court of Appeals for the Second Circuit—five judges concurred, three dissented, and one judge concurred in part and dissented in part. He would felicitate but thought that best wishes was too effusive.

I wish I could bring you the greetings of the President of the United States but we are not that close. Just four years ago tomorrow I addressed the Hibernian Society of Savannah, Georgia. My day started with a breakfast meeting of the Sinn Fein Society of that city. Another guest and I, after being introduced to the members, were escorted to a table for two in the basement lest we overhear whatever sinister plots the green-jacketed Sinn Feiners were hatching upstairs. The other guest, my breakfast companion, was Jimmy Carter, former governor of the state and a recently announced candidate for the presidential nomination of his party. His chances were obviously considered slim then even in his home state since we were seated in the basement out of touch with the electorate and also out of reach of the bourbon which flowed freely upstairs. Our conversation was hardly sparkling; his southern drawl was pronounced and for same reason my unaccented pristine Bronx diction was equally difficult for him. The finest English spoken in the world is said to be in Dublin, but surely The Bronx must be in second place. I concluded that he was slightly deaf and I am sure he made a similar judgment about me. Had I known what the future held forth for him, I would have ordered hominy grits instead of corn flakes. I could have been so much more affable, charming, and encouraging. Instead of "Governor" and "Judge," it could have been "Jimmy" and "Billy." After breakfast we walked together to High Mass at the Cathedral and sat in the front pew. Now when I am asked if I know the President, I say, "Not really well, although we used to go to Mass together."

Last summer I had the privilege of attending the Red Mass at St. Patrick's. My partner in the procession was a bewigged and gaitered English judge from Liverpool. Fellow Friendly Sons, the English still do not understand the Irish. After Mass I introduced the English judge to Governor Hugh Carey. Upon hearing where the judge presided, the governor said "My grandfather sailed from Liverpool." "Oh" said the Englishman, "Was he a yachtsman?" Between 1810 and 1910 some four million Irish yachtsmen sailed from Ireland to America, never returning to the clubhouse. What a pleasure it is tonight to address not only the descendants of kings but yachtsmen as well.

I, for one, have not been a part of the new hysteria which has gripped millions of Americans with the exhibitions of the treasures found in the tomb of Tutankhamen. However, certain circumstances have compelled me to change my mind. I have recently received intelligence from a confidential but reliable source that when King Tut's mummy was unwrapped, a Sacred Heart badge was found pinned to his BVD's. I also understand that when the golden wine jugs buried with him were unsealed they were found to contain, not wine, but Guinness Stout. I can tell you in the confidence of this room that my research now persuades me that Tutankhamen was in fact Timothy Hanlon, a young Irishman from Connemara.

Egyptologists have persistently made the error of assuming that anyone interred in an Egyptian tomb is necessarily Egyptian in origin. Our own experience exposes the fallacy. Not everyone resting in Gate of Heaven was born in Westchester County. In fact, they come from as far away as Naples, Sligo, and even Poughkeepsie. For all I know, there may even be a couple of Egyptians up there. You may recall a comparable mistake by eminent historians who facilely assumed that a sea captain who lived in Genoa was necessarily an Italian.

It is an accepted historical fact that the amount of rock required to erect the pyramids far exceeded the supply in Egypt.

A natural source of rock as well as stonemasons, builders, and bricklayers was, of course, Ireland, particularly Connemara. Moreover, Ireland, as any traveler knows, has a shortage of sand and chronic unemployment. It was indeed natural that a reciprocal trade agreement be entered into between the two countries; soon barges of sand from Egypt and barges of rock and workers from Ireland were traversing the Atlantic Ocean and the Mediterranean Sea. I attribute the success of the Irish in America in the barge and towing business to this early experience, which made towing bricks up the Hudson and through the Erie Canal child's play. The pyramids still stand, a tribute to Irish engineering skill—in fact, after the Irish left, the Egyptians built very little over two stories high. The broad golden strands of Dingle Bay are further evidence of Irish enterprise and Egyptian sand. Among the itinerant workers was Timothy Hanlon, an unemployed bricklayer, who soon became a foreman on the job. It is not at all unreasonable to imagine that the pharaoh's daughter, coming out to visit the job site, would fall in love with Tim. Except for the ugly ones, the Irish are the most handsome people on earth. After a whirlwind courtship, Tim married the princess and became king when the pharaoh died of a heart attack, undoubtedly overcome by joy that his daughter had married so well. Tim, the boy king, died shortly thereafter, probably of snake bite. There were no snakes in Ireland, and Tim mistook an asp for an eel. He was buried in unconsecrated sand but with royal honors.

The Egyptians at that time spoke pre-Coptic Egyptian, and Tim, of course, spoke Gaelic. Although it is admittedly difficult to find modern philologists equally skilled in both ancient tongues, in fact, Timothy Hanlon in the mouth of an Egyptian translates freely into Tutankhamen. This is not quite so apparent to those of us who speak English, but remember that that language had not yet been invented. The people who lived in England still communicated by grunting.

In any event, aided by a generous grant from the Israeli Government, I am detailing all of the facts in a forthcoming book entitled "King Tim, or, Setting the Record Straight." Unfortunately, if they sign a peace treaty, my book will never see the light of day—the Egyptians have understandably been adamant about that from the beginning. Let us hope that cooler heads prevail and that academic freedom triumphs over the concept of peace at any price. Incidentally, my linguistics consultant on this project is a professor of modern languages at Iona who tells me that, for some unexplained reason, Brother Driscoll has determined that Polish be a required course at that school.

And now to the lighter side. Each year at this time we are delighted to hear recalled the charm and beauty of Ireland matched only by the charm and beauty of its people. Although I have visited Ireland many times, I cannot reminisce as a native about growing up in a thatch-roofed cottage warmed by a pleasant peat fire. I grew up not in Cork or Kerry but in The Bronx. Not in a cottage but in an apartment house, which I now understand is properly referred to as a townhouse. Our heat was steam and not peat, and we had it when the boiler was working and the super was sober, conditions which seldom coincided.

We have heard many stories of the cruelty and inhumanity of the absentee English landlords in dealings with their Irish tenants. I am unmoved—I can assure you that the landlords we had in The Bronx were at least as ferocious. My mother was forced to learn more Landlord and Tenant Law than that known to all of the Municipal Court judges in The Bronx put together. My mother's maiden name was Donahue, and her mother, born in Cork, had the maiden name of Scriven, not typically Hibernian. I was also told that my grandmother had a brother named Samuel. There is a Samuel Scriven listed in the yellow pages of the Cork phone book as a tobacconist. Correspondence ensued, and on my first trip to Ireland I met Sam Scriven at a local pub in Cork. He took me to the alleged family homestead, a magnificent castle of concrete block with a rusted tin roof, surrounded by mud. The drawbridge must have rotted away. He even showed me my granduncle's unmarked grave in the cemetery in Macroom. There must have been several changes in management at the church, since in the graveyard the Catholics were on the left and the Protestants on the right. Sam was almost in the middle. How many Irish Americans have a cousin named Sam who runs a candy store in Cork? When I asked Sam if he wanted anything from the States, he said he would like an autographed photograph of Abe Beame. He also asked me if I could check out the singles weekend rate at Grossinger's. It was at this juncture that I discontinued my genealogical studies. When I related all of this to my mother on my return, she told me that my grandmother had gone to Uncle Sam's funeral in New York and that he was now resting peacefully in Calvary Cemetery. God knows who is in that grave in Macroom; it might even be an Egyptian.

We all have read about and most of us have seen the devastated areas of my native county, The Bronx. I was shocked, however, to read that one of the areas scheduled for rehabilitation was the Grand Concourse. When I was a boy the Grand Concourse was more magnificent than the Champs Élysées and more impressive than O'Connell Street. Poe Park rivaled St. Stephen's Green. The most majestic edifice on that great Boulevard was the Loew's Paradise, a veritable Taj Mahal. Although its architecture and decor displayed a somewhat discordant blend of ancient Roman and Egyptian influences with Hollywood and Miami Beach overtones, the total effect was somewhat awesome. Every Irish American boy in The Bronx who did not have a vocation to be a priest or a policeman aspired at least to become an usher at the Paradise. Even the lowest ranking wore a uniform that would make a Mexican general envious. The military training and bearing of that elite corps was at least equal to that of the West Pointers. Appointment as an usher came not from Congress but from a higher authority, the North End Democratic Club. The most memorable feature of the Paradise was its ceiling, which at all times had a bright full moon, twinkling stars, and slowly, softly moving white clouds. It was always moonlight and roses on the Grand Concourse. Years later when I was stationed in Texas learning how to make night marches in the desert using a compass, my instructor, a native Texan looking up at the stars shining so brightly practically on top of our heads, asked me if I had ever seen anything so beautiful. "Yes," I said, "Loew's Paradise—especially if you sit in the balcony." Incidentally, I never found that course to be particularly helpful in my later career.

In those days we were proud to be from The Bronx and to be known as New Yorkers. The Big Apple was a somewhat grotesque dance which lasted only for a season and a half at Roseland. The historical, cultural, or even agricultural relevance of the Big Apple to New York City has never been apparent to me. Can you imagine a proud Roman if he was suddenly advised that his hometown was to be known as the Big Olive—or the revulsion of a Dubliner who was told by the Lord Mayor that he now lived in the Big Potato? This is, I suppose, the "time of the troubles" for this city and The Bronx. But we will survive—after all, we did live through the occupation of the British, the great fire, and the Lindsay Administration. It all depends upon our leadership, and I am hopeful that Mayor Kevin Koch will be up to it. During the British occupation we did have Hercules Mulligan, George Washington's personal spy whose exploits I covered in a previous homily. When the British left New York and Washington entered, it is reliably reported that General Washington had his first breakfast in this town at Mulligan's home. I was not the first Mulligan to have breakfast with a presidential candidate.

Although the flight of the Irish from Ireland to America has been amply covered by historians, very little has been written about the post-World War II hegira of the Irish American from the city to the suburbs. Those in Queens and Brooklyn fled to Long Island, those in The Bronx to Westchester, those on the West Side of Manhattan moved east, and those in Staten Island stayed home. Their social and cultural patterns suddenly changed. Bingo gave way to backgammon, stickball was abandoned for golf, and beer drinkers became addicted to martinis. The social and cultural assimilation of the Irish American into the mainstream was not entirely successful. The transition from caboose to cabana is not simple. Bingo depended on luck, while backgammon demands a modicum of skill. The luck of the Irish is thus severely discounted in this new diversion.

Undoubtedly, through the genetic influence of the early Irish in America, who were employed to drive spikes into railroad ties, Irish Americans can swing clubs or bats magnificently if the stroke proceeds in a downward direction. We also managed to swing a bat, a broomstick, or even a tennis racquet laterally. However, the underhand swing in golf is most unnatural and uncomfortable, and most American Irish are doomed to be perpetual duffers. Even the consolation shot is called a Mulligan, significant of our ineptitude. The transition from beer to martinis was, of course, disastrous. Martinis are like impure thoughts for us—we can't help having them, but when we begin to enjoy them, we get into trouble.

Gentlemen, the Irish have became more or less assimilated into the American mainstream whatever that may be. If it is what we see so often on the television screen and the modern motion picture, we better assemble the yachts and return to the clubhouse. However, the pendulum still swings, and I detect a growing recognition that the exercise of personal freedoms demands the correlative observance of personal responsibility lest liberty become license. We are a government of laws which recognizes that its function was never to create the rights we have as children of God but rather to protect and foster them. It was such a concept that nurtured our forebears, and we their descendants must never forget that. Jim Farley once said that the only time we stand together was at the Last Gospel, but, alas, that has been eliminated. It is good for us to stand together tonight on the eve of the Feast of St. Patrick to respond to the toast to the United States which we unabashedly love and cherish. For the liberties and opportunities it has provided us and others like us. To the United States—God bless!

SECOND CIRCUIT
BAR ASSOCIATIONS DINNER
HONORING
CHIEF JUDGE IRVING R. KAUFMAN
April 10, 1980

Chief Judge Kaufman, distinguished members of the bench and bar, ladies and gentlemen:

On May 27, 1971, I was nominated by the President and, with the advice and consent of the Senate, was appointed to sit on the United States Court of Appeals for the Second Circuit. The Congressional Record accurately reported that I was to fill the vacancy created by Judge J. Edward Lumbard's decision to take senior status. Since he was then the Chief Judge of the Second Circuit and I was appointed to take his place, it seemed crystal clear to me that it was intended that I was to become the new Chief Judge. My mother, who didn't even have the benefit of a law school education, had the same understanding.

Through some maneuvering not clear to me even to this day, a comparative unknown, Henry J. Friendly, who had never even been a professor of law, much less the dean of a fully accredited law school, was instead named Chief Judge. I fully reported my dissent on this issue at the Annual Dinner of the New York County Lawyers Association on December 9, 1971, so that this is a matter of record and not peevish hindsight this evening. Rather than create a major issue, I have faithfully served as a member of the court fully convinced that justice would eventually prevail. It was indeed shocking for me and my family to learn that by some further skullduggery, Henry the Pretender, was succeeded in 1973 not by me but rather by Irving the First, your honoree this evening. There are even further rumors that unless clearer heads prevail he will be succeeded by Wilfred the Second! This, of course, is not the first time in our history that the will of the President has been thwarted by a small group of willful men.

I think that all of you can appreciate how embarrassing and frustrating it has been for me to carry on under these circumstances. However, even more humiliating was the request of this evening's committee that I pay public tribute tonight to the Chief Judge—particularly when it was without any suggestion of an honorarium. I was not at all disposed to accept the assignment until it was emphasized that the enthusiasm of the organized bar and the law schools with the imminent departure of Irving R. Kaufman as Chief Judge was so pronounced that a sellout crowd was expected here this evening—indeed had it not been for the transportation strike, Yankee Stadium could have been filled on this occasion.

The committee advised me that I was allotted seven minutes to discuss the personality of the Chief Judge. I demurred—I said it could not be done in that time and asked instead for a minute and a half.

When speaking of the Chief Judge, adjectives such as humble, reticent, self-effacing, do not come readily to mind or trippingly on the tongue. Nor should they. That is not his style. He is a mover of mountains, a man of broad vision, unbounded enthusiasm, and remarkable accomplishments. He is, of course, a highly competent and hard-working judge. But his concerns are not simply with judicial decision-making or even the administration of our court. He is vitally concerned with the administration of justice generally. His involvement in this broader field will be discussed by those who follow me.

I note that tonight is the eve of the feast of another pontiff, Pope Leo the First, one of only three popes to be called the Great. I am confident that the committee had this feast day in mind when they selected this date to celebrate Irving's thirty years on the bench. You all will recall that in the fifth century, in the year 452, this fearless man, Leo I, single-handedly stopped the advance of Attila the Hun at the very gates of Rome and forced his retreat beyond the Danube. Irving would have issued an injunction and expelled him from Europe.

Irving R. Kaufman is a tireless and dedicated member of our profession who is not afraid to ruffle feathers. We use initials in our court to designate judges—his are IRK, and if you don't do something you are supposed to do, you will be irked until it is accomplished.

Irving's public image is well known—but there is another facet of his personality which is not known generally and which deserves consideration. IRK is essentially and primarily a family man—totally dedicated to his wife, Helen, to his children, and to his grandchildren. In the bosom of his family, the lion is indeed a lamb. A visit to his home reveals an atmosphere of warmth and affection which is most impressive. His personal relationship to the members of his court is particularly close and intimate. Judges of the court tend at times to become afflicted by ills real or imaginary, and the Chief is always available for advice, assistance, or at least consolation. He is not a fair weather friend; in times of adversity he indeed is most approachable and understanding.

To really understand IRK, one must first realize that all of his higher educational experience in college and law school was directed by the Jesuits at Fordham. Combine this with a native quality best captured in Homeric Greek expression—chutzpah—and indeed you have a very formidable figure to deal with. After a quarter of a century of negotiating with the Jesuits, I have learned certain techniques of survival. I stay a respectful distance away. I am the only judge of the court who maintains his chambers in a separate building. A couple of years ago IRK tried to persuade me to occupy chambers adjacent to his on the twenty-fourth floor of the courthouse—I refused the offer and told him I didn't like the neighborhood. Judge Timbers who had nothing but a log cabin in Maine accepted the offer.

In the world of whimsy which I highly prefer to the one in which we live, I have often taken liberties with Judge Kaufman, even on occasions as public as this, and he has never been irritated or annoyed. In fact, he gets the biggest chuckle. I am very proud to be a member of this otherwise distinguished court—it has known some great Chief Judges, but I am confident that Irving R. Kaufman will rank among the very best.

To be frank, I never really wanted the job anyway.

MEMORIAL SERVICES, JUDGE MURRAY I. GURFEIN

September 15, 1980

Chief Judge Feinberg, members of the court, Eva Gurfein and members of his family, and friends of Murray Gurfein:

When Chief Judge Irving R. Kaufman delivered his warm eulogy for Murray Gurfein at the funeral chapel last December, he made a perceptive comment, he said, "I never knew a man or woman who didn't like Murray Gurfein. I knew many who loved him." His colleagues on this bench were emphatically in the latter category—we loved him.

This afternoon I would like to speak briefly about Murray's service on this bench. Not his opinions—they are published and available for study—but rather the values he brought and the inspiration he provided. His curriculum vitae is well known to this audience of family, friends, and colleagues. It is sufficient to say that he was a scholar long before he entered law school, that he had a magnificent scholastic record at the Harvard Law School graduating *magna cum laude*; that he excelled as a prosecutor both at the state and at the federal level, and that for twenty-five years he maintained a broad and successful private practice of law in this city. He volunteered his service in World War II and became a highly decorated officer in Military Intelligence and O.S.S. He was separated from service with the rank of Lieutenant Colonel. After three and a half years in the Counter Intelligence Corps—I must say, in more prosaic circumstances than Mr. Hyde has indicated that he and Murray enjoyed—I was discharged as a technical sergeant, so that Murray's military career was particularly impressive to me.

Even this bare recital of achievement reveals that Murray Gurfein was extraordinarily well qualified for service on the district and circuit courts. But it was not simply his technical skills, his professional excellence, or his rich experience which made him a great judge. It was, of course, his human attributes—his love of the law and his love of his fellow man, his courtliness, his

gentility, his sense of compassion as well as justice, which made
him a superlative jurist.

Despite all of the laurels and achievements, while Murray
took his assignments seriously, he never took himself that seriously. By no means did he consider himself superior to his colleagues or to counsel who appeared before him. He was a fellow
worker in the vineyard of the law seeking to find a way to
achieve justice, sometimes through tangled facts and conflicting
legal authority.

I did not meet Murray or his beloved Eva until 1971 when we
appeared together before the Senate Judiciary Committee
which considered our credentials. When he joined the Circuit
Court he took chambers adjacent to mine in the Customs Court.
We were the only circuit court judges in the building, and our
friendship flourished. I had the unique opportunity of working
closely with him, often lunching together, and, like all lawyers,
forever talking together. Murray never tired of discussing his
own cases—a characteristic which is hardly uncommon among
judges. However, he had the ability to listen to the problems of
other judges, a much rarer judicial trait. He not only listened
but was helpful—from his vast practical experience as well as his
phenomenal memory for cases, he was able to provide assistance
to those less blessed than he was.

Murray approached every appeal, no matter how flimsy it appeared to be, with great gusto and a meticulous attention not
only to the arguments presented but to those he thought *should*
have been presented. Once he satisfied himself as to the law and
the facts, he had the ability to set forth his views succinctly but
felicitously, and sometimes unforgettably. In particularly difficult cases he was always anxious for the views of his colleagues
and indeed the arguments of his law clerks. While he never
lacked the courage of his convictions, he had the greater courage to change his mind if he determined that his original reasoning was flawed. Murray was particularly effective when a
panel was divided. He had the ability to plot a course which
was consonant with the law and somehow brought together his
colleagues. He sometimes brought order out of what could have
been chaos.

Not only was Murray widely read in the law but he demonstrated the value of a broad classical education. His conversation
was certainly not limited to the law. He was an acute observer of
the business, social, and political scene. He was a close friend in
whom you confided without fear of any trespass on your pri-

vacy. He was a thoughtful and charitable man—charitable not only in the sense of private philanthropy but, more important, he did not harshly judge any man no matter how much he might disagree with his views. He loved not only to tell a good story but again to listen to one—his memory for ancient jokes in point was as reliable as his memory for cases in point. He was, of course, totally devoted to Eva and their family. He was, in sum, a man for all seasons, not only a superb judge but a superb companion whom I sorely miss.

One sometimes wonders what observances such as this accomplish. We cannot bring him back and we provide small solace to his dear wife and family. However, in reciting the litany of his virtues, it is indeed good and profitable for each of us as judges and as human beings to realize our own shortcomings. It is obviously easy to recognize the flaws of our colleagues but to appreciate our own now is indeed difficult. Thomas à Kempis once commented that if men were able to sort out just one evil habit each year, eventually we would reach perfection. None of us know how many years are left—certainly, not enough to attain perfection—but if each of us would recognize some quality of Murray's in which we have failed, then all of us would be better judges and better men.

Requiescat in pace.

GOVERNOR ALFRED E. SMITH
MEMORIAL FOUNDATION DINNER
October 16, 1980

Mr. Silver, Your Eminence Cardinal Cooke, President Carter, Governor Reagan, Senator Javits, Senator Moynihan, Governor Carey, Governor Byrne, Governor Wilson, Mayor Koch, and all the Angels and Saints:

It is indeed an honor and privilege to be invited to speak this evening. In view of the company and the eminence of those who will follow me, I will not trespass upon your patience for more than a brief period. I do note, however, that the engraved invitation to this dinner indicated that there would be only one speaker this evening—me. It is therefore fair to conclude, at least on the only record before me, that this enormous gathering, the galaxy of notables and celebrities both on and off the dais, the presence of the media and the press, radio, and television, are for the most part due to my presence. My mother who will be 91 next month put it well the other day, "Billy, isn't it a wonderful thing that President Carter and Governor Reagan, who have so much on their mind now, would take this time to come to New York tonight to hear you speak." "Yes, Mom," I said, "but the cardinal must have heard me too often." I agree, it is indeed flattering—I had never even met Governor Reagan before and I did not realize how much I had impressed President Carter when we had breakfast together in Savannah, Georgia, on the early morning of March 17, 1975, on the occasion of the annual meeting of the Sinn Fein Society of that city, a group obviously circumscribed in number and circumspect in behavior. After breakfast, before the St. Patrick's Day Parade, we walked together to Mass at the cathedral in Savannah. When people ask me now, "Do you know the President of the United States" I reply, "Not really well, although we used to go to Mass together."

Ladies and gentlemen, I know well the rigors of political campaigning—about thirty years ago I ran for the office of the Vil-

lage Trustee of North Pelham. Many of you, I am sure, will recall
what an active, arduous, and at times bitter campaign that was.
The office, in addition to its obvious prestige, also involved an
annual salary of $250—which is now roughly equivalent to the
salary of a federal judge. In that campaign, I had to travel back
and forth from the New Rochelle line to the Bronx City line and
from the Hutchinson River Parkway to the boundary of Pelham
proper. For someone who couldn't drive a car, you can imagine
how fatiguing this was, especially in view of the great issues
which had to be addressed. I do not remember now what they
were, but I do remember the results. I ran for office in a village
which had a Republican registration which was three times
greater than that of the Democrats. I ran as a Republican and
lost by a two-to-one margin. That election night I cried for the
first time since 1928 when Al Smith was defeated by Herbert
Hoover. That occasion gave me the first inkling of my true vocation for the federal bench, which is attained by presidential appointment with the advice and consent of the Senate for a
lifetime tenure. This eliminates the intervention of the electorate—it is a decent and gentlemanly method of carrying out matters of this import.

However, I harbor no ill feelings for the electorate of North
Pelham—time has eroded any bitterness. Those rotten people
voted against me because I was born and brought up in The
Bronx. Even the Republicans voted against me because they
could not believe that anyone named Mulligan from The Bronx
was really a Republican. In any event, I moved my wife and
family out of North Pelham and have never returned even for a
haircut.

My choice of a topic this evening is quite limited—I have already spoken at this dinner in 1973, about Al Smith's career. As
a federal judge one is afraid to comment about anything in public lest, after post-prandial pontification, the very issue you have
decided at the Waldorf comes up on appeal. Since I have written
several hundred opinions in my judicial career, I thought it
might be fascinating to discuss those holdings—oh, not all of
them—but perhaps the fifty most significant. I suggested this to
the cardinal and his shogun, Charlie Silver, and discovered a
somewhat curious coolness, an almost hostile reaction. I can
only assume that this is because the opinions are published and,
presumably, you are familiar with the compelling logic of the
adjudications.

Instead I thought I should give you in the privacy of this

room my reaction to what I consider to be somewhat anomalous phenomena which have afflicted American society in the past two decades. We are living in a period of self-proclaimed love—everyone seems to have a compulsion to assert his love of neighbor, friends, and even enemies. Those embarked upon demonstrations, even those reasonably characterized as violent, carry placards announcing "Love," and sometimes in a frenzy of affection, the love signs are bounced on the skulls of those suspected of disaffection. In churches we see embroidered banners enjoining upon us the virtue of "Love." At Mass we have brought back the ritual of the kiss of peace or at least a subdued version—we shake hands with our neighbor and announce peace and love even to total strangers. We have experienced the Ice Age, the Stone Age—we are now living in the Love Age.

Despite all these protestations of love and affection we have experienced at the same time in America the greatest increase in litigation, both civil and criminal, in the history of this or any other civilization. Aside from the enormous growth of crime, we are suing each other in civil actions with a ferocity and vigor unmatched in history. All the ills of mankind, real or imaginary, as well as some recently discovered by Congress, apparently are considered capable of resolution only by an action in the federal courts. The old adage "Don't make a federal case out of it" has been transmuted into "Please do make a federal case out of it."

People who used to go to confession or visit a psychiatrist are now persuaded that the only method to obtain spiritual surcease, as well as temporal gain, is to bring an action in the federal court not only on behalf of themselves but also for all of those similarly afflicted. You can be a plaintiff in a lawsuit today without even knowing it. People who used to be playing bingo or running electric trains have a new pastime—bringing lawsuits. Someday when you are shaking hands in church you may be passed a summons and complaint. If you truly loved, you wouldn't sue. No matter what the condition of the rest of the economy, the law profession is flourishing. The law schools are filled—every one who graduates from college wants to be a lawyer and start to practice at $37,000 per year. New law schools are being opened at a record rate, and even those built a few years ago are being expanded. Soon we will be building only jails, law schools, and courthouses.

Despite the tremendous growth of litigation which is crippling the courts and choking the judiciary, a strange myth has gained popular credence—that the law profession is not accessible to the public and that we must do something to promote its availability.

The bar associations, with judicial sanction I admit, have thus permitted lawyers to advertise their services and their fees. You cannot read the daily press, watch television, or even ride the subway without seeing advertisements heralding the services of lawyers at modest fees. Even lower prices for Columbus Day and Washington's Birthday may be in the offing. I fully expect to leave the subway station at Foley Square some morning and find, next to the street vendors of pocketbooks, umbrellas, and costume jewelry, lawyers seated on the sidewalk on portable chairs and desks hawking wills, closings, and uncontested divorces at bargain rates. Any policeman who attempts to serve a summons will undoubtedly be served with a complaint returnable in the Southern District Court alleging a violation of the constitutional rights not only of the attorney but of all others similarly situated.

The flood of litigation shows no sign of abating. On the contrary, *The New York Times* reported a couple of weeks ago that New Jersey has adopted a new plan of cooperation between the New Jersey State Bar and the United Jersey Banks which will permit a prospective client to fill out a loan application at his attorney's office. The attorney will then forward the application to a bank. If it is approved, the bank will immediately pay the attorney 95 percent of the fee, keep 5 percent as a service charge, and the client will pay 18 percent interest annually on the loan. The newspaper quoted a spokesman or, more properly, a spokesperson for the program who said that "The plan would make legal services more accessible, result in quicker payments for lawyers, many of whom find credit cards demeaning and long waits for payment a threat to their practice." Of course, if the client fails to pay the loan to the bank and is sued, presumably he can apply for another loan at another lawyer's office.

When I was a boy in The Bronx during the Depression, you used to be able to get a set of dishes if you went to the movies long enough. Now you can get the same set if you make a deposit at the bank or even keep one there for six months. I predict that soon you will be able to get the same set if you retain a lawyer.

Thus we live in an age which cries for peace and love but is suing at a rate which continually escalates and which seems to believe that the solution of the problem is to make more lawyers available to more people so that more litigation will follow. If we had a five-year moratorium on civil litigation in this country, it could only benefit society. Judges could attend to criminal cases with greater speed and efficiency. Prospective clients would soon realize that with the passage of time most of their problems would evanesce anyway. Those which didn't disappear could be settled amicably with the aid of counsel. Blessed are the peacemakers, not the litigious. For those who still want to join action, perhaps trial by wager of battle would provide an interesting alternative. William the Conqueror introduced this Norman custom to England—the accuser fought the accused, and the survivor was deemed to be in the right. Understandably, there was little litigation in England at that time. Laws authorizing dueling or at least fisticuffs in these situations might be enacted. Certainly, money would be saved, honor preserved, and speedier justice accomplished.

This modest proposal, I must admit, does not represent the views of my court or any other for that matter. It may not even represent mine but now perhaps at least the Cardinal and Charlie Silver will recognize that it would have been better if I had discussed my opinions. I thank you for your patience and forbearance.

UNITED STATES of America, Appellee,
v.
Janet Leslie Cooper BYRNES, Appellant.
No. 822, Docket 80–1359
United States Court of Appeals, Second Circuit.
Argued Feb. 9, 1981.
Decided March 17, 1981.

Defendant was convicted in United States District Court for the Northern District of New York, Neal P. McCurn, J., on two counts of false declarations before the grand jury, and she appealed. The Court of Appeals, Mulligan, Circuit Judge, held that defendant's perjury in stating before grand jury that illegally imported swans and geese were dead when she received them and that she buried them at municipal dump was "material," where such testimony shielded from conspiracy charge defendant's employer, who was target of grand jury's investigation, and delayed discovery of identity of person to whom the birds had in fact been delivered pursuant to arrangement with defendant's employer.

Affirmed.

Gustave J. DiBianco, Asst. U. S. Atty., Syracuse, N. Y. (George H. Lowe, U. S. Atty., Syracuse, N. Y., of counsel), for appellee.

Richard M. Heimann, Walnut Creek, Cal. (Tonsing & Heimann, Walnut Creek, Cal., of counsel), for appellant.

Before MULLIGAN and TIMBERS, Circuit Judges and DUFFY,* District Judge.

*United States District Judge for the Southern District of New York, sitting by designation.

MULLIGAN, Circuit Judge:

Who knows what evil lurks in the hearts of men? Although the public is generally aware of the sordid trafficking of drugs and aliens across our borders, this litigation alerts us to a nefarious practice hitherto unsuspected even by this rather calloused bench—rare bird smuggling. The appeal is therefore accurately designated as *rara avis*. While Canadian geese have been regularly crossing, exiting, reentering and departing our borders with impunity, and apparently without documentation, to enjoy more salubrious climes, those unwilling or unable to make the flight either because of inadequate wing spans, lack of fuel or fear of buck shot, have become prey to unscrupulous traffickers who put them in crates and ship them to American ports of entry with fraudulent documentation in violation of a host of federal statutes.[1] The traffic has been egregious enough to warrant the empanelling of a special grand jury in 1979 in the Northern District of New York to conduct a broad investigation of these activities. Even the services of the Royal Canadian Mounted Police were mustered to aid the inquiry.

A principal target of the grand jury investigation was Kenneth Clare, a Canadian, who was believed to be in the business of shipping exotic birds into the United States, misrepresenting on import documents the value, the species and even the number of birds in the containers, thus avoiding the payment of United States Customs duties, inspection and quarantine. When one learns that an adult swan stands some four and a half feet tall and is normally ill tempered, the reluctance of a border inspector to make a head count is understandable. In this case Clare even had the audacity to pass off as Canadians, birds whose country of origin was England! Another target of the investigation was a California attorney, Edward R. Fitzsimmons, whose hobbies included the collection of horses, llamas and exotic birds. It was believed that Fitzsimmons and Clare worked together hand or claw in glove.

In February 1975, Fitzsimmons allegedly purchased from Clare four trumpeter swans and two red-breasted geese.[2] The

---

[1] E.g., 18 U.S.C. §§ 43 (transportation of wildlife taken in violation of state, national or foreign laws), 542 (entry of goods by false statements), 1001 (false or fraudulent statements to federal agencies); Food & Drugs Act, 21 U.S.C. § 111 (prevention of contagious diseases); Endangered Species Act, 16 U.S.C. § 1538 (regulating import and export of endangered species).

[2] No birds have been indicted and there is no indication in the record that they were even aware of, much less participated in, the criminal activity un-

crated birds were brought from Canada through Massena, New York, a Port of Entry in the Northern District of New York. Their entry papers were spurious. The trumpeter swans (cygnus buccinator) were described in the shipping documents as mute swans which are a less valuable variety. The birds were then airlifted to San Francisco by the Flying Tiger Lines where they were picked up by Janet Leslie Cooper Byrnes, the appellant, who was employed as a secretary by Fitzsimmons. Byrnes was a *quondam* zoologist at the London Zoo and knowledgeable about ornithological matters. When called before the grand jury on February 7, 1979, Byrnes testified that she did pick up the birds in 1975 but further stated that after driving away from the airport for ten or fifteen minutes, she heard no noises from the crates.[3] She stated that she stopped at a gas station, pried open the crates and discovered that all the birds were dead and in fact so stiff that she assumed they had been dead for some time. (D.O.A.). She promptly drove to a municipal dump where the birds were interred in unconsecrated ground.

By reason of this testimony the appellant was indicted on May 8, 1980 on four counts of false declarations before a grand jury in violation of 18 U.S.C. § 1623.[4] After a three day jury trial before Hon. Neal McCurn, Northern District of New York, Byrnes was convicted on two counts on July 18, 1980.[5] She was sentenced to be committed to the custody of the Attorney General for a period of six months and fined $5,000 on each count. Execution of the prison sentence was suspended and the defen-

---

earthed by the grand jury. They were at least as innocent as the horses whose jockeys were bribed to discourage their best efforts at Pocono Downs. See *United States v. DiNapoli*, 557 F.2d 962, 964 n.1 (2d Cir.), cert. denied, 434 U.S. 858, 98 S.Ct. 181, 54 L.Ed.2d 130 (1977).

[3] The trumpeter swan makes a noise described by a trial witness, Cherie Perie, as *"weird."* The appellant, on the other hand, in her grand jury testimony stated that the male trumpeter during courtship "struts around with his neck and head held high and makes this marvelous little trumpeting sound." Transcript at 29. *De gustibus*. The mute apparently courts in silence.

[4] Title 18 U.S.C. § 1623(a) provides in pertinent part: "Whoever under oath . . . in any proceeding before a grand jury of the United States knowingly makes any false material declaration . . . shall be fined not more than $10,000 or imprisoned not more than five years, or both."

[5] Two of the four counts of the indictment, including appellant's testimony that the swans were mute rather than trumpeter (Count II) and that Fitzsimmons had no business relationship with Clare (Count IV) were dismissed by the trial court prior to submission to the jury. The remaining counts related to appellant's testimony that the swans and geese were dead (Count I) and that she disposed of the allegedly dead birds at a landfill (Count IV).

dant was placed on probation for a period of one year on each count, the sentences to be served concurrently. This appeal followed.

I

Appellant does not challenge the sufficiency of the Government's proof to support the conviction. Ida Meffert, who had emigrated from Germany and had obvious difficulty with the English Language was one of four government witnesses brought from California to Syracuse, New York for this momentous trial. She testified that she was a collector of Australian parrots in Hayward, California and described these parrots as "citizens." The court interjected: "A citizen bird?" The witness answered: "Yeah, the whole birds is citizen."[6] More pointedly Mrs. Meffert testified that in February 1975 the appellant delivered four live swans and two live red breasted geese to her pursuant to an arrangement with Fitzsimmons whereby Mrs. Meffert and her husband provided room and board for some of his exotic wildlife. Mrs. Meffert was subjected to a grueling cross examination by counsel for appellant that was apparently aimed at her ornithological qualifications.[7] Mrs. Meffert testified that

---

[6] There are various record references to "citizen" birds which was confusing since those at issue here were aliens. We are persuaded, however, that the word spoken was "psittacines" (parrots) and not citizens. The confusion of the scrivener is understandable.

[7] On direct examination, the following testimony was given:

"Q. Mrs. Meffert, do you recall testifying yesterday about your definition of birds?

A. Yes.

Q. And do you recall that you said that the swans and geese were not birds?

A. Not to me.

Q. What do you mean by that, 'not to me'?

A. By me, the swans are waterfowls." Transcript at 399.

Shortly thereafter, Mrs. Meffert was cross examined as follows:

"Q. Are sparrow birds?

A. I think so, sure

Q. Is a parrot a Bird?

A. Not to me.

Q. How about a seagull, is that a bird?

A. To me it is a seagull, I don't know what it is to other people.

Q. Is it a bird to you as well or Not?

Q. To me it is a seagull. I don't know any other definition for it.

Q. Is an eagle a bird?

after a few days one of the swans died and she preserved his leg in her freezer to establish his demise.[8]

"Man comes and tills the field and lies beneath,
And after many a summer dies the swan."
Tithonus, Alfred Lord Tennyson

[1] The principal argument on appeal is not that Byrnes had truthfully testified to the grand jury, but rather that her testimony was not "material" within 18 U.S.C. § 1623(a). That statute is violated only when the false statements bear upon issues under investigation by the grand jury. Appellant argues that her testimony that the birds were dead upon arrival and buried rather than delivered to Mrs. Meffert, was totally irrelevant to the grand jury investigation. The District Court rejected this contention and we affirm its finding of materiality. The leading case in this circuit addressing the question of materiality of false declarations before a grand jury is *United States v. Berardi*, 629 F.2d 723, cert. denied,—U.S. —1, 101 S.Ct. 534, 66 L.Ed.2d 293 (1980). See also *United States* v. *Mulligan*, 573 F.2d 775 (2d Cir.), cert. denied, 439 U.S. 827, 99 S.Ct. 99, 58 L.Ed.2d. 120 (1978). Both parties rely upon Berardi, as did the District Court in finding the materiality of Byrnes' declarations. All of the elements of materiality set forth in *Berardi* are met here. As we explained in that case, the Government has the burden of establishing that the perjury was committed in response to a

A. I guess so.
Q. Is a swallow a bird?
A. I don't know what a swallow is, sir.
Q. Is a duck a bird?
A. Not to me, it is a duck.
Q. But not a bird.
A. No, to other people maybe.
Q. Where is your husband now, ma'am?
Q. Up in the room" (Transcript at 400-01).

[8] The difficulty of establishing that swans and geese were birds, a proposition not accepted by Mrs. Meffert, was obviated by a Government stipulation that both were birds.
"Let the long contention cease!
Geese are swans, and swans are geese."
The Scholar Gypsy, *The Last Word*, Stanza 2,
Matthew Arnold.
The trial judge, perhaps to relieve the tension, observed that while he had enjoyed goose dinners he had never consumed swan—some indication of the limited cuisine available in the Northern District. The Swan leg was not offered in evidence as an exhibit.

question within the purview of the grand jury investigation. That nexus need not be established beyond a reasonable doubt. 629 F.2d at 727. It is normally satisfied by introducing into evidence the grand jury minutes or the testimony of the foreperson of that jury. This enables the district court to determine the scope of the grand jury investigation and the relationship of the questions which elicited the perjury. *Id.* Here Judge McCurn had the benefit of the minutes as well as the testimony of the deputy foreperson and the United States Attorney in charge of the investigation.

[2] Materiality is broadly construed:

> "Materiality is thus demonstrated if the question posed is such that a truthful answer could help the inquiry, or a false response hinder it, and these effects are weighed in terms of potentiality rather than probability. Thus, in applying this gauge to specific situations, it is only the question, at the time of its asking, which is considered. It is of no consequence that the information sought would be merely cumulative . . . or that the matters inquired into were collateral to the principal objective of the grand jury. . . ."

United States v. Berardi, supra, 629F.2d at 728 (citations omitted).

[3] Measured by this broad test it is clear that the appellant's perjury here was material. The grand jury investigation was prolonged and broad in scope. Appellant's argument that it was simply limited to the importation of wildlife and had nothing to do with matters subsequent to importation is not accurate. Fitzsimmons was a target of the investigation and appellant's testimony that he had not received the birds shielded Fitzsimmons from the conspiracy charge relating to his role in the transactions in which he and Clare were allegedly involved. Moreover, had the truth been told Ida Meffert would have been identified months before her role in the matter was actually discovered. Appellant's false testimony clearly impeded and hindered the investigative efforts of the grand jury. Her perjury was therefore material within the meaning of the statute. See *Carroll v.* United States, 16 F.2d 951, 953 (2d Cir.), cert. denied, 273 U.S. 763, 47 S.Ct. 477 71 L.Ed. 880 (1927).

II

[4] Appellant's remaining arguments are even less meritorious. In his opening to the jury, while explaining the background of

the case, the prosecutor stated that Kenneth Clare had pleaded guilty to falsifying shipping documents. Appellant immediately moved for a mistrial; Judge McCurn denied the motion, but admonished the jury to disregard the prosecutor's remark, pointing out that "the guilt or innocence of any of these parties is not binding on the young lady." In the three day trial that followed, the Government never mentioned Clare in its case or on summation. In view of the strength of the government's perjury case, it is apparent that even if any error was committed it was harmless and did not warrant the granting of a new trial. *United States v. Frascone*, 299 F.2d 824, 828 (2d Cir.), cert. denied, 370 U.S. 910, 82 S.Ct. 1257, 8 L.Ed.2d 404 (1962).

[5] Finally, appellant urges that the trial judge committed reversible error by not taking judicial notice of Migratory Bird Permit Regulations, 50 C.F.R. Part 21 (1979) which require the registration of trumpeter swans and the obtaining of permits for their possession and disposal. Mrs. Meffert admitted that she had never registered the swans but also stated that she was unaware that any such regulations were in existence. Appellant argues that since they were not Mrs. Meffert never possessed the trumpeter swans. The argument is totally unpersuasive. Count II, charging appellant with false testimony that the swans were mute rather than trumpeters, was withdrawn from the jury. Thus, the relevance of the registration was minimal. Furthermore, Mrs. Meffert admitted that the swans weren't registered. Therefore, the point was made and her conceded ignorance of the Migratory Bird regulations hardly establishes that she didn't possess the swans which she didn't consider birds in any event.[9] The existence of the regulations was irrelevant and whether or

---

[9] For a liberal construction of the term "birds," by a Canadian court *see Regina v. Ojibway*, 8 Criminal Law Quarterly 137 (1965-66) (Op. Blue, J.), holding that an Indian who shot a pony which had broken a leg and was saddled with a downy pillow had violated the Small Birds Act which defined a "bird" as "a two legged animal covered with feathers." The court reasoned that the statutory definition "does not imply that only two-legged animals qualify, for the legislative intent is to make two legs merely the minimum requirement. . . . Counsel submits that having regard to the purpose of the statute only small animals 'naturally covered' with feathers could have been contemplated. However, had this been the intention of the legislature, I am certain that the phrase 'naturally covered' would have been expressly inserted just as 'Long' was inserted in the Longshoreman's Act.

"Therefore, a horse with feathers on its back must be deemed for the purpose of this Act to be a bird, *a fortiori*, a pony with feathers on its back is a small bird." *Id.* at 139.

not Mrs. Meffert violated them would only confuse the issue before the jury. The trial judge has broad discretion in these matters and he committed no abuse of discretion in refusing to take judicial notice of the regulations or submitting them to the jury. See *United States v. Albergo*, 539 F.2d 860, 863 (2d Cir. 1973), cert. denied, 429 U.S. 1000, 97 S.Ct. 529, 50 L.Ed.2d 611 (1976); *United States v. Bowe*, 360 F.2d 1, 15 (2d Cir.), cert. denied, 385 U.S. 961, 87 S.Ct. 401, 17 L.Ed.2d 306 (1966).

The judgment of conviction is affirmed, justice has triumphed and this is my swan song.

The Lawyer
1981–1989

CONFERENCE OF METROPOLITAN DISTRICT CHIEF JUDGES, WINTER PARK, FLORIDA
March 27, 1981

The subject assigned to me this morning, the relationship between the courts of appeal and the district court, is indeed multifaceted. We are now restructuring our circuit courts to allow district court representation. What will eventuate is not clear, and I think that this aspect of the relationship will develop over the next few years, so that comment now is premature and not particularly helpful. I can only say that the one part of the job I will not miss is attendance at council meetings. My last will be on Monday.

I would prefer to speak briefly of the sometimes positive relationship which comes into play by virtue of the very nature of our work—judging and judicial review. This relationship, in my view, basically depends upon the personal attitudes of the judges involved. Since there can be no doubt that the function of the appellate court is to review the work of the district judge, there is obviously some basis for hostility or resentment when a reversal or, even more realistically, when a remand is ordered by a Court of Appeals. We all have pride of authorship and scholarship as well, and any correction by another tribunal, no matter how gently phrased, is liable to cause some resentment dependent upon the thickness of the epidermis of the jurist involved.

The following observations are in order: From the very nature of the judicial process, and the proper functioning of an appellate court, the fact that a trial court might be offended to some degree or another can certainly not enter as a factor in the decision-making process. By the same token, there is no need for an appellate court to couch its opinion in unnecessarily strident tones, except where egregious conduct is involved—and this is indeed a rare case. Appellate judges must recognize, and generally do, that evidentiary rulings made in the heat of litigation, while not necessarily off the cuff, are nonetheless not usually made with the extensive briefing by counsel and clerks which is the luxury of a three-judge appellate tribunal. Oddly enough, the appreciation of the problems of the trial judge may be more fully appreciated by one directly appointed to the Court of Appeals than by those who rose from the ranks. There may well be a tendency on the part of former district judges to believe that they would have done something differently and therefore what was done constituted reversible error. I have found this tendency among district court judges appointed to sit on the Court of Appeals for a particular sitting.

The attitude of trial judges to the review process varies among judges, depending primarily upon their own concept of the process and their own confidence in their own abilities.

Some perhaps outwardly at least profess no concern at all, taking the view that after I rule what is done upstairs is of no concern to me. While they may say this, I often note that they send a clerk up to hear the argument and report back on the results. Some few agonize, particularly young judges—one of whom wrote me a personal note even on an affirmation because he thought there was some implied criticism.

I think a second observation is that if the trial judge knew what panel would review his work when he was trying his case, the percentage of reversals would drop considerably. Charlie Brieant in the Southern District has suggested that when the district court judge is selected from the wheel, it should also select the panel.

Trial judges must also understand that appellate judges often disagree among themselves not only where dissenting opinions exist but where a judge assigned an opinion finds that it is mutilated by suggestions for amendments from his colleagues. The written intramural memos in this situation are much more destructive of one's ego than opinions reversing or remanding.

The term "judicial temperament" is most usually ascribed to the attitude of the judge toward the litigants and counsel who appear before him. However, it has another dimension equally important—the attitude of one judge to another. In my view, that can only be one of mutual forbearance—a recognition that each has a job to do and that no one is infallible. Certainly not the Supreme Court. The fact that one judge sits at one level and the other at one presumably lower in the judicial hierarchy is not because of greater ability but more accurately by reason of the accidents of age, geography, coincidence, or politics.

In any event I have never found any serious problems in this area. Any mature judge recognizes that today's hero can be to-morrow's villain, whether he be a member of your own court or another. Obviously, we all have much more in common than other-wise. There is primarily an intangible—the camaraderie of the federal judiciary. Will Rogers is alleged to have said that he never met a man he didn't like. He was not the first to make that statement. In our religious tradition we are enjoined to hate the sin but love the sinner. Unfortunately, I am among those, like most, who appreciate the sentiment but cannot adhere to it. All that I can say is that in my ten years on the bench I have met hundreds of federal judges, and I have greater admiration and affection for them than any group of men with whom I have ever been associated.

We are engaged in the challenging and indeed vital work of administering justice as well as humans can make it work and thus probably enjoy a mutual understanding and respect for what has to be the highest vocation in our profession. The fed-eral bench by and large is provided and equipped superlatively to carry out this task. We have ample chambers, library facilities, physical equipment, clerks, and staff. We have a highly efficient Advisors' Office at judicial center. Much of this is due to the efforts of Chief Justice Burger, who, in my view is the staunchest supporter the federal judiciary has had in modern times. At the same time we are drawn together, oddly enough, by adversity (misery loves company), and I refer, of course, to the grossly inadequate salaries and survivors' benefits which in my case made my demise as a federal judge inevitable. In the army the soldier who griped was not necessarily disaffected—it was part of the misery we all felt and, surprisingly, it created some sort of morale. I made my reasons for leaving the bench clear and definitive and deliberately so. I, frankly, did not realize that this would engender far more publicity than anything I had ever done either on or off the bench. You may be interested in some of the reactions. My judicial colleagues both in New York and throughout the country, while regretting my departure, fully understood its motivation and applauded my voicing my rea-sons for the move. It has been indeed a wrench, and I would not have done it were it not compelled by financial considera-tions. After thirty-five years at law school and on the bench, what I had thought initially was adequate financial support for my family became continually eroded by double-digit inflation which could not have been reasonably anticipated.

The reaction of the legal profession and the press in New York was also understanding—in fact, both *The New York Times* and the *Daily News* printed editorials calling upon Congress to remedy the situation. Of course, there were some dissenters—principally Harry Reasoner on radio who couldn't understand how a judge could not live on $71,000 a year—as well as a few letters from obscure attorneys who obviously would be happy to go on the bench; the most positive reactions have been a resolution from the American Judicature Society calling for a congressional investigation of the J.S.A.S. as well as a letter from two congressional members to the Chief Justice promising to introduce such legislation.

This is hardly an audience which needs to be persuaded that we are sorely mistreated by the Congress. The Chief Justice has appointed a committee headed by Irving Kaufman which is pursuing these issues vigorously. My recent experience has led me to believe that we have a much better chance to improve the J.S.A.S. than to obtain a salary increase. *The New York Times* reported that the widow of Congressman McCormick is receiving an annual pension of $91,000—at our former $57,500 salary, the maximum for the survivor of a district court judge was $21,800. My widow would obtain $23,000, and I would have to live to be 81 before that was payable. That would entail thirty years of judicial service, not counting three-and-a-half years of military service. It is quite clear that there is some inequity present.

The salary inequity is quite obvious to those of us who live in metropolitan districts; my commuting bill alone for one month is $74, none of which is paid for by the government and none of which is deductible. The New York law firms now pay $37,000 for entering students fresh out of law schools. Within ten years they are making much more than federal judges. Soon only those lawyers who have extensive independent means will be able to afford the luxury of the bench. I don't have to emphasize to this group how disastrous this will be for the bench.

The difficulty, as I view it, aside from the drive to curb federal spending, is that the Congress, which has a decidedly low public image, cannot believe that federal judges with lifetime tenure should make more than they do despite the considerable fringe benefits available to them and not to us. They may well consider themselves underpaid, but they realize that their constituencies are revolted at any vote to increase their own salaries. We must remember that at our present levels we rank in the top one-percent income bracket in the United States. We are rated, according to the press, not simply as affluent but as rich. The error, of course, is to equate judges with the general public. The comparison must be made not with the public but with our professional peers. The difficulty for the congressman is that he is elected not by attorneys but by those who for the most part make far less than he does. Since re-election is on his mind, he will not jeopardize votes by voting himself a raise. The linkage between the Congress and the bench in salary matters must be broken if we are eventually to succeed. Under the leadership of the Chief Justice and the Kaufman Committee, I am hopeful that this will be accomplished. When I leave the bench in a few days, I hope to be able to devote some time to this enterprise which is close to my heart.

I thank you for your invitation to be here and I wish you all well.

FEDERAL BAR COUNCIL PRESENTATION OF LEARNED HAND MEDAL FOR EXCELLENCE TO THE HONORABLE WALTER MANSFIELD

May 4, 1981

Distinguished members of the bench and the bar, Circuit Judge Walter Mansfield, Tina, and members of the Mansfield family:

For some eighteen years the Federal Bar Council has been bestowing the Learned Hand Medal for Excellence in Federal Jurisprudence to distinguished members of our profession. Judge Mansfield, this year's recipient, adds even further luster to the list of eminent members of the bench and bar who have been so honored on prior occasions. I am myself honored this evening to be designated to make this presentation to him on your behalf.

I should like to begin my brief homily by recalling an interlude in Walter's life which was not legal and which in fact interrupted his professional career. However, it epitomizes qualities of courage and moral conviction which have marked his professional service. In World War II Walter Mansfield left the firm of Donovan, Leisure, Newton & Irvine, which he had joined after his graduation from Harvard Law School in 1935, to enter the military service of our country. Unlike many lawyers who became chair borne, he volunteered to become air borne. He joined the Marine Corps and volunteered for service in a parachute battalion, eventually making some twenty-three jumps. The most daring of these was after his assignment to the O.S.S. when he parachuted behind German lines to spend six months with the guerrilla forces of Mihailovich in the mountains of Yugoslavia. His departure was equally bizarre. He was picked up by a British submarine off the Dalmatian Coast. His next field of operation was equally risky. He served behind Japanese lines in

China, where he spent a year organizing the guerrilla forces of Chiang Kai-shek. He planned and conducted successful raids on Japanese supply lines. He was in China at the end of the War, having risen to the rank of major. I must say that I was entirely unaware of Walter's deeds of derring-do when I first joined the bench, and typically it was not the Judge who revealed them to me. I happened to read a history of the O.S.S. and learned that my serene, placid, and soft-spoken colleague was, in fact, a trained guerrilla fighter. My dissents from his opinions thereafter grew fewer in number and more gentle in tone.

My own military career was astonishingly similar to Walter's, and I presume that this is why I was selected to make this award this evening. I too left a large firm, three partners, to enter the military service, albeit with the active encouragement of my draft board. I too became involved in Intelligence as an agent in the Counter Intelligence squad. After three-and-a-half years of active service in most of the boroughs of this city, I had risen rapidly through the ranks to the level of technical sergeant. I never even boarded a plane and certainly would never have been tempted to jump out of one. I too traveled over dangerous waters—New York Harbor, commuting by ferry to Governor's Island and even occasionally to Staten Island where I was assigned to the Port of Embarkation. Walter Mansfield won the Bronze Star, the Legion of Merit, and the White Eagle Award of Yugoslavia. I was awarded the Good Conduct Medal in a split opinion.

Walter's private practice of law was with the Donovan, Leisure firm, with a three-year hiatus from 1938 to 1941 when he served as an U.S. Attorney prosecuting and trying a wide variety of criminal cases. When he rejoined his firm after the War, he specialized in litigation, including the trial of heavy corporate antitrust and unfair competition cases. As the firm grew larger and more prosperous, he was forced to devote more of his attention to law firm administration. In 1966 he became a judge in the United States District Court for the Southern District of New York, where he gained the plaudits of the bar for his thorough, equitable, and reasonable conduct of the trial of cases. In 1971 he was appointed to the Second Circuit Court where he joined his former partner and dear colleague Judge J. Edward Lumbard, who has also been the recipient of this prestigious medal.

The record of a circuit court judge is preserved for professional and public scrutiny but only to the extent that his opinions are published. A discussion of these opinions is impossible in view of the time frame this evening. Actually, the opinions of a judge constitute only the tip of the iceberg. The business of judging is multidimensional, and the best opportunity for observation of a judge's contributions to a court is to serve on the same bench with him. I was fortunate indeed to have that opportunity for the past decade. It goes without saying that Walter is, of course, an able and scholarly jurist. The principal virtue, in my view, which he brought to the bench was his meticulous and sophisticated study of the record. I never knew him to be unprepared for the argument of any appeal, no matter how voluminous the record. His most persistent question on the argument is—where does it say that in the record? He recognizes the critical issues of fact and he wishes to be assured that the record supports the sometimes colored statements of fact in the brief. After the argument, when we would occasionally discuss the merits of the appeal before our more formal voting conferences, I would often express my views as to how we should go. His usual response was—let me take another look at the record. Having come to the bench primarily with a background of law teaching, my observation of Walter's insistence on familiarity with the record was indeed an educational process. His experience as a prosecutor, private litigator, and trial judge made him ideally suited for the Appellate bench.

There is another facet of judging which is not usually fully appreciated even by the practicing profession. I refer to the service of the judge to the administration of justice. While a Chief Judge and the Circuit Executive and his staff may be able to handle the bulk of administrative detail, there are nonetheless rule-making and regulatory functions which are best supervised by an active judge. Walter served gratuitously and generously on more of these committees than any other judge on the bench. He served indefatigably with his characteristic close attention to detail. I did come here to praise him but not to bury you with further detail. I can say, in sum, that he has brought a quiet style and grace to all his judicial tasks. There are obviously many other virtues of Walter's which I could dwell upon. The Second Circuit Court has enjoyed, and still does, a reputation for excellence. It is because of jurists of the stature of Walter Mansfield that this reputation persists. It was indeed an honor for me to have been associated with him.

We wish him, his beloved Tina, and his family all the best of health and happiness as he takes on senior status. I thank the council for affording me this opportunity to make this award on its behalf.

BIRTHDAY DINNER FOR THE HONORABLE EDWARD WEINFELD

May 18, 1981

Chief Judge McMahon, Judge and Mrs. Weinfeld, my brothers and sisters of the bench:

It is indeed an honor and privilege for this separated brother to be invited to participate in this special proceedings this evening. Many of you are familiar with Irving [Emeritus Chief Judge] Kaufman's widely publicized open letter to President Reagan on judge picking. Irving indicated that the ideal judge should possess not only extraordinary intellectual capacity and a thorough grounding in the law, but a grasp of history, philosophy, poetry, economics, sociology, psychology, and selected sciences as well. You also need, he says, worldly common sense, the ability to communicate effectively and to write precisely and powerfully. These are only a few of the attributes of the ideal judge. I would add the ability to see thunder and hear lightning. Judge Kaufman further advised the President to use his power to appoint wisely since the President would never be able to discharge the judge he has appointed. While this may not have been the purpose of the open letter, it occurred to me that I fell so far short of all these ideals, except perhaps for poetry, that the only appropriate step to take was to resign from the bench. I, therefore, wrote to the President, not an open letter, but a private letter tendering my resignation from the Second Circuit bench. The President was so overwhelmed by emotion and the pain of loss that he was unable to collect his thoughts and did not accept until this morning! He must have somehow learned about my comments here this evening. I also wrote to Senator Moynihan advising him of the step I had taken. After a month, he responded asking me to consider somebody for a clerkship in 1982. Senator D'Amato hasn't answered either. In the immortal words of the poet Dangerfield, "I don't get no respect." If I were asked the question as to what the ideal judge should be, I would say to the President: Get somebody like Eddie Weinfeld. I don't know if they make any like that today, but a reasonable facsimile would do. Irving did say that the President should pick people who will not be overcome by all the trimmings and trappings of the office. Eddie certainly never has been. He usually describes himself as just another soldier in the ranks.

I never thought much of the trappings either until I lost them to enter the private practice of the law. In the world outside, my friends, there is no private elevator, no private john, no personal law clerks, and no calendar prepared in advance. You recognize your advancing years. The average age of a partner at Skadden is the average age of the children and even the grandchildren of my former colleagues on the bench. I am the second-oldest partner—the only people I meet who are my own age are the messengers and the porters. When I asked what their policy would be when I reached 70, they said they had no policy since they had so infrequently faced the problem. If you don't die in service, they make you a messenger. When I came in one morning at 9:15—the earliest I have been up since I left the army—I found a young lady sleeping on the couch in my office. She had been working all night. When I came in, she asked me what shift I was on.

My entire adult life has involved positions with little or no salary but always a title—Sergeant, Commissioner, Professor, Dean, and Judge. Now even the summer associates call me Billy. I have taken to wearing my robes in the office since I still haven't been able to afford new suits. Actually I am adjusting fairly well to my new surroundings. The lawyers are top-flight, work hard to support me, and I expect to be out of intensive care shortly. Charlie Brieant asked many of Ed's former clerks to supply me with anecdotes about him. They did, but none was really new to me. His opinions and the cases he has tried have been reported time and time again. We all know that he is the first to arrive and the last to leave the courthouse. I always asked my law clerks to emulate that practice. On the Sunday that the air lift was attempted at the Metropolitan Correctional Center, Ed was the only judge in the building, working as usual. The F.B.I. considered the possibility that he was somehow involved in the attempted snatch. I told them that if some others of my colleagues had been found present there at that time that this would be a good lead—but not in the case of Eddie.

Ed is noted for his addiction to physical exercise—for walking, playing tennis, and, for all I know, weight lifting. I personally find the reading of poetry much more exhilarating. When I joined the firm, I was told that I could use the facilities of a new athletic organization called the Vertical Club. I responded that I was more interested in the Horizontal Club. The most courageous thing I ever did for the ten years I spent on the bench was on one occasion to reverse Eddie Weinfeld. If Henry Friendly had not concurred, I probably would have gone the other way. Seriously, Judge Weinfeld made appellate judging a pleasure. He had worked on the case so hard, prepared it so diligently, and written it so well that those attorneys rash enough to appeal always felt some extra pressure. I recall one diversity case involving Pennsylvania tort law. The losing side retained eminent counsel on appeal, a former New York Court of Appeals judge, who claimed that the trial judge had committed reversible error in his charge. The record revealed that on the weekend before the charge Judge Weinfeld not only had received submitted written requests for charges but had spent an entire Saturday going over the charge with counsel for both sides, all of whom had agreed to the charges as given. No exceptions were requested. Another easy appeal. In his address at the courthouse this spring, Ed referred to the old saw about the Hands: quote "Learned" but follow "Gus." In the case of Weinfeld you can both quote him and follow him.

Aside from his obvious professional abilities, his diligence, his impartiality, his often expressed view that every case is important, we remember Eddie best because of his gentility, his grace, his humility, and his good fellowship. The last day I sat in the court a number of district court judges were good enough to attend. That afternoon I received a telephone call from Eddie, who apologized for not being present. I said, "I know you must have been busy in the court." "No," he said, "I am calling from Arizona." I asked what he was doing out there and he said: "Oh, they gave me some sort of an award." His innate modesty, his thoughtfulness on that occasion as on many others was typical. Ed Weinfeld deserves every award he has received and will receive in the future, but his charm lies in the fact that he doesn't really believe that he merits any of them.

There is a great deal of camaraderie on the federal bench. Although we all have had differences and sometimes have expressed them rather vehemently, nonetheless a sense of common dedication to the cause of justice brought us all together in the long pull. For many, and I think I speak for all of you, Eddie Weinfeld typified the very best of all dedication and fellowship.

He has well earned the complete trust and respect of the profession which practices before him as well as of his colleagues on the bench. He has been at the bar for more than sixty years, on the bench more than thirty years, and on the earth more than eighty years. We are all fortunate to have shared some part of those years with him.

GALA ROAST FOR
MAYOR EDWARD I. KOCH,
SHERATON CENTRE
September 15, 1981

Senator Moynihan, Vice President Mondale, Mayor Koch, distinguished guests, and friends all of the mayor:

It is indeed a great honor and privilege, I think, to be invited to appear here this evening for the avowed purpose of insulting the chief executive of the City of New York in public and in his presence. There was no shortage of volunteers for this honor. This is an art form with which I am unfamiliar. Gentlemen normally assault their friends privately—behind their backs; they attack their enemies in public but not quite as enthusiastically.

In any event, since the mayor has been constantly asking "How am I doing?" I suppose he deserves a frank response. Why he has selected two vice presidents to do this to him is a sign of his humility. Most of you know that Senator Mondale was formerly Vice President of the United States—and certainly you know that I am presently Second Vice President of the Friendly Sons of Saint Patrick. In fact, in November, absent a primary fight or the intervention of a federal three-judge court, I will become First Vice President of that great organization.

Since the mayor is supported by both major parties, I assume my role here is that of a Republican spokesman. My credentials in this respect are hardly spectacular and, in fact, suspect. Any Irish Catholic born and brought up in The Bronx who nonetheless becomes a registered Republican hardly displays political acumen. After the War, I moved to Westchester where I thought Republicans were more acceptable.

In 1954 I became the Republican candidate for Village Trustee of North Pelham which had a four-to-one edge in registrations over the Democrats. I don't have to remind this sophisticated audience what a bitter campaign that was and how important the issues were. I was defeated by a Democrat by a three-to-one margin. Since that time the Republicans have been noticeably cool to any political aspirations I might have had. However, I held no grudges and bear no animosity to the Republicans of North Pelham. Those rotten people voted against me because they thought that anybody named Mulligan who came from The Bronx had to be a Democrat. According to political analysts that was the biggest political upset until the presidential elections of 1980.

I have interviewed the mayor and asked him what he considered the biggest problem facing him as mayor. He answered promptly—"Solving Rubik's Cube." I then understood why among his intimates he is affectionately known as Edsel—an indication of the stature he commands among those who know him best.

In addition to his honesty, I admire the mayor for his courage—not only because of his infantry service in World War II where he served both in the European theater and in Loew's Paradise (he is the only G.I. in World War II to receive a Purple Heart from the Loew's Management), but also for riding a camel in Egypt with an Arab headdress. His courage is tempered by discretion, however. I learned, for example, that one night, unable to sleep, he rode his camel out into the desert. They arrived at the edge of a precipice, the camel balked, and the mayor was catapulted into an abyss. He grabbed out and miraculously caught on to a tree that was growing sideways out of the cliff. He called out in desperation—"Is anyone up there?"—and once again—"Is anybody up there?" "I am," came the response. "Is that God?" said the mayor. "Yes, Edsel," came the response. "Are you the God of Abraham and Moses?" "I am," said the voice. "Do you trust me?" said God. "Oh, yes," said Ed. "Then let go of the tree," said God. After a few minutes' reflection, and viewing the abyss, the mayor responded, "Is there anybody else up there?"

Ed is a great innovator. He is the first mayor in the history of New York to choke on a Chinese egg roll in Chinatown some weeks ago. I asked him to explain—he said "I never ordered an egg roll; I ordered an egg cream. Why do you think I was using a straw?"

The mayor, in order to give me an idea of his campaign style, brought me with him to a home for the aged in Brooklyn. We met three old ladies playing cards in a lounge. "How am I doing?" said the mayor. The first said "Oy"; the second said "Oy veh"; and the third said "Oy viz mir." "Do you speak Spanish?"

said the mayor to me. I admitted I did not. He said "Let me translate—they said 'fantastic,' 'marvelous,' and 'superb.' " I was duly impressed.

I was most flattered when the mayor asked me if I would like to return to government service. I told him I would have to ask my partners at Skadden, Arps—"Don't worry about that" he said, "Joe Flom, your senior partner, suggested it to me." "What do you have in mind?" I said. "How do you like to cook?" he said. Since that job would last only six months, I was not interested. In a public statement commenting on the rapid turnover of chefs at Gracie Mansion, the mayor said that he enjoyed simple food. I asked why the turnover. He told me that his favorite restaurant was a place called Lundy's, which used to advertise, "The fish you eat today slept last night in Sheepshead Bay." One night the mayor visited Lundy's and ordered fresh flounder with a bialy on the side. I assumed that this is a cocktail of some sort. When the fish arrived, the mayor viewed the fish and the fish stared back. Never at a loss for words, the mayor said "Do you come from Sheepshead Bay?" "Yes, Mr. Mayor," said the fish. "Did you know my friend Horowitz?" said the mayor. "Why should I know him?" said the fish. "He drowned in Sheepshead Bay," said the mayor. "When?" said the fish. "Last month," said the mayor. "I didn't know him," said the fish—"I had already been caught." The mayor promptly left. The next morning he directed his chef to provide him with a fresh flounder that evening for dinner at Gracie Mansion. When he arrived home, the fish was served. He looked familiar. They stared at each other and the fish said, "Mr. Mayor, how come you no longer eat at Lundy's?" That was the end of the chef. I must say frankly that I do not intend to vote for Ed Koch—I don't live here anymore. If I did live here, I would give him serious consideration.

I conclude by saying that only someone who admires, respects, and enthusiastically supports Mayor Koch could be this disrespectful. I have a great empathy for the mayor because he is the quintessential New Yorker—open, able, forthcoming, hardworking, visible, and totally honest. I wish him well and I plan to register soon as a full-time student at the Culinary Institute.

ST. JOHN'S UNIVERSITY
LAW ALUMNI ASSOCIATION
December 5, 1981

I am indeed honored to be invited to participate in the Annual Homecoming of the Law Alumni of St. John's University. Many of you may have wondered why I left the prestigious Second Circuit bench to go into private practice. Some skeptics have questioned my public confession of impending financial disaster and concern for a long-suffering spouse and children. It is about time that I revealed the real reason for my decision—it was inspired by fear.

One of the perquisites of a federal judge is the right to use an official plate—U.S.J. followed by a numeral. When I joined the court in 1971, I was U.S.J. 52; six years later I was U.S.J. 27; in 1979 I was U.S.J. 22. The declining number was dependent upon my seniority. Since judges seldom, if ever, resigned, the declining number actually reflected the death rate of my colleagues. Every year I received an annual intimation of my own mortality, and it was quite disquieting. I gave the statistics to a doctor friend of mine and after careful study he reported to me that the license plate statistics were as accurate a mortality table as any he had encountered. I asked him what his advice was— instead of orange juice, aspirin, and bed rest, he told me that when I got down to U.S.J. 5 I should sell my car. He didn't claim that this would make me immortal, but he did say that the declining plate number undoubtedly expedited the aging processes of the judiciary and was psychologically debilitating. In 1981 I reached the age of 63 and also received a new plate— U.S.J. 7. The effect was somewhat traumatic: in seven years I would reach the biblical term of three score and ten, and U.S.J. 1. The message was clear and compelling. Rather than sell the car, I decided to quit the bench and get back to a three-digit number which will, I hope, ensure me of a greater life expectancy. I realize this was a rather drastic remedy and did not mention to the press the real reason for my decision to leave the bench. I trust you will keep it in the confidence of this room.

Life as a practitioner is quite dissimilar from the orderly, scholastic, and almost monastic life I enjoyed on the bench, and the transition has not been easy. After thirty-five years working for the Jesuits and the United States, two institutions which have many characteristics in common, a theme which I will not develop this afternoon, I found relative affluence a most difficult status to accept. The habits of a lifetime are tough to shake, and relief from the vow of poverty is difficult. I discovered that taxicabs were vehicles which accepted passengers and were not simply quickly moving objects to carefully avoid while walking to the subway. I discovered that there were men's stores other than Sy Syms's; I now look in the windows at Brooks Brothers and in another few months I expect to get up enough courage to actually enter the store and eventually even make a purchase. I may require the assistance of a psychiatrist.

There are other psychological adjustments which have to be made. As practicing attorneys, you realize that while the judge does not enjoy a large income he does have other compensations. He comes to the courtroom in a private elevator; his gown is placed on him by a bailiff; when he enters the courtroom he is announced, all stand, and he is for the most part fawned upon, called "Your Honor" or at least "Judge." When he returns to his chambers, he is greeted by three law clerks, two secretaries, and a spacious suite of three or four rooms plus a private john, some with showers. For the most part he arranges his own calendar, knows where and with whom he will be sitting for the next six months. The judge knows that all of this attention and all of the amenities are due not to him personally but out of respect to his office. However, the longer they continue to be accorded the more difficult it becomes to make the distinction between the office and the man. I always considered myself to be a democratic fellow whose head would never be turned by the trappings of the office and the continuous obeisance paid. It was only when I left the bench that I began to appreciate that I had not at all been immune to the flattery. I have given up wearing the robe in the office. I no longer call my partners counselor and no longer tell them that they may approach the bench when they come to my office. I do have the robes in a nearby closet and when I feel depressed I close the door of my office and walk around in them for a while. I am gradually beginning to become acclimated and within a few years I hope to be a normal practicing attorney.

As you know, I spent most of my adult life teaching and deaning at Fordham Law School. Fordham and St. John's obviously have much in common, and I don't know if our contribution to the profession has ever been fully appreciated by the bar at large or even our own alumni. Both institutions were founded under and operated under the aegis of Roman Catholic religious orders—and yet both from the beginning, and before the concept of ecumenism was even thought of, opened their doors to people of all races, creeds, and colors. There was never any thought of discrimination. Both schools initially recognized the obligation and indeed the opportunity to educate the sons of immigrants who had not yet acquired the funds to support full-time education at Ivy League prices. Both had and continue to have evening divisions to accommodate those who have to support themselves by working in the daytime. I remember well as Dean of Fordham when the suggestion was made by a fortunately short-lived administration that we should drop the evening division because no Ivy League school had one and thus we would somehow be transmogrified into somebody's concept of a first-rate law school. We successfully resisted the suggestion, denied the allegations, and defied the allegators.

My view continues to be that a law school depends upon the intellectual quality of its faculty and students and upon their willingness to work long and hard. Where their parents come from and what church, if any, they attend or how much material wealth they have acquired has nothing at all to do with this concept. Unfortunately, this for many, many years was not appreciated by the New York bar establishment. All of us at one or another time in our lives have experienced some covert or even overt discrimination because we did not attend so-called national law schools. When I first became Dean, there were firms which either did not interview Fordham graduates or if they did would relegate them to the managing clerk's office. The situation was even more difficult for St. John's. I am happy to say that the professional success of our alumni has succeeded in changing the picture. The law firms are now vying for top people even though they come from an urban school with an evening division. People sometimes ask me, "Why did you pick Skadden, Arps?" I tell you quite frankly that aside from its professional quality and material success, I was impressed with the fact that we have more Fordham Law alumni than any other New York firm. I have three St. John's partners and about fifteen St. John's associates. The success of the venture did not and does not depend upon whose diploma hangs on the wall but upon the ability and energy of the person who sits behind the desk. It has been a long and at times discouraging battle to persuade the profession of our virtues but the tide has turned and as our alumni become better placed and more influential, I think we will achieve what we always deserved—the opportunity to have our alumni be judged on their merit and not on the supposed standing of their schools.

We in turn owe a continuing obligation to our law schools not simply to make an annual financial donation but to try to help those students who follow us by opening doors and creating opportunities.

This school has been blessed with a top-flight faculty and deans such as Tinnelly, McNiece, Murphy, and Rohan. I have known and worked with all of them. I wish all of you well and I thank you for inviting me.

THIRTY-FIRST ANNUAL TWELFTH NIGHT CELEBRATION OF THE ASSOCIATION OF THE BAR OF THE CITY OF NEW YORK
January 18, 1982

Judge Markewich, Judge McLaughlin, distinguished members of the bench and bar, friends all:

Had I known this was an English custom, I would not have come.

I am advised by counsel that it is a great honor and privilege to be publicly humiliated and embarrassed by a bunch of thespians at this otherwise civilized bar association. I view this sellout crowd with mixed emotions. Why are so many friends and colleagues willing to pay for the privilege of witnessing my ordeal. I am now of the opinion that my funeral services, which, to the best of my knowledge, will be held without admission fees, will attract an even greater number of my followers. St. Patrick's Cathedral will not be big enough, but Shea Stadium will do. This will disappoint the Cardinal but elate Bill Shea and accounts for his presence here tonight.

I must also thank the Committee for inviting my wife and family to be present here as the guests of the association; otherwise they might have missed this tribute. Thank God, my mother, who is in her 93rd year, had another date—her bowling team is competing this evening. But, after all, I did agree to become the sacrificial lamb here this evening. It reminds me of Whitney Seymour's story of the miscreant who was tarred and feathered and ridden on a rail out of town. When later asked for his reactions, he said, "It would have been painful and uncomfortable had it not been for the honor of it all."

I deny all of the allegations made this evening and defy the allegators.

I have no resentment and bear no animosity toward those attorneys who wrote, composed, and otherwise participated in the performance this evening. If the dramatic and musical skills displayed by the cast are on a par with their legal ability, then I feel sorry for those families dependent upon them for support. With respect to the participation of Judge McLaughlin, I must say that I have long since felt that it was entirely inappropriate for a jurist, particularly one with such limited experience, to participate publicly in the humiliation of a humble member of the practicing profession. This is not a suddenly acquired view but one which I have held persistently for at least the past nine months. Judge McLaughlin could not resist any invitation to participate in a party which promised lavish refreshments and a jazz band. Joe started out his musical career with the Fordham University Marching Band. He found it impossible to learn to play any instrument except the drum and that only with one hand—he therefore naturally became the drum major. He will undoubtedly apply for a conducting job with the jazz band this evening, and I will support his application with enthusiasm. Joe is now in a career making decisions—something he has failed to do for the past ten years.

After twenty-five years teaching and deaning and ten years on the bench, it is a rather frightening prospect to have to go to work for a living for the first time in my life. It is complicated further by the ethical questions which arise when an ex-federal judge appears before his former colleagues on the bench.

I refer, of course, to the clear prejudice and bias which sitting judges may have against their erstwhile colleague. After all, he has emerged from his previous condition of servitude, which may provoke their envy and hostility rather than pride that one of their own has made it. There is also, particularly in the case of a former judge of the circuit court of appeals who appears in a district court, the grave possibility that the trial judge was on one or more occasion reversed in an opinion which I authored. What is even more disastrous, I may have used language which now appears even to me to be infelicitous or even strident. It becomes even more complicated when I may have to appear before my former colleagues on the Circuit Court. How often did I dissent in bitter tones, such as "I dissent for the reasons given by the majority," or even "I concur in the result"—which freely translated means, the majority somehow reached the right conclusion despite their faulty reasoning.

The proper approach to these concerns of course is to face them honestly, squarely, and manfully—if that adverb is still permissible. I propose a footnote in a memorandum or brief to the court indicating that since leaving the bench I have had the opportunity to review my prior opinions and was shocked to find that on one or two occasions (hopefully no more) I had unfortunately reversed the learned district judge. I would candidly indicate that maturity and experience have persuaded me to confess error and to regret any inconvenience or embarrassment my prior opinion may have caused. Of course, if the record reveals that I had affirmed the trial judge, the same ethical considerations would compel disclosure, together with some indication of pleasure in seeing how sound we all were. In fact, I believe 1984 would be the ideal time for a total review of all my opinions with a *nunc pro tunc* rewrite which would eliminate any possibility of bias by the district judges.

Handling these problems in a footnote when appearing before the Second Circuit becomes rather difficult in view of the three-judge panels. In my ten years on the circuit there was only one circuit judge with whom I never had any disagreement, the Honorable Sterry Waterman, who is present here this evening. I assume he came to praise me and not to bury me.

Of course, there is another side of the coin. Despite all the evidence to the contrary, some may feel that his former colleagues might be prejudiced in favor of the ex-judge litigator. While I consider this to be only a remote possibility—my solution to the problem is quite simple: I solemnly pledge to all federal and, for that matter, all state, local, or municipal judges, magistrates, justices of the peace, and notaries public before whom I shall ever appear that I will not represent any client unless his cause is eminently just, supported by overwhelming authority and uncontradictable facts. In this fashion justice will be achieved without fear or favor, and I will be enabled to live in a style to which I have not been accustomed.

Seriously, I appreciate the honor which you have accorded me and thank all of you who participated in making this a memorable evening.

NEW YORK STATE BAR ASSOCIATION PRESENTATION OF GOLD MEDAL TO WILLIAM HUGHES MULLIGAN

April 30, 1982

President Williams, Officers and Members of the New York State Bar Association, distinguished members of the bench and bar, ladies and gentlemen:

I am, of course, honored and flattered to receive the Gold Medal for Distinguished Service in the Law which is awarded annually by this Association. It marks a high point in my professional career, and I am deeply indebted to the Executive Committee and the Association for the honor. I am humbled to be in the excellent company of the past recipients of this medal, which includes two of my former colleagues on the Second Circuit bench, Harold Medina and Henry J. Friendly. While the judgment of any group which gives me a Gold Medal is open to question, I nonetheless, on my own behalf as well as my family's, thank you for your generosity and friendship.

I have made it a practice in my professional career to give serious messages in the classroom, in my written opinions, and, now, to the clients of Skadden, Arps. On occasions such as this I prefer a somewhat lighter tone. Whatever the current problems of law reform, calendar congestion, legal ethics, and international affairs, they will have to continue thus. I do not propose to solve them this evening. Rather than reflect upon my career in the law, I thought you might have some interest in what was happening to me forty years ago this spring when I was admitted to the bar of this State.

I graduated from Fordham College in 1939, during the Depression, and, being unable to find a job, like many of my contemporaries, I discovered that I had a vocation for the law. I applied for and was admitted to the Fordham Law School. In those days admission to law school was comparatively easy, even at the most prestigious institutions. The ability to pay a modest tuition, to shave and own a suit, tie, and at least one shirt was sufficient. Having achieved an A average in my first year at law school, I was encouraged to take a part-time job in my second year as a book-boy at the New York County Lawyers Library on Vesey Street. There I found it possible to brief my law school cases and shelve books at the same time with a reasonable degree of success. My reward for five half-days and a full day on Saturday, when I also operated the elevator, was indeed generous: $8.00 a week in cash, the free use of a linen coat, and a magnificent view of the cemetery at St. Paul's Church.

In my third year, one of my professors, apparently impressed with my grades, advised me that he had recommended me for a clerk's position with a New York law firm. I assumed that it was either Sullivan & Cromwell or White & Case but instead it was Casey & Caddell at 154 Nassau Street. I had never heard of the firm, but I was assured that it was an up-and-coming organization with a great future. In addition to the two named partners, there was one associate and one employee who answered the phone, took dictation, and served process. I later learned that he was a graduate of a state penal institution who was being rehabilitated by the firm, which had also organized a quasi-religious group called "The Order of Michael" with the laudable purpose of succoring those who had unfortunate experiences with the penal code. When I joined, he thought that I had entered the firm under similar circumstances. He was extremely disappointed to learn I was simply a law student. Before I was retained I was interviewed at considerable length by the senior partner, Casey, who was then in his early thirties. I was questioned in great detail about my grades and mental and emotional stability. After full deliberation he advised me that he was willing to meet the $8.00-a-week salary I was then earning. I pointed out that I was reluctant to leave that eminent position without an increase and that in any event I thought the free use of a linen jacket was of some value. After further questioning and even more rumination, he agreed to pay me $9.00 a week but emphasized that I was to be placed on probation for one year until he could be assured that I could live up to the rigorous standards of that firm which had been in business for two years.

In addition to The Order of Michael, the law firm also operated a civil service school at night in a loft building on East 12th Street. The loft contained one classroom, an office, and an alleged gymnasium—a bare floor, a mat, two dumbbells, and three strength machines purchased secondhand from Coney Island. The school was named "The Columbian Institute" which had created some legal unpleasantness with another institution of higher learning founded a couple of hundred years before. When the director of physical education of the Institute absconded, taking with him the tuition money, as well as most of the soap and towels, I was offered the newly created position of registrar at an additional $7.50 a week. In addition to clerking in the afternoon I administered the Institute at night, collecting $3.00 a week tuition and renting towels and soap and selling sneakers to aspiring trackwalkers and sanitationmen. I also administered eye and hearing tests to applicants. Casey himself administered the heart test using a secondhand stethescope. The applicants for admission were a surprisingly healthy group. I can recall no one who ever failed the physical, which was fortunate for both the Institute and the law firm since their continued existence depended primarily upon the regular and prompt collection of tuition.

In my senior year I was attending law classes from 9:30 to 12:30, clerking at the law office from 1:00 to 5:30, and administering the Institute from 5:30 to 9:30 P.M. At the same time I was class president and an editor of the *Law Review* and was struggling to maintain my A average. My free time was devoted to meditation and whatever dating was possible under the circumstances.

While Pearl Harbor was considered generally to be a national tragedy, it actually provided me with a glimmer of hope that I could somehow gracefully escape my somewhat rigorous schedule.

In view of the War, senior law students were permitted to take the March 1942 bar exam, which gave me the opportunity for yet another job as a salesman for a cram course. In my spare time I applied for a commission in all branches of the armed forces, but in spite of my intimate familiarity with the eye charts, I was rejected because of my myopia. I passed the March bar, graduated *cum laude* in June, and in the same month was admitted to practice at the beautiful courtroom of the Appellate Division, First Department. Exactly one month later I was admitted as a private in the United States Army in a not so beautiful tent at Governor's Island. Nearsightedness apparently posed no problems for enlisted men. After one week in a tent at Fort Dix I was shipped by train with a group of recruits to the Brooklyn

Army base. We were lined up at the pier and heard the fatal order "Prepare for Embarkation." While we knew that troops were needed overseas, we had not realized that the demand was so immediate. Not only had we not heard gunfire, we had never even seen a gun. We were marched onto a seagoing tugboat and we sailed out into the harbor, but then made a sharp left to Fort Hamilton, which could have been easily reached by subway. We were stationed in the Overseas Staging Area, fully convinced that the next move was to a troop transport. Within twenty-four hours I boldly entered the office of the Commanding Officer at Fort Hamilton, introduced myself to a somewhat surprised warrant officer, and advised him that I was a law school gradu- ate, admitted to practice in New York, and was ready, willing, and able to accept a direct commission in the Judge Advocate General's Corps. My presentation evidently made some impres- sion. It was not favorable. Two days later I was shipped by truck—back to the Brooklyn Army Base where I was given a cot, together with some two hundred other unfortunates, on one floor of a warehouse which had it been a prison would have been closed today by even the most conservative federal judge. By virtue of my law degree, my physical dimensions, and my Irish ancestry, I was assigned to the military police detachment. Armed with a nightstick and a Colt 45 I patrolled the local wa- terfront taverns keeping the peace among servicemen of all branches as well as the resident ladies auxiliary which had a pro- fessional interest in the war effort.

One day while taking hand grenade practice, which I consid- ered a rather extraordinary method of preserving law and order in Brooklyn, I was summoned to an interview in the company of some twenty or thirty other lawyers who were then stationed at the base. The interviewing officer told us that we were being asked to volunteer for what he characterized as the most dan- gerous branch of service, Intelligence. It was indicated that any- one who wished to leave the room was free to do so. It was a great tribute to the bar that no one left. Actually, we all lacked the courage to make the first move toward the door. The inter- viewing officer was destined a year later to be indicted in the Southern District for aiding and abetting draft evasion. I was interviewed, investigated, and finally summoned to service in the Counter Intelligence Corps just in the nick of time since I was then stationed at the Staten Island Port of Embarkation. I was still an M.P. patrolling the sands with a rifle and I am proud to say that that island was never invaded during that period.

In the C.I.C., known by its members as the Corps of Indignant Corporals, I sought in vain to apprehend Japanese spies in the metropolitan area. Either there were never any around or they were too clever to be caught by a nearsighted lawyer. My only triumph in that service was the wooing and winning of Roseanna Connelly, the colonel's secretary, the mother of my three children (two of whom are members of the New York bar) and the grandmother of my four and a half grandchildren. Rosie was in charge of the shipping list at C.I.C., and some cynics have attributed my extended service on Manhattan Island to our relationship.

After three years, six months, and eleven days, most of which were spent in civilian clothes, I was discharged as a technical sergeant and given a good conduct medal, the only medal I received before this evening.

In the waning days of the War I sought a position teaching law at Fordham. When Dean Wilkinson asked for my work experience I told him of my intelligence activity. He advised me that if he were running a detective agency he might hire me but that since this was a law school I was not qualified. I sought refuge with Lorenz, Finn & Lorenz where I started as an associate at $50.00 a week. The rest of my professional career is somewhat better known, but I think I earned the medal in 1942.

Suppose, ladies and gentlemen, that I was graduating from law school in 1982, rather than in 1942, and had managed to achieve the same scholastic record. It would indeed be a world I never knew. Although now they can afford them, law students never wear coats and ties, or shave a beard, until a job interview. Their discomfort then is not because they hold you in awe, but because they are unused to the costume. Although the tuitions are considerably higher, government loans and scholarships were never heard of forty years ago. Most of the students have apartments or pads near law school to avoid the rigors of commuting, a fate reserved for their fathers. I would not have to go out and look for a job, the law firms would be romancing me, not Casey & Caddell, however. All personnel went to war and the only survivor, Jim Casey, managed to have the army send him to medical school. He is now a practicing psychiatrist in New York and is present this evening, claiming full credit for the gold medal. With him is the young professor who recommended me to him, Joe McGovern, who is a former Chancellor of the Board of Regents of New York.

In fact, if I were in the class of '82 I probably would have been a summer intern last year trying to live on some $800 a week with free lunches at French restaurants, dinners at the Plaza, or the palatial residences of senior partners. I remember that Casey did take me to a bar in The Bronx for beer and a ham sandwich on the eve of my departure for the service. The entertainment programs today are quite spectacular, and Mediterranean cruises are not completely out of the question. After this experience I would have been offered a permanent job unless I had assaulted a partner during the summer. I would have been interviewed by a legal periodical asking me to rate the competence of the firm, the ability of the partners, their concern for young lawyers, the entertainment program, and their pro bono activities. All of this would be duly reported in the periodical and read avidly by the hiring committees of the various large firms, each of which would vow to be more pleasant and generous to future summer classes. If I was unhappy with the quality of the lifestyle of my summer firm, I would interview others asking such questions as—Can I have my own office? Can I have my own Lexis? How many paralegals are available to me? When can I become a partner? Are conjugal visits permissible? Are courses in English composition available? Can I use dial-a-cab to the health club where I do my cardiovascular exercises? The starting salary would be about $43,000 or $44,000 per annum plus moving expenses and a color T.V. set for your mother.

Incidentally, when I joined Skadden, Arps I was asked if I would like to join a health club. Of course not, I replied angrily—I know all about those places—Casey and I ran the first one in New York.

In sum, the legal world has completely changed in forty years. If someone would ask me today would I have rather graduated in 1942 or 1982, I would have to say in all honesty, of course in 1982. With the single proviso that Rosie Connelly be somewhere in the wings. Thank you again.

PRESENTATION OF THE HERBERT H. LEHMAN AWARD TO JOSEPH H. FLOM, THE AMERICAN JEWISH COMMITTEE FOR HUMAN RELATIONS

May 11, 1982

It is a great honor and privilege to be invited to speak this evening on the occasion of the presentation of the Lehman Award to Joe Flom.

I am proud to address the members and friends of the American Jewish Committee, which is devoted to the cause of combatting bigotry and ensuring the civil and religious rights of all individuals. As a member of a minority group which has experienced historically the evil and pernicious effect of religious and ethnic prejudice, I agree that we must never assume that these obscenities have disappeared even in these supposedly enlightened times. The price of political and religious liberty is constant vigilance, and this gathering this evening is tangible evidence that the vigilance continues, and indeed it must.

The program indicates that I am to give a keynote address. I assure you that I do not intend to make any major pronouncements here this evening either on the state of the nation or on the state of the economy. I will leave that in the competent hands of Joe Flom. While I have known *of* Joe for a considerable number of years as an ever-growing figure in the legal profession, I have known him personally for just over a year and I became his partner on April 1, 1981.

I should like to give you some insight into the man, perhaps one which is generally unknown to the public, the press, and, in fact, most of his partners. When I joined Skadden, Arps a year ago I had been teaching law and deaning at Fordham for twenty-five years and judging on the Second Circuit for ten years. After thirty-five years of employment with the Jesuits and the United States I had naturally obtained a wealth of experience and a concomitant shortage of capital. While blessed with holy cards, mitzvahs, indulgences, honorary degrees, plaques, and certificates, I suddenly discovered that they were not acceptable as legal tender in any of the meat markets or pool halls which I frequented. My only portfolio was an expanding cardboard envelope provided by the government in which I could carry my briefs. I turned it in when I left the bench. I had no idea that the term portfolio had a tertiary meaning until I joined Skadden. I even thought that billable hours was the name of a race horse.

I began to feel on the bench that, in view of my experience, wisdom, and reputation in the profession, I should leave to join a very successful law firm and even increase the wealth of its members. When I joined Skadden, Arps I felt that I would attract so much business and attention that Flom would be pushed aside as the principal figure in the firm and that I would soon replace him. After living so long in the convent and in chambers, isolated from the real world, I was told that outside it was dog-eat-dog. Flom would just have to take care of himself. Well, ladies and gentlemen, I confess in the privacy of this room that my expectations did not materialize. Since I have joined the firm, Flom has not only maintained, but increased, his stature in the firm and in the profession generally. Instead of becoming a rainmaker, I have succeeded only in creating a few clouds. I must admit that some of his success is attributable to natural ability and prodigious energy, admittedly fortified now by my financial and business acumen, to which my career amply attests. My message this evening is that his ability to generate even more business is due not simply to his talent but also to his concerted efforts to ensure that my emergence on the scene would have minimal impact. I realize that this is a serious charge but I would like to detail just a few of the protective devices that he has utilized.

After joining the firm I noticed that my phone was not ringing at the office with the frequency I had anticipated. In fact at first I thought it was disconnected. However, it was not until a few weeks ago that I discovered that my name and business address are not even listed in the Manhattan phone book. Flom of course is listed—twice. My home phone is unlisted so that now telephonic communication with me is virtually impossible. Even when I was on the bench I was listed in the Manhattan phone book, and at that time I didn't even want to talk to anyone, especially to those convicts who disagreed with my opinions.

When I checked on this at the office I was told that it was a
question of cutting down expenses, a subject which I had never
heard raised before in this firm, which takes over the Radio City
Music Hall and the Lincoln Center for the Performing Arts for
dinners for its lawyers. We are even thinking of buying the
Statue of Liberty to house the paralegals. Incidentally, I am very
pleased to see so many Skadden partners present this evening
who have come here to hear me speak.

There are two other William Mulligans who are listed in the
Manhattan phone book. One is a friend of mine who is a divorce
lawyer, and he has told me that his business has surprisingly
expanded and increased tremendously in the past year. The
other William Mulligan is my son, who is not even a partner, but
an associate, at another New York firm, which apparently has
the funds to pay for his listing. I haven't been able to talk to my
son about this. All I know is that this year he purchased a big
new house in Westchester and is now on a Mediterranean cruise
with his family. He occasionally passes on some business to me
which he considers trivial, but he also insists on a forwarding
fee.

Not only am I not listed in the phone book, but on the directory board at 919 Third Avenue, in the lobby of our building, I
am listed as having an office on the 35th floor—actually I am on
the 47th floor. As you may have suspected, Flom is on the 35th
floor. Anyone asking for me on that floor, except for creditors,
escaped convicts, or relatives, is undoubtedly ushered in to see
him. When I asked the reason for this misinformation, they said
it was a security precaution—Flom's security, not mine.

Aside from the telephone and the building directory, there is
yet another mechanism employed by Flom to ensure his continued leadership of the firm. Almost every law firm, no matter
how small, has a letterhead listing the names of all the partners.
Skadden, Arps had such a letterhead from the first day it
opened. However, on April 1, as soon as I joined, a decision was
made to abandon this practice and now only the firm name—
Skadden, Arps, Slate, Meagher & *Flom*, appears on the station-
ery. In short, ladies and gentlemen, I have been rendered
completely anonymous and impotent.

I am sure that many of you read a recent article in *Fortune*
magazine which discussed our firm at considerable length. Indeed, it included a group picture of the firm. Since they couldn't
keep me out of the picture, I was able to get in the second row
after arm wrestling with several associates. They also had a pic-

ture of Joe Flom having breakfast at the Regency Hotel with somebody named Marty Lipton, who is not even associated with our firm. I think he is in the tea business someplace. I submitted a picture of myself having breakfast with Cardinal Cooke but that was rejected by *Fortune* and has appeared only in the *Observatore Romano*, the official newspaper of the Vatican. If New Yorkers can't find me, you can imagine how difficult it is for the Romans. What I have told you is factually correct. I have been effectively sheltered from prospective clients. I am now limited to those people I meet on the street or that business which the other two Mulligans have no interest in. If your Committee thinks that a man like this deserves a medal for "human relations," that of course is your own business.

I, of course, have tried some counter measures. I did think seriously of changing my name to Skadden, which would have really created a problem for Joe. However, my 93-year-old mother has objected and can't understand why I want to change my name at my age and if I did, how about O'Shaughnessy? I am having a sign painted for my window. It says "William Hughes Mulligan, Attorney—Abogado." Since I am 47 flights up, it probably would attract only the iron workers on the buildings now being constructed on Fifth Avenue in the 50s. I did think of a green neon sign with arrows going up the side of my building to the 47th floor, but the building agents have rejected this modest proposal. You can imagine who was behind that decision. I have other plans, but I hardly think that this is the occasion for announcing them. Time is on my side. In ten years he will be in his mid-60s slowing down and I will be only 74, at the peak of my powers.

Actually, Joe and I have much in common, and he looks up to me like a father. We both smoke pipes and do the daily crossword puzzle in *The New York Times*. We both were enlisted men in World War II, and both came from very wealthy families who never let us know lest we become spoiled.

Enough for my serious remarks. It is quite obvious that Joe Flom is an exceptionally bright and able lawyer, but there is no shortage of bright lawyers in this town. He is also a very hardworking lawyer, but again this is not unusual in New York. Joe has other characteristics which have ensured his success—he is a resourceful and inventive lawyer who considers every possible contingency and opportunity for the client he represents. However, in addition to corporate and litigation experience, he has great business acumen. From my own experience I can attest that Joe is a knowing observer of the human condition—he has the ability to accurately estimate human motivation and aspiration and make decisions accordingly. He is the principal architect of a very successful firm but at the same time recognizes his responsibility to the profession generally. I have been personally concerned with the inadequate salary and survivors' benefits of the federal judiciary. I can tell you that from my experience as a member of the Judicial Conference Committee on Judicial Relations that he has, without any fanfare or publicity, made available without stint his time and financial support to this cause. There are other private charities and interests which have come to my attention that again emphasize his interest in those less fortunate. Again, his participation has been without publicity and extremely low key, which is a typical Flom characteristic. I do not wish to imply that he is without professional flaws—his knowledge of Latin is practically nil. When he questions me about some issue of law in which I have no knowledge, and I can assure you that these areas are not difficult to find, I resort to Latin, which holds him at bay. Now that Claire has become a Trustee of my alma mater, Fordham University, I predict that she will coach him and I may have to turn to Greek.

There is much more I could say about our honoree, but let me sum it all up by stating that I am extremely proud to be a partner of Joe Flom's. I congratulate him on this recognition of his worth to the community and the profession. I wish Claire and Joe and all the Floms all the best *ad multos annos*.

TRIBUTE TO THE HONORABLE MILTON POLLACK
June 17, 1982

It is indeed an honor for my wife and me to be invited to join this good company. Although I never had the honor to be one of his law clerks, I did spend a great deal of time working for Judge Pollack when I was on the bench. I know that the fifteen years have passed quickly for him, but a member of the bar recently said to me that he thought Pollack had been on the bench at least twenty-five years or more. I guess it depends upon your perspective. For some reason which is unknown to either one of us, we see eye to eye on most political, social, and particularly legal issues. Since he and I agree with each other on so many issues, understandably we each have a high opinion of the ability of the other. When I was on the bench I recall no case where he was reversed by a panel when I was sitting. There was only one remand and, as you can imagine, I never heard the end of that. When he sat on the Circuit Court with us we never disagreed. I hope he will always remember these statistics now that I have entered the private practice of law. Our only major disagreement relates to papal infallibility—I believe the pope is infallible when he speaks *ex cathedra*. Milton, on the other hand, says that everything he says is infallible.

In preparing this talk this evening I decided to review all of Judge Pollack's opinions and discuss perhaps just a handful of the most significant. Believe me, it was a formidable task, and the unbillable hours of partners and associates and paralegal time was indeed staggering. After considerable study, I found one which was so succinct, clear, and persuasive, and so typical that I must call it to your attention. It is the best he has ever done. It is Judge Pollack's recipe for "twenty-minute pound cake" which appears in the *Legal Aid Cook Book*, vol, 2. 1969, at page 229. It has been Lexised and Shepardized and, I can assure you, it has never been reversed, distinguished, or even cited—whether it was ever used I cannot tell, except to say that it was called to my attention this morning by an anonymous lady lawyer who apparently was impressed by it. She called from Beth Israel's intensive care unit. I should tell you that in the same volume at page 100 appears Dean Mulligan's recipe for "Hobo Stew." I did not research that one, but I can tell you that I was never again asked to submit material to that learned journal.

Milton Pollack needs no eulogy from me this evening. Someone once said that no gentleman has any secrets from his valet; never having had one, except my mother, I cannot comment. However, I do know that judges can hide no weaknesses from their law clerks. Therefore there is no reason for me to tell this group how patient and long-suffering the judge is, how gentle he is even with the brashest attorney. As he said to me once, "Bill, we are all public servants, and if counsel needs more time, more discovery, or wishes to make repetitive or frivolous motions, it is better to err on the side of leniency." Of course, since I have been off the bench so long, I may have him confused with some other judge. In any event, rather than speak about him, I thought you might appreciate hearing about me because you don't know me as well as you do him. I will be brief.

You may have heard the story about the Irishman who complained bitterly at the local pub about the inordinate length of the Sunday sermon by his pastor. "What was it about?" said a companion "I don't know," he responded; "he never said."

The transition from the bench to active practice was not easy. Judges are given every courtesy, great attention, and deference, and afforded almost all the amenities, except for salary, commensurate with their ability and experience, and survivors' benefits, which are less than those of a bus driver.

One of my first problems was what I should be called by my colleagues. I find that all former law clerks no matter for whom they clerked felt entirely comfortable calling me "Judge." Others who never served in the courts, particularly young lawyers, believe that all their brothers should be called "Citizen" or "Comrade." A few weeks ago a messenger boy on the elevator said to me, "Are you really a judge or is that your nickname?" I said that I had been a real judge but I guess now it is just a nickname. Frankly, I prefer to be called "Your Worship," but it is not catching on.

My only serious comment: A couple of weeks ago I was invited to attend a meeting at the Bar Association where representatives of four bar groups were gathered to discuss Rule 0.23 of the Second Circuit rules which permits the disposition of appeals by summary orders which are not published and which cannot be cited in unrelated cases. The theory is that the court is inundated with meritless appeals which raise no issues of jurisprudential value, and the purpose of the summary order is to apprise counsel in cursory fashion of the reasons for the court's decision. In an ideal world every dispute that comes to the court will result in an opinion available to the public and the profession, but we do not live in such a world.

When I joined the bench in 1971, the Second Circuit entertained 1,423 appeals, and when I left in 1981, it had 3,058. In every other circuit there is machinery to screen out frivolous appeals without argument. We are the only circuit to permit argument in every case in which counsel seeks it. If our court is to continue its reputation for scholarship and also for speedy decisions, the summary order techinque must be adhered to. The average time for the disposition of a civil case is 5.7 months from the notice of appeal to final judgment. That is less than half the time of the average circuit in the United States. I believe that my continued support of the rule is not because I have not taken the robe off but because my experience on the bench is such that no other approach is feasible. If we had eleven Milton Pollacks on the bench of the Second Circuit, the time would be cut down to 5.7 weeks with opinions in all cases. However, the millenium has not been reached.

I thank you for inviting me because I have long since been an admirer of the dedication, the ability, and the experience which Judge Pollack brings to the bench. He is totally devoted to the evenhanded administration of the law, and I have always welcomed his friendship. I also congratulate him for having the taste and discretion to woo and win Moselle. She really earns all the honors that Milton wins. She probably wrote his best opinion.

TRIBUTE TO THE HONORABLE WILLIAM H. TIMBERS, PRINCETON CLUB OF NEW YORK CITY

June 13, 1983

It is indeed a great honor to be invited to be with you this evening to pay tribute to Judge Timbers. The Timbers family, of course, includes the law clerks; all of you here in fact know the Judge far better than I, and yet you have requested me to speak—perhaps that is understandable. I agreed to speak after the committee advised me that no active or senior judge in this circuit found it convenient to be present here this evening.

The Judge and I sat together for a decade on the Second Circuit and became not only colleagues but close friends and on occasion conspirators. We rarely differed in our opinions when we sat together; but on those few occasions when we did dissent from each other, particularly when the third judge agreed with me, Bill never said an angry word. He never upbraided me; he simply did not speak to me for weeks thereafter. In fact, in one case he even forbade Charlotte to speak to me.

One thing that Bill never found out about me—and I am revealing it only this evening—is that I never shared his enthusiasm for dogs. Bill loves all kinds of dogs, but particularly those that are huge and vicious. He likes them better than most lawyers and even some judges. He even opened a bank account for Loki Timbers—and Internal Revenue agents who came to investigate Loki's failure to file tax returns were introduced to the alleged recalcitrant taxpayer and never returned again.

When I was a small child I was attacked by a Norwegian Elkhound; I beat him off, hitting him over the head with my bottle—I believe it was a fifth of gin—it must have been in the summertime.

Some months ago Bill invited me to dinner at the Board of Directors of the Westminster Kennel Club. It was a formal meeting with many of those present wearing white knit vests with their tuxedos—knitted so as to portray a portrait of their favorite dogs. I was fairly comfortable that evening until one of the members said we are all so much interested in hearing your remarks this evening. Of course, the judge had never advised me that I was to be the featured speaker, and when I brought this to his attention, he said "You never needed any preparation to make a speech, so what difference does it make?"

The last time I appeared at the Princeton Club was when Judge Timbers had arranged a dinner here upon my resignation from the bench. It was attended by the judges of the Court. The occasion was memorable because that afternoon President Reagan had been shot, which undoubtedly accounted for his absence that evening. He had planned to be present so he could publicly reject my tendered resignation. However, in the confusion following the assassination attempt nothing was done, and Judge Timbers got me a job with his old firm.

Judge Timbers and I were in part drawn together by our religious convictions, which reminds me of the recent floods in the South. A man's home was becoming flooded. He was standing on the front porch when a rowboat came and offered to take him away. He responded, "No thanks, I put my faith in God." A little later when the water had reached the second floor, a rowboat appeared again. The owner refused to leave saying, "No thanks, I place my faith in God." The water rose still higher, forcing him to the roof. A helicopter then circled overhead, throwing down a rope. He again refused to leave, saying "No thanks, I place my faith in God." A little later he drowned. He went to heaven. Upon his arrival he castigated St. Peter, saying, "I placed my faith in God, and He deserted me." The Lord responded, "Let me check the record." He pulled out a book, looked at it, and said, "Look, I sent two rowboats and a helicopter, but you failed to cooperate."

Judge Timbers and I were further bound together by our love of the law. I recall the first year I was on the bench when we had to decide the Cambodian bombing case. A district court judge in Brooklyn had decided that the President, the Secretary of State, and the Chiefs of Staff should stop bombing Cambodia immediately instead of on August 1st, the agreed-upon date. In the middle of the tense argument the Judge disappeared from the bench—I thought he was calling the White House. About five minutes later he returned with an old Supreme Court Reporter under his arm—with a slip of paper marking a case. I grabbed the volume and read the case—it was an admiralty insurance case which had no relationship to the appeal before us. I realized then that Timbers, having mastered the case before us, was bored with the argument and had to be titillated by some other interesting problem of the law.

Aside from his known expertise in securities law, Judge Timbers has become known for his prisoners' rights opinions. I sat on many with him where irate prisoners complained of serious constitutional deprivations—two fried eggs for breakfast instead of three, insufficient billiard tables in the rec room, the unavailability of Lexis in the prison library, and so on. However, this year the Seventh Circuit was faced with the ultimate in police brutality. The appellant named Madyun was a state prisoner in Pontiac, Illinois. He was serving a 100-to-300-year sentence for murder; I believe, however, that he was eligible for parole after 125 years—so that he was not that bad off, after all. Madyun, who had been in the slammer for twelve years, had committed only twenty violations of prison rules, which, he argued, was not a particularly bad record. In any event, in 1978 he had a visitor at the prison, his wife, but before he was allowed into the visitors' room a female guard asked him to submit to a body-frisk search. Madyun was understandably shocked at her boldness and refused, thus incurring a penalty for refusal to obey a direct command. Obviously, this was a case of great moment, so much so that the Seventh Circuit imported Judge Timbers to sit on the case and write the opinion. It is reported, at 704 F.2d 954, that the Judge had to define such delicate issues as the scope of genital and anal area searches—the First Amendment, Fourth Amendment, and the Fourteenth Amendment. He is still a tough man—he held that Madyun was not protected and had to submit to the indignity of a female search, although he carefully pointed out that male guards had no right to make comparable searches of female prisoners. I leave it to you and legal scholars generally to study and appraise the opinion. The male prisoners have generally applauded the decision, but the male guards have asked me to represent them on appeal.

Obviously, I am, like all of you, a Timbers fan. Now that I have left the bench I realize how much I miss my colleagues—but most of all Bill Timbers.

GROUNDBREAKING CEREMONIES, FORDHAM LAW SCHOOL ADDITION
September 28, 1983

It is indeed a privilege to appear here this morning on the occasion of the groundbreaking for the addition to the Law School. It is indeed a great tribute to John Feerick's leadership and fund-raising abilities as well as the confidence of the University in the Law School and its Dean that this project has proceeded with such celerity. This occasion brings to mind the initial groundbreaking of this Law School in May of 1960. I should like to recall very briefly some unwritten but accurate history of that event.

I was then Dean of the Law School, but my role in the ceremonies was quite limited. My principal function was to go to LaGuardia Airport in a limousine to pick up the Chief Justice of the United States, Earl Warren. For that occasion I had been persuaded by Professor Eugene J. Keefe to purchase a black homburg. Apparently he thought that this would give me at least an external decanal appearance. The Chief Justice took the 7:00 shuttle from Washington, D.C., and I met him at ten minutes to eight at LaGuardia. I had arranged for a substantial breakfast at the Lotos Club. However, the Chief Justice advised me that he had already had his breakfast and would prefer to go directly to the site which was then a vacant lot. This decision, of course, totally upset my timetable. The chauffeur left us in the rubble of the armory which had once stood there. No one was in sight, and the only object we could see was a lonely steam shovel. I thought of inviting him for a ride, but then I couldn't even drive a car. The only building around was the Power Memorial High School where we were to vest in the gym at nine o'clock and process in formation for the ceremony. I escorted the Chief Justice to the side door of the gym and after several raps a face emerged announcing angrily that we couldn't enter until nine. I asked if we could at least take a workout, and the answer was to slam the door in the face of the Chief Justice. I was thinking of taking him to Mass at St. Paul's when the Chief

Justice suggested we take a walk. I quickly agreed, although the area was hardly attractive. We walked up Amsterdam Avenue and finally ran into a group of law professors who did not recognize me in the homburg until I was on top of them. I introduced the Chief Justice, and one of the professors took a step back, his foot hit the gutter, and he fell awkwardly. This was the first case in history of a Fordham professor rolling in the gutter while sober.

The ceremony proceeded without a hitch, and then it became my responsibiiity to escort the Chief Justice to the luncheon at the University Club. The next event was totally unplanned: my introduction of the Chief Justice to Cardinal Spellman. This ordinarily would be of no great moment except that the place of the introduction was the men's room of the University Club. I even removed the homburg to show my proper respect at this summit conference. I must say that even the sophisticated members of that club were impressed. Incidentially, I never wore the homburg again. Its only use since that time has been as a receptacle for me to toss playing cards, the only card game in which I excel and the only form of exercise I have indulged in, in the past twenty years.

By the end of the day the Chief Justice and I were fast friends, and our sole topic of conversation on the way back to LaGuardia was the subject of course in which we had mutual interest and considerable expertise: baseball. In the course of our discussion of the 1927 Yankees, the Chief mentioned that Tony Lazzeri was probably the first Italo-American to play in the major leagues. I respectfully dissented citing the case of Ping Bodie. I must say that this citation without research or briefing really impressed the Chief. In fact, he made me stay with him in the VIP room at LaGuardia until he actually boarded his plane. In later years when I got to know the present Chief Justice Warren Burger rather well I thought I would impress him, and during a lapse in conversation I mentioned to him that Ping Bodie was the first Italo-American to play major league baseball—for some reason the Chief was totally unimpressed and in fact he looked at me rather sharply. Scholarship apparently in these days of calendar congestion is not always recognized and appreciated.

ROAST OF WILLIAM A. SHEA AND MILTON GOULD AT THE ASSOCIATION OF THE BAR OF THE CITY OF NEW YORK THIRTY-THIRD ANNUAL TWELFTH NIGHT DINNER

January 6, 1984

It is indeed an honor to be invited to actively participate in this annual roasting. Having been the victim two years ago, I relish the opportunity to deride and humiliate Bill Shea and Milton Gould this evening. Had this event been publicly advertised, we could have filled Shea Stadium despite its lack of facilities. Gould, as you know, had gone to extraordinary lengths to avoid this confrontation. He wrote this note to me today.

My credentials to judge Shea are quite impressive. Some thirty-five years ago I was at the same time on the full-time faculty of Fordham Law School and a part-time associate at the firm of Manning, Hollinger & Shea, making a very modest living. I was offered a partnership in the firm with the enthusiastic support of Bill Shea, who assured me that I could still keep my full-time faculty position at Fordham while a partner of the firm. I accepted the offer but at the end of the month I received no check. I timidly asked Shea what the problem was, and he said it had been decided to raise the salaries of the associates and to accomplish this the partners would have to skip some draws. I cite this only to indicate how selfless Shea has been to his associates. That tradition continues—in a front-page article in the *Legal Times* last November, Milton Gould was quoted as follows: "Our people are very generously compensated. At the end of the year Bill Shea and I decide what everyone will get and that's what they get." That story illustrates not only the innate generosity and humility of Shea & Gould—Shea & Gould is in fact not a partnership but a duopoly. It also explains why Gould waited until just after the end of the year to undergo surgery.

Shea is highly regarded as a negotiator and conciliator. These traits were of course inherited from his grandfather, Mick Shea, a short man, known in his hometown in Cork as Mick the Small. He was a friend of my grand uncle Snowshoes Mulligan, so called of course because he had flat feet. It was the custom of Mick Shea to ride his donkey down to the local pub every night for a few pints of Stout. He always tied his donkey to a post behind the pub. One night after several pints with the locals, Shea left the pub and found that someone had painted his donkey bright green. Infuriated he rushed back and yelled, "Who is the blatherskite who painted my donkey?" At that point a huge man, Gallagher the blacksmith, arose and said "I did. What are you going to do about it?" "Well, sir," responded Shea, "I just wanted to tell you that the first coat is dry." It was freely predicted then that if any descendant of Shea's got to America, he was destined to become an attorney skilled in the arts of negotiation and diplomacy. The term "power broker" had not yet been coined.

Gould's ancestry is equally revealing. Gould's grandfather was a rabbi and noted Talmudic scholar. In his congregation lived a poor illiterate peasant, Shorenstein, whose major asset was a handsome dray horse which was coveted by a Cossack whose love of horses was exceeded only by his hatred of Jews. The Cossack stole the horse, and Schorenstein tearfully reported this to the rabbi. Rabbi Gould said, "Come with me to the Cossack's stable this evening." When they arrived, the rabbi said, "Take your horse and go home, and don't worry." The rabbi stood in the stall in place of the horse. The next morning when the Cossack came down to inspect his new horse, he found instead the rabbi. When asked where the horse was, the rabbi said, "I am your horse." The rabbi explained: "Two years ago I cheated a peasant. God punished me by changing me into a horse for two years, and last night my term was finished." The Cossack was astounded and he said, "Go home; I cannot use you." Several weeks later, the Cossack ran into Schorenstein driving his handsome horse. The Cossack rushed up to the horse and yelled in his ear, "Well, rabbi, I see you've been cheating again." The inventiveness of the rabbi was told and retold in the village, and it was freely predicted that if any of his descendants came to America he would surely be a lawyer. Every time Milton Gould argued in the Second Circuit pointing out that the convicted felon he was representing was really a paragon of virtue and probity, I used to think this is the grandson of the rabbi who persuaded the Cossack that once he had been a horse. Alas, poor Milton, there are no Cossacks in the Second Circuit.

It was of course inevitable that these two—predetermined genetically to be attorneys—would meet in the great melting pot that is New York. In fact, they were classmates at George Washington High School. It is some indication of their brilliance that they were partners in a law firm for five years before they realized that they had been in the same high school class. Shea was a noted truant who came to school only when the basketball team had a game. Gould seldom attended classes—he was always in the library poring over dictionaries looking for words like hubris, which of course is a derivative of the Greek word "chutzpah." To give you some idea of the caliber of that class, the valedictorian was Howard Cosell.

In his book *The Witness Who Spoke with God*, Gould recounts that fifty years ago in New York it was rare indeed for a Jew or an Irishman to get a job in a so-called white shoe or Ivy League firm. The Jews, he said, went to Jewish firms and the Irish joined Irish firms—I assume he means the F.B.I. It was natural that eventually Shea and Gould would form a firm which was just about exclusively Irish and Jewish. The firm motto is "We shall make no Wasp a partner before his time." Shea was quite hesitant about joining with Gould until Gould "explained to me," says Shea, "that the Israelites are one of the ten lost tribes of Ireland." Shea was further convinced of this when he learned that the president of Israel, Chaim Herzog, was born in Ireland. As the president of the Friendly Sons of Saint Patrick, which is two hundred years old this year, I can state that President Herzog is eligible for membership but, Milton, the fact that you are Shea's partner is not enough.

The Shea, Gould firm is noted for its political clout, and I am told that its new television spot-announcements this year feature a string of sitting judges, commissioners, and councilmen who will attest "I did not get my job through *The New York Times*; I retained Shea and Gould and I am now on the public payroll." The success of the firm is now widely known—they managed to have their partnership numbers published for all the world to see. Gould does so well that his chauffeur is reported to have a chauffeur, and Shea, dissatisfied with a mere stadium, is negotiating for the purchase of Staten Island, which he is planning to resell to John Marchi at a handsome profit. Wait until he finds out that Joe Flom has bought the Verrazano Bridge. Since Gould is a prolific author, you may wonder how he gets time to practice law. After much research I discovered that he really has a ghost writer—Louis Nizer. Nizer had used Howard Cosell for his own book. Gould claims he could never have tried a case if he had not read Shakespeare. Most litigators I talked to said they preferred Jack Weinstein or Joe McLaughlin. One asked me if Shakespeare lectured at P.L.I.—"Not recently," I replied.

In any event their success was ensured—not only their genetic synergism but also their training by Talmudic scholars and the Jesuits. The Jews and the Jesuits have much in common—at one time or another each has been banned in most of the countries of the old world. In addition, I quote from Chaim Bermant—the *London Jewish Chronicle* of May, 1983.

> "The Irish," says Dr. Johnson, "are a fair people—they never speak well of one another"; which is something they have in common with the Jews. They also have the same fractiousness, the same tenacity, the same religious fanaticism and tendency to extremes, the same love of words and overeagerness to use them, the same sense of grievance with the same tendency to be aggrieved, and the same long memory for the shortcomings of others; and, like the Jews, are more inclined to recall their misfortunes than their triumphs.
>
> Irish songs, like Jewish ones, are sung to a minor key even when they are merry. The Irish have a tendency, uncommon among Jews, to get drunk on liquor, but then Jews get drunk on food. . . .

In any event we also share a sense of humor and can take all of these insults without any resentment or bitterness. Time erodes all rancor. I cannot forget, however, what this lousy cast of alleged actors and alleged attorneys did to me two years ago, and I can assure you that I will get each and every one of you some*how*, some*where* when you least expect it.

God bless!

BICENTENNIAL DINNER OF THE SOCIETY OF THE FRIENDLY SONS OF SAINT PATRICK IN THE CITY OF NEW YORK

March 17, 1984

Your Excellency Bishop O'Keefe; Ambassador Kane; Your Honor the Mayor; Your Honor Justice Meskill; Monsignor Murray, and our distinguished guests from Ireland: Minister Barrett, and our Consul General Flavin: distinguished members on the dais; Friendly Sons of Saint Patrick, and your guests:

Two hundred years ago this evening, on this very night, we held our first dinner at Cape's Tavern on Broadway. Before dinner our founding fathers held a business meeting at the home of Daniel McCormick, our first president, who lived on Wall Street in a house with a front stoop, where he used to sit greeting his friends.

The first seat on Wall Street was a rocking chair.

Daniel McCormick was a staunch Presbyterian, a trustee of the Brick Presbyterian Church, and served as our president for fifteen terms. He died at age 91. But, remember, there were no doctors then.

The records of the first dinner are rather skimpy. But more than twenty attended; the vast majority were Presbyterians and Episcopalians. Things have not changed. There may be twenty Protestants here this evening.

The absence of Irish Catholics at our first meeting is understandable. The first Catholic Church in New York City, St. Peter's, was not to open for two more years.

Under British law, not yet repealed, any Catholic priest found in New York was subject to imprisonment for life. In fact, under the New York State Constitution, no Catholic could hold office unless he took an oath renouncing allegiance to the pope.

In some respects, Irish Catholics were treated like American

Indians. But, we never were given any reservations—with the possible exception of Rockaway Beach.

John Leary, an early member, solved the religious problem by joining Trinity Church. But, he still went to Mass and communion in Philadelphia every Easter. His example has influenced many Catholics today, who, similarly, attend Mass only on Easter. The more zealous ones also make it on Christmas.

To those pastors who wonder where all the extra Catholics come from on Easter and Christmas, I can only suggest Philadelphia.

A local paper reported on our first Dinner as follows: "The day and the evening of the 17th were spent in fraternity and mirth, and a number of suitable toasts were drunk on this joyous occasion."

We have no list of those in attendance. But, I should note that Hercules Mulligan was a founding member and lived nearby on Pearl Street, over his tailor shop. Although his back was bent and his palms permanently calloused by reason of the frequency of his rowing over and back across the Hudson with secret messages for Washington, Hercules was, undoubtedly, present, despite his infirmities. He did not miss a single toast.

The records do show that although it must have been terribly difficult for him even to thread a needle, much less to sew, he made a velvet suit for George Washington in 1779, and a pair of breaches in 1792. The cost of the suit was twenty-nine pounds, and it took fourteen and a half yards. I believe it was a two pair of pants, wash-and-wear model.

Mulligan was a great spy. And in the unbiased opinion of Bill Casey, given here in 1981, he was far superior to Nathan Hale. He was never caught.

Mulligan was a great friend of Alexander Hamilton, who was our first president McCormick's attorney. It is too bad that Hercules never taught Hamilton how to shoot.

Mulligan was not a good businessman. The records indicated that at one point he became insolvent. I think Washington "stiffed" him. But that is only a private opinion.

Mulligan died of a Tuesday at age 85, and he now sleeps peacefully in the Trinity Churchyard waiting for the Resurrection Day, when he will run down to Cape's Tavern for a fast one.

The first Dinner, fully reported, was in 1824 where seventy people were in attendance. Thirteen formal toasts to the States were drunk, plus twenty-three volunteer toasts, proposed by any member who felt in the mood and could stand up.

The party began at five P.M and lasted until midnight. There were several near drownings that night. Statistics will prove that the death rate of members is particularly high in late March and early April. I attribute this to the Lenten fast.

In 1831, this Dinner grew to one hundred, including Philip Hone, the former mayor of the City, who proposed a toast in which he effusively stated his strong admiration and affection for the Irish.

However, he was also the author of a diary, which was published long after his death. In his diary, the mayor confided, "Irishmen are the most ignorant and obstinate men in the world. And I have seen enough to satisfy me that ignorance and vice go together."

Since that time, no mayor of New York has kept a diary. Or, if he did, it was never published, certainly not in his lifetime.

Our Centennial attracted two hundred members, and among the featured speakers were Chauncey Dep and the Reverend Henry Ward Beecher, who was a great pulpit orator, and one of the most sought-after public speakers of his day. He was witty and eloquent, and he praised the Irish so extravagantly that he was made an Honorary Member of this Society. He was 71 at the time of the Dinner, and he actually offered to speak at the Bicentennial. I am sure he would, if he could. But he died, I think, of acute laryngitis.

I recently visited 115 Broadway, which was the site of our first Dinner two hundred years ago. And there is still a restaurant there, a Japanese restaurant. It was too small for tonight's dinner. Even though the manager did promise a few bottles of Saki at every table, I did not think that this would be conducive to the general health and welfare of the Society, particularly the Life members. He also promised to produce Reverend Moon as speaker.

I should point out to you, gentlemen, in the spirit of ecumenism, that not only is today St. Patrick's Day, but at sunset tonight our Jewish colleagues will celebrate the feast of Purim. This is most appropriate, because as the *Encyclopedia of Judaica* emphasizes, there is ample evidence from Jewish scholars—and I quote—"on this day a man is obliged to drink so much wine on Purim that he becomes incapable of knowing whether he is cursing Haman or blessing Mordecai." And that calls for a lot of wine.

So, while we Christians may be inhibited this evening by the laws of fast and abstinence, for our Jewish friends, this is a Holy

Day of Obligation, an obligation to imbibe, and where better
than with us for those who are still capable of distinguishing
Mordecai and Haman.

I suggest visiting the Shea suite, known tonight as Vec Shay,
which will be open until sundown on Sunday.

It is my view that the Israelites indeed are one of the ten lost
tribes of Ireland.

Judge Milton Pollock claims to be a direct descendant of
George Pollock who was our president in 1796.

Gentlemen, time precludes any further exposition of our glorious past. Suffice it to say that despite the Irish proclivity for
combat, and to suffer mightily for slights—real or imaginary—we have stayed together as a Society for two hundred
years.

I believe our faith in God and our sharing in a common Irish
heritage, plus our sense of humor, combined with a certain ir-
reverence about things mundane are in good part responsible
for our success, and I hope we last for at least another two hundred years.

TRIBUTE TO THE HONORABLE DAVID EDELSTEIN, UNIVERSITY CLUB OF NEW YORK CITY

June 28, 1984

Judge Edelstein, Florence and friends, Your Excellency Bishop Broderick, Very Reverend Monsignori. Archbishop O'Connor couldn't be here because he is in Rome to visit the pope. The pope isn't here because Archbishop O'Connor is visiting him.

It is indeed an honor and privilege to be invited to speak here this evening to say a few words about the man we celebrate, Judge David Edelstein, who was appointed as a District Court Judge on November 1, 1951, the Feast of All Saints. Indeed a fortuitous and felicitous day for the ascension of a man who earned three degrees—A.B., M.A. and L.L.B.—from a Jesuit university. In the words of the Introit for the mass on that day, "Gaudeamus omnes in Domino, diem festum celebrantes sub honore sanctorum omnium"—"Let us all rejoice in the Lord as we celebrate the feast in honor of all the saints." St. David actually entered upon duty on November 14, 1951—which, as you all recall, was the feast of St. Josaphat, the archbishop of Polotsk, who was beaten to death in a riot in 1623. Why David selected that day is a matter, of course, between him and St. Josaphat.

In the thirty-three and more ensuing years David Edelstein has dispensed justice fairly, firmly, and indefatigably and sat in fact as Chief Judge of the Southern District from July 1, 1971, until February 18, 1980. I do not have the time to discuss the religious significance of these dates, except to note that February 18 was the fortieth anniversary of David's marriage to Florence Koch. She, of course, is the true saint of the Edelstein family. It was suggested to me by a certain person who prefers to remain anonymous that this evening I discuss Judge Edelstein's opinions and their impact on the law of the Second Circuit or any other circuit I might select. I responded, "No, David, this is an evening for celebration not cerebration. I will leave that for a law review article at some future date when I have finished my primary task, rebuilding, expanding, and enriching Skadden, Arps, Slate, Meagher & Flom—generally known as the Mulligan firm."

The only opinion I would like to discuss this evening was the first case I ever sat on—it was a three-judge court in the Southern District of New York. The bench was William Hughes Mulligan, Frederick Von Pelt Bryan, and David Edelstein. Fred had four names, I had three, and David two, but despite these obvious differences, we got along reasonably well. I was so inexperienced and new to the bench that I even left my wallet in my jacket pocket in the robing room while sitting on the bench. Since I had just left Fordham, it only had holy cards in it anyway. Even before we approached the bench, David and Fred had persuaded me that this litigation involved two of the heaviest constitutional issues ever to surface in the Southern District or any other district in the country. They both said that only a law professor and a law school dean could address these issues and that, in fact, my reputation as a constitutional scholar would be made overnight by this opinion. It was intimated that Chief Judge Henry Friendly had held the case up until I had ascended the bench to write the opinion. My clerks had not thought much of the case, but I assumed they were as green as I was. I, of course, agreed to write the opinion, confiding to Roseanna that my career was only beginning. When I circulated the draft opinion, Edelstein said Part A was satisfactory but Part B was not, Bryan liked B but could not buy A. Neither sent me a concurrence tab—and neither mentioned the caliber of the opinion. I changed a few adverbs and adjectives which provoked grudging tabs without further comment. The opinion *Kiernan v. Lindsay* is reported in 334 F. Supp. 588. I cite it now because it has never been cited anywhere before this evening. It was affirmed without opinion by the Supreme Court. I thought initially that the opinion was so good that the Court could not add anything. It was only many moons later that I realized that the case was as pedestrian as my clerks had thought and that I had been gulled by two professionals into writing the opinion. It was a lesson I never forgot.

Rather than speak of David Edelstein the scholarly judge, I thought it would be more appropriate to discuss his personal qualities. After all, his opinions are available to all and are published by the West Publishing Company, which pays him and all of us such lavish royalties. David is a great conversationalist particularly in the judges' dining room where he brings his own can of tuna fish. He prefers his own brand to that served by the government, a real indication of judicial independence. If the judges' dining room on the fifth floor of the courthouse were located in the Metropolitan Correctional Center, it would be held unconstitutional. When David and I were alone there he used to speak to me in Latin but always lapsed into English when some Yale or Harvard judge not blessed with a Jesuit education would join us. A sign of judicial discretion. When another Jesuit product Irving Kaufman (a/k/a Irving I) would come in, St. David would speak in Greek, which even Irving couldn't understand. David who enjoyed literature once advised me that Henry James had said that the two most beautiful words in the English language were "Summer Afternoon, Summer Afternoon." When he asked me to comment, I said that while Summer Afternoon was pretty good, "Open Bar" had a lot going for it.

David, of course, was and is a boon companion—he can be prevailed on to leave his beloved law books to visit a pub, cafe, or even a discotheque. I spent many an hour with David at the Gas Light Club or on safari in the Hamptons discussing the rule in Shelley's case as applied in the Second Circuit. It was on one of these occasions that I observed the sharp legal mind of Judge Edelstein. We had just finished two scotch and sodas, and the waiter came back, pointed to the glasses, and said, "Will you have two more of these?" David immediately responded, "And what would we do with two empty glasses?" Accurate findings of fact are as essential to the judicial process as they are to the pursuit of social pleasure. David also is a keen student of national and local politics. I understand that he turned down an invitation to have an audience with Senator Mondale in St. Paul to be with us this evening. It has been suggested that a Finestein-Edelstein ticket might have some appeal.

David Edelstein, as this gathering of luminaries of the bench and bar indicates, is a man who has a great capacity for making friends. He is an authentic New Yorker who knows what is going on not only in the Court but in the marketplace. He has a quality of enthusiasm and freshness which is unique and which prevents him from ever getting old—he is a stylish, sophisticated student of the human comedy as well as the human tragedy. And he has been around the block often enough to know the difference. We all value his friendship. His principal asset, of course, is Florence, who has been and remains his sweetheart, his wife, and the mother of the sons he cherishes. We all feel close to David and we wouldn't take such liberties with him were it not for our appreciation that he enjoys the lighthearted banter which has always been characteristic of the bar. David, as we Jesuits say, *ad multos annos*. For those who did not enjoy the training we had, it is freely translated, "God Bless David and Florence and Jonathan and Jeffrey."

HOLY CROSS COLLEGE ALUMNI ASSOCIATION, WORCESTER, MASSACHUSETTS
September 28, 1984

Ladies and Gentlemen, it is indeed an honor and privilege to be invited to speak here this evening. I may be the first Fordham alumnus to be invited to appear here. Incidentally, I bring you the warm greetings of the Fordham University Board of Trustees; the resolution was passed by a vote of 16 to 6—all the dissenters were Jesuits. One said he would switch his vote if we would delete the word "warm" before "greeting." To the average Fordham man all other Jesuit colleges are fungible. Not to me. I salute you; any school that can produce Tip O'Neill and Doug Flutie can't be all bad. We also distinguish Georgetown, which caters to the cream of Catholic youth—the rich and the thick. Seriously though, I did hear a T.V. broadcast in which one commentator, who, I believe, was a former priest, stated that Mario Cuomo was a graduate of Holy Cross College, an outstanding Jesuit institution. Actually, of course, Monsignor Cuomo is a graduate of St. John's College where his exposure to theology was limited to memorizing Joyce Kilmer's "Trees."

Like Ed Williams, I use three names: William Hughes Mulligan. When I was elected president of Senior Week at Fordham, which was destined to be the highest political office I ever attained, *The Bronx Home News* announced that I was a direct descendant of Archbishop John Hughes, who was the founder of Fordham. Actually, poor Irish boys in the Bronx, and there are no others, either become cops or ushers at the Loew's Paradise; failing to pass the physical for either, they enroll at Fordham. One of them, Joseph O'Hare, will be inducted as Fordham's new president tomorrow.

Someone asked me why at my advanced age and busy life I agreed to come all the way to Worcester, Massachusetts, to give a talk to a group of non-clients. I responded that I had never been here before and, besides, Edward Bennett Williams had invited me. Moreover, Ed said that if I accepted, he would make a deal: if I ever needed a speaker, he would do it. I could not resist the offer, but afterward I thought about it—when would I ever need a speaker? I concluded that only at my funeral Mass and then it would be most difficult for me to hear his message. I spoke to Ed, and he suggested that if I became ill I should let him know and he would send me a copy. This, he said, gave me the opportunity to edit the work; in fact, he said, I could even send him a first draft. Now you can understand why Ed is such a successful advocate.

I have adhered to one principle in public speaking, and that is to avoid serious messages. All my serious views appear in my written opinions which lawyers may find in the Federal Reporter, Second Series from volume 450 to 644, *U.S. v. Byrnes*, my swan song, dated March 17, 1981. I attended a Jesuit college which at the time was overwhelmingly populated by Irish Americans, most of whom claimed to be descended from Irish kings. Actually, their forebears like mine and yours probably came because of the famine. Many of them were hungry, and most of them were thirsty as well. Historians often discuss the potato famine, but I suspect that there was a long strike at the Guinness Brewery which contributed to the hegira of the Irish. Ethnic humor is condemned by *The New York Times*, which is also known as the New Testament in some quarters, but as president of the Friendly Sons of Saint Patrick of New York, which is two hundred years old this year, I can hardly be accused of ethnic bias. However, a New York *Daily News* columnist has accused my Society of being anti-feminine or sexist. In defense I suggested that while on the bench I believed in upholding the Constitution of the United States, and as president, I equally believe in upholding the Constutition of the Friendly Sons of Saint Patrick, which is actually three years older than the American Constitution but which has received considerably less publicity.

Henry James once said that the most beautiful words in the English language were "Summer Afternoon, Summer Afternoon." I asked a friend of mine for his comments, and he said he preferred "Open bar, Open bar." Certainly, the most beautiful question in the English language is "Will you have another drink?" I answered that question in the negative only once, but that time I had misunderstood the question.

There are Jesuits in Ireland—at least enough to picket President Reagan when he paid a visit. But many years ago an Irish Jesuit who became overly enamored of Irish Whiskey was exiled to a remote parish in Cork. While he was there, he was approached by an Irish farmer who told him that his only horse, his prize possession, had been stolen by the local English squire. The Jesuit promised to get it back. That night the farmer led the Jesuit to the Englishman's stable and pointed out his horse—the priest said lead him away to your farm and don't worry. The priest stood in the stall taking the place of the horse. The puzzled farmer left. The next morning the English squire entered his stable to check out his new and prized possession. He found instead the Jesuit. The priest explained, "I am a Catholic priest; I committed the sin of gluttony in drink, and the Lord as punishment changed me into a horse for six months. Last night at midnight my full time was served and he changed me back into a priest." The Englishman was completely startled but not completely unconvinced that miracles like this could happen in Ireland, the land of leprechauns. He sent the priest away.

Several weeks later the Irish farmer entered his horse in a race. The Englishman was there and, recognizing the horse, he ran over and whispered in his ear, "Well, Father, I see you have been hitting the bottle again." This Jesuit was highly regarded and esteemed by the Irish villagers—but the English viewed him and the society with great suspicion.

The major reason for my presence here is that for reasons that have never been clear to me I have always had a great reverence for the Jesuits. They saved me from the police and possible head ushership. After seven years of Fordham College and Law School, I taught law and deaned at Fordham Law School for twenty-five years. I left rich in experience and with a sizable portfolio of indulgences, plenary and partial, holy cards, and a half dozen honorary degrees. Ever since Martin Luther, the market value for indulgences has been considerably depressed, but I persevered and defended the Law School and my faith as well against the onslaughts of the Society of Jesus. When I decided to resign the deanship of the law school, it was perhaps one of the most popular decisions I ever made—applauded by the Jesuits, the law school faculty, the student body, the Alumni Association, and the accrediting agencies; it was the first time that all these constituencies ever agreed on anything. The Jesuits even gave me a six-month terminal leave with salary, but I joined the Second Circuit Court of Appeals instead and that six months is still owing. After ten years on the bench, I resigned to join Skadden, Arps, and for the first time in twenty-five years, I was making a living wage. The Law School immediately announced a building expansion campaign, and made me chairman of the annual giving drive, and vice chairman of the Board of Trustees of Fordham University. I am still making a living despite the Jesuits, but they have not made things any easier.

I thank you for all your attention and your devotion to the Society of Jesus, which has so influenced each of us.

PATENT LAW BAR ASSOCIATION
March 29, 1985

It is indeed an honor and privilege to once again be invited to address the Patent Law Bar Association at your annual dinner. When I was on the bench, invitations to this dinner were always accepted with alacrity. Perhaps some of my colleagues came because of the opulent pre-prandial refreshments and vintage wines at a fine dinner. But I came only because it gave me the opportunity to discuss file wrapper estoppel, the latest advances in microbiology, and nuclear mathematics and physics with those of you who, like me, were scientifically trained and are au courant with star wars and other fascinating developments. The only one I could discuss these problems with sensibly in the courthouse lunchroom was Judge Conner. I do admit that after several jars at this party some of my other colleagues displayed a remarkable eloquence in these esoteric matters. In any event your receptions were always appreciated. Henry James once said that the two most beautiful words in the English language were "Summer Afternoon, Summer Afternoon." When I told this to a judicial colleague, he dissented and suggested instead "Open Bar, Open Bar." Certainly, the most appealing interrogative sentence is "Will you have another drink?" A faculty colleague once said he answered this question in the negative only once and that time he misunderstood the question.

Despite my chemical, mathematical, and related scientific skills and interests I never discussed these subjects with you at dinner. The topics I wished to cover were after all highly technical, would require audio-visual aids, and even so in an audience which consisted of wives, guests, and federal judges, I was not sure I would be understood.

One astute observer once remarked that both the British and the Irish had violated a fundamental principle of physics—the English had elevated themselves by their gravity and the Irish had depressed themselves by their levity. Being Irish I tried to continue that tradition here. My first speech here was in 1973 and I was tempted to repeat it tonight on the theory that your junior partners were still in law school, the seniors had forgotten, and the associates were out protesting on some campus. However, I spoke at that time on opinion writing—this is a subject upon which my views have changed considerably in the past four years and I found my comments rather trite. In 1978, in my second appearance, I discussed the different types of attorneys who paraded before the Second Circuit and found them all rather amusing. Again I see nothing humorous about that dissertation; I am now part of the procession, a supplicant, a mendicant—an oracle no longer.

Some of you may recall that, many years ago, a baseball player, Mike Delehanty, is alleged to have said "Isn't it great to be young and play for the New York Giants!" Of course, in those days players had no agents, and such wonderful sentiments are not permitted today. I truly wish I had said in some speech after I had joined the bench—"Isn't it great to be young and play for the Second Circuit!" Alas, I became known for something much less ebullient—I had no agent, I was forced to become a free agent, and on departure in referring to the financial benefits of the federal bench, I said "I can live on it, but I can't die on it." That, on reflection, while undoubtedly accurate, was as lachrymose and lugubrious as a lead editorial in *The New York Times*.

I don't intend to provide you with my autobiography this evening; that will be serialized in a scholarly journal next year, *Cosmopolitan*. I should point out that to some extent we are all products of our genes—this audience will appreciate this particularly. The Irish all claim to be the descendants of kings and to have royal tastes. Although Mulligan in Gaelic means "the bald-headed servant of the priest," I am inclined to think that something is lost in the translation. I admit, however, that although I did work for the Jesuits for twenty-five years and was in effect a servant, I did leave with most of my hair. My thesis is that if I was not born to the purple, my inclinations were certainly in that direction. When I started deaning at Fordham Law School in 1956, the Doctrine of the Divine Right of Deans was still generally accepted. The law school dean usually had lifetime tenure. He was looked upon not necessarily with affection but at least with respect and sometimes with awe. Why not? He selected the entering class, hired and fired the faculty, fixed the curriculum, and set the schedule. That was a wonderful era, and I enjoyed it immensely. If not infallible, I acted as though I were.

The first subversive movement in higher education was the theory that the faculty, the community of scholars I had thought, should share in the governance of the institution. Faculty committees were to do all of the things that the dean had once done—in fact, appointments to committees were made by the Committee on Committees, which in turn was appointed by the faculty. This stage was soon followed by one even more obnoxious—the doctrine that the governance of the educational institution was truly vested in the student body, to be shared with the faculty, preferably the younger faculty who were more attuned to the lifestyle of the student body. The dean's function was to raise funds, attend wakes and weddings, the latter only if invited. The students were very uncomfortable, and I thought that their discomfort was due in major part to their tight jeans, braided hair, beards, and pointed shoes, and that a shave, a haircut, and larger pantaloons would do much to alleviate their unrest. One of their principal demands was the elimination of examinations, grades, and class standings. The purported reason for the elimination of exams and grades was that they lead to competition among students which, they alleged, was unhealthy. Moreover, examinations do not really test a student's knowledge of the law. In one issue of a law student newspaper at that time the student editor pointed out the following weaknesses of the examination system: (1) the student may not have felt well on the day of the exam; (2) he may not have understood the question; (3) he may have forgotten the answer; (4) his answer may differ from the professor's and, believe it or not, in an effort to pass an exam, the student may be forced to permanently borrow books from the library. Thus, one of the reasons seriously proposed for the elimination of exams was to cut down the book thefts which were plaguing the law school libraries. At the same time incongruously they began to mark the teachers and publish the grades in the student papers. This drove the professors crazy, although in the case of academics it was at times difficult to discern. Their philosophy was that since they were the only segment of the community of scholars which was paying any money to the enterprise, they deserved to be heard. My response was that the women who shopped at the A&P were the only ones who paid in that enterprise, but I thought the management should run the store and not the clerks, and certainly not the shoppers. I also suggested that if they didn't like the A&P, they should go to Gristede's. Enlightened sentiments such as those fell on deaf ears, and the students at many institutions displayed their intellectual capacity and administrative talents by picketing, violence, and physical takeover of facilities.

This surely was no atmosphere for a person of royal antecedents; I felt as comfortable as Czar Nicholas living on a commune.
I fled into exile and joined the Second Circuit Court of Appeals.
It was indeed a wonderful, wonderful world. It was a totally
structured and ordered society, and the circuit court judge was
at the top of the heap. There was no nonsense at all about equal-
ity; district court judges and lawyers as well knew their place.
The mantle of infallibility was now real—a long black robe. Your
ascending the bench was proceeded by the bellowing of a bailiff,
raps of the gavel, and all in the courtroom, even law students,
stood at rapt attention. I thought that the blare of three trumpets would add further class but the democratic judges rejected
this, Chief Judge Kaufman dissenting. I found that every word
you said was seized upon, and if you yawned, or even hiccuped,
an associate in a big firm would take a note or go check Lexis.
The unruly young men of the '60s now barely recognizable appeared in gray flannel suits, white button-down shirts, and
striped neckties. All had been members at the time of a variety
of British regiments and not the stickball players from The
Bronx and Brooklyn I had always assumed them to be. It was
then I realized that the campus revolution had failed and that
sanity had returned to the campus; perhaps literacy will follow.

I found on the bench that I was viewed not only as a scholar
but as a wit as well. Jokes that my wife and children ignored
were treated with huzzahs and guffaws by attorneys. Sometimes
they even laughed when I was serious or even nodded soberly
when I was kidding. Life was beautiful. I had magnificent chambers which would house the five most senior partners of the
largest New York firms. The government provided me with all
the creature comforts and amenities except for one—money—
and, believe me, fellow members of the profession, to para-
phrase St. Paul, without cash all the rest is clashing cymbals and
tinkling brass. In any event I renounced the throne four years
ago and became something I really had never been, a practicing
lawyer. I recall renting a house that summer and I explained to
the owner, a fellow war veteran but of the German Navy, that I
had been a law school dean and then a judge but now I was
practicing law. He responded, "At this age why do you want to
start working for a living?"

The transition from the bench to the bar was, frankly, most
difficult. Of course, I brought my robes with me to my new office, which is about the size of a large closet in my chambers. I
wore them only when I was in the office, not in the corridors

lest I frighten the associates. When one came into my office, I would say "You may approach the bench." I also brought a gavel, and instead of pushing a button for my secretary, I banged the gavel.

The choice of a title created quite a problem. I had been "Professor," "Dean," and "Judge" for thirty-five years. My only title now was President of the Friendly Sons of Saint Patrick, and for one of royal blood, "Mr. President" was not suitable to me. My partners, on the other hand, thought it pretentious. The problem was solved quite accidentally, although I preferred "Your Worship." One of the young messengers said to me one day, "Judge, are you a real judge or is that just your nickname?" I had to admit to myself for the first time that I was not a judge. I was not even a lapsed judge or a retired judge; I was an ex-judge. I said, "It's just a nickname." In any event I found it preferable to "Baldy" or "Fatso," and so now when I am called "Judge," I don't know whether its a term of respect or an indication of intimacy—but I have found it acceptable.

Another new venture for me was the necessity of keeping a diary. I soon found out that my entries, which covered the weather, the achievements of my grandchildren, and the New York Giant football scores, were not really what the firm was interested in. I was asked if I knew about billable hours. "Yes," I said, "I think he is running in the Fifth at Aqueduct." I also found an age problem. On the bench, for the most part, my colleagues were my age or older. I mentioned Judge Crater to an associate at the firm one day, and he asked me what circuit he was sitting on. I mentioned Sacco and Vanzetti to a junior partner, and he said that he preferred classical music to rock and roll. I told a story that was hilarious to another associate when I was on the bench and at the end he asked me soberly, "To whom shall I bill the time?"

Going back to the courthouse through the front door and in a public elevator is another new experience. When I get in the courtroom no one stands up even to let me get by to sit down with the spectators. Appearing in a federal court requires additional research. Did I ever reverse the district court judge and if so was it done pleasantly? Did I ever dissent from panel members in a circuit court case? I felt that the only way to handle this was to be honest and announce to the court that to spare any and all embarrassment, I would appear only in those cases where the facts and law were so clearly on my side that no problems at all would arise.

Most of all I found that the public perception of lawyers is hardly encouraging. The Italians have a saying, "Sta meglio un sorcio in bacco del gatto che il cliente in mano dell'avocatto." Judge John Canella, although Sicilian and not Italian, with the aid of the great Danny Fusaro, translated this to mean "It is better to be a mouse in the mouth of a cat than a client in the hands of a lawyer." I first saw that motto framed in Admiral Rickover's office. Incidentally, when I asked someone at the courthouse if I was missed, he said, "Yes, but not as much as Dan Fusaro."

I am beginning to accept my current condition and may even begin to enjoy it. At least I appreciate the first day of the month. I have one new pastime—I have six grandchildren, and when I can assemble a quorum at my house I get out my robe and gavel and we play judge. I can even wear my academic black velvet cap with the gold tassel and wear a few old hoods depending on what color appeals to them. We have active calendar, sentence offenders, and reward the just. I am treated with dignity and respect. If they forget to call me "Judge," they use the best title I ever had—"Grandpa."

Thank you.

TWENTY-FIFTH ANNIVERSARY
OF THE HONORABLE
WILLIAM H. TIMBERS,
PRINCETON CLUB OF NEW YORK
April 9, 1985

It is indeed a great honor to be invited once again to make a few remarks at Judge Timbers's Annual Dinner—this year marking the twenty-fifth anniversary of his ascent to the bench. I congratulate Charlotte for putting up with him for an even longer period. I am delighted that Judge Timbers's alumni now include graduates of the Fordham Law School, and I am sure that Judge Kaufman joins with me in thanking him for his recognition of our alma mater. I am proud to be included in an inner circle of Judge Timbers's colleagues which he calls the "Irish Mafia." The term is, of course, a misnomer—the Mafia never had the power of the federal bench, although I believe it did take better care of its members. The term "Irish" is also quite misleading— the capo di tutti, Don William H. Timbers, is a Wasp, member Van Graafeiland is obviously a Dutchman, Judge Pollack is an Hungarian—the only Irish are Meskill and Mulligan, and I sometimes suspect Meskill. Now that I have left the bench I prefer to be called "Consigliere."

I suppose no one knows Judge Timbers's professional worth more than his law clerks. The fact that you are here in such numbers attests to your continuing loyalty and devotion. My law clerks never gave me a dinner, only a lunch in an Italian restaurant in Chinatown. I believe it was owned by another family, the real Mafia. Once I left the bench I never even got a lunch; instead I gave a dinner for them at a country club in Westchester but it didn't give them any ideas. In fact, one asked me if I was going to make it an annual event.

I would like to tell you a true story about your Judge which I have never revealed before. After I had been on the bench about two months, *Newsweek* magazine ran a story on possible successors to Judge Harlan on the Supreme Court. In addition to those of several well-known Circuit Court judges, my name appeared in the story. A few days later I received a handwritten note from Judge Timbers marked personal and confidential in which he said he had read the article, thought it was a great idea, and was willing to do anything to make my appointment a reality. He said that although I had sat with him only a couple of weeks, he had detected the signs of genius and thought I was fully qualified. I showed the letter only to Roseanna and I told her that Bill Timbers was an excellent judge of character and ability. In fact, ever since then I have been his close friend and champion. It was not that he had flattered me, of course, but simply a recognition of his ability to make accurate judgments.

I must say that there have been times when things became a little sticky. I remember when he prepared an opinion in a criminal case expecting a visiting judge to concur. I dissented, and the visiting judge changed his mind and agreed with me. It took months of delicate negotiation to get the opinion published—in fact, the Timber opinion was published first, and only a close reading would indicate that the dissenting opinion was really the majority opinion. Another incident I recall was a dissent in a securities case where my views were contrary to the *amicus* brief of the S.E.C., an agency to which Judge Timbers has been known to pay a modest respect. In a footnote I indicated that while the S.E.C was *amicus curiae*, the friend of the court, it was not the father of the court. I made the mistake of putting this in Latin which the Judge felt was somewhat unfair. The Supreme Court reversed the Second Circuit, which did not make the Judge any better disposed toward me.

Another incident I recall which affected our relationship was when he invited me to be his guest at a formal dinner of the board of directors of the Westminster Kennel Club. It was held at the Brook Club and was very fancy. I arrived before he did and was brought into a beautiful wood-paneled room where drinks were being served. I knew it was elegant when I noted that most of the assemblage, which, of course, was in formal attire, also sported knitted sashes where they had embroidered portraits in color of their favorite dogs. I, frankly, hate cats and barely tolerate dogs. When I was a boy on the farm we used to periodically control the cat population by putting cats and an appropriate number of rocks in feed bags which were tossed into the Wallkill River. You can imagine my chagrin when one of the members, an Irish Retriever, said that they were looking forward to my speech. This was something no one had told me about. I remonstrated to Timbers, who said that I was such a great speaker he had no doubt that I could rise to the occasion. I was introduced by the chairman, a Great Dane, I believe, as a former colleague of Judge Timbers's and a great dog lover. The only dog story I knew was about my brother-in-law the veterinarian, Jim Flannery. He had been called by a local farmer whose dog was trapped beneath a truck in the farm yard. When Jimmy got there, he could see the dog was *in extremis* and told the farmer he would have to shoot him. The farmer got a rifle and invited Jimmy to perform the coup de grace. Jimmy, an infantry veteran, went prone, took aim, and succeeded in putting the bullet in the rubber tire of the truck which then settled down and killed the dog. The audience did not appreciate the story. I got few laughs and a few barks.

I do miss my colleagues on the bench—now and then I looked forward to meeting your judge at the Yale Club bar. One night after Judge Timbers had downed a bourbon on the rocks, the bartender pointed his finger at the glass and said, "Judge Timbers, will you have another?" He responded immediately, "And what would I do with another empty glass?"—again a sign of his acute attention to the facts in the case.

I find that while I was younger than most of my colleagues on the Second Circuit, I am one of the oldest partners at Skadden, Arps where the average age of a partner is very early forties or, possibly now, even less. The only people my age are the messengers, and I think I will be joining them when I resign as a partner; at least I will get more exercise and more visits to the Court. Last October I made an argument to the Second Circuit Court—at least at the time I thought I was making an argument. I would have done better at the Dog Show. In any event on the way back to the office I said to a young associate who had been a law clerk to a district court judge that it was indeed a nostalgic experience. I remembered with fondness the robes, the deference of counsel, the majesty and dignity of the courthouse—it all made me wonder I said if I make a mistake going to Skadden, Arps. "Oh no, Judge," said the young woman;, "think of how good it will look in your résumé."

Actually, I have kept rather close to the bench because I am a member of the Judicial Conference Committee on the Judicial Branch and thus am familiar with the financial welfare or lack of it which still plagues the bench. Actually, in the four years since I left, the take-home pay of the federal judges has decreased. This is because of the Social Security taxes which they

are now required to pay as well as the legislation which precludes a pay raise unless the Congress votes affirmatively. The
imposition of Social Security taxes provides no real benefits for
the bench—the vast majority of judges has already qualified for
coverage by reason of prior employment. Some advanced in
years actually cannot serve long enough to obtain coverage. The
passage of the bill without any study of the judges' peculiar
status also had the bad effect of killing any chance of increasing
the survival benefits (the widows' mite) since the Congress argues that Social Security actually has that effect. In sum, the
judges continue to be underpaid, and as practicing members of
the profession we have some obligation to rally to their support.

If they ever do get a raise, I may go back—assuming I can
reclaim my seniority. This will permit me to retire immediately
at full salary and open a vacancy for someone more deserving.

I congratulate Bill on his silver jubilee, which will be celebrated, I am sure, by other events perhaps greater in numbers,
but the sponsorship of this dinner by you, his clerks, I am sure
will mean more to him.

MY FRIEND, JOE CROWLEY

Joe Crowley and I were close friends for over fifty years, and yet it was not until his death that I fully appreciated his virtues and how fortunate I was to have him as a friend and colleague. I never attended a dinner or any kind of testimonial which was given in his honor. He was completely self-effacing and managed to sublimate his own ambitions and aspirations for the sake of others. He always seemed content to remain in the background and advance the cause of his friends. In the legal profession this is indeed a rare characteristic, probably looked upon askance by those whose lives are devoted to their own preferment. But Joe was living the true Christian life—love of God and neighbor come first. Joe's neighbors were not simply his wife and family but every student who ever set foot in Fordham Law School, even if he was the last man in his class or in fact had flunked out. The more hopeless the case the greater champion of the cause was Joe. It was not easy to be a Dean when he was the advocate of the student who was in academic difficulties; Joe always said that the student involved was a "good person." Even if he weren't, Joe would be at his side.

A great deal of this goes back to Joe's initial vocation to the priesthood. I first met him in 1931 when we both entered the minor seminary, Cathedral Preparatory School, and became fast friends. After four years I discovered that I did not have a vocation and left to go to Fordham College. It took Joe three more years to make a similar decision, and he joined me in senior year at Rose Hill. At the end of the year Joe had compiled an excellent scholastic record and, typically, had made a host of friends.

While I was in law school, Joe was working in the labor department at Todd Shipyards, where he had his initial exposure to the laws in which he was to become an expert. During the War Joe was an intelligence officer in the Air Corps, and I was an enlisted man was in the Counter Intelligence Corps. When he married Mary Duffy at the Lady Chapel in St. Patrick's Cathedral, I was proud to be the best man. After the War, Joe entered the Law School, and I was one of his teachers. It was a challenging assignment, and he sometimes asked unanswerable questions, interspersing his inquiries with the Latin tags he delighted in so much. Joe's true values as a serious student of the law were not only concealed by his innate modesty but shielded as well by a robust and indeed at times outrageous sense of humor. Although I have tried to retell some of his antics, I find it impossible since you had to be there and understand him to fully appreciate his sense of the ridiculous.

Joe kept people laughing from the time I met him until the end—my parents, my wife, as well as my children and grandchildren, all appreciated his humor.

When I became Dean of the Law School, I knew that Joe Crowley not only possessed a top-flight legal mind but I knew as well that he had all the instincts of a good teacher. He had been clerk to Judge Gregory Noonan in the Southern District Court of New York and later was a litigator in the Satterlee, Warfield firm. I persuaded him to leave practice and become a full-time teacher at Fordham Law School. It was probably the best thing I ever did for the school. Not only did Joe teach Labor Law and Remedies, but when John Finn died, he volunteered to teach his New York Practice Course. He also started our Corporate Law Institute which thrives and flourishes. He was totally devoted to the School, but I believe his greatest value was his devotion to the students. He was the pastor of the student flock—he shared and respected their confidences and left no stone unturned to assist them not only in their professional careers but in their personal lives as well.

Joe had a wide variety of interests—he had a natural talent for foreign languages and what he didn't know he faked superbly; he was an amateur theologian but probably more knowledgeable than some alleged professionals. He was interested in traveling, particularly to Ireland, where he was widely known and fully appreciated. He was a Trustee of St. Joseph's Seminary where he had been a student, and his advice was highly regarded by the Archdiocese.

The great crowds of students and alumni at his funeral mass at his home parish and at the memorial Mass at St. Peter's were tribute not only to his professional achievement but in greater measure to his personal virtue and selflessness. Fordham Law School has had great teachers and administrators in its history, but no person in my experience could match Joe's devotion to students. We mourn him and we pray for his family who sorely miss him, but what a great privilege to have known him so long and so well. God bless, Joe.

PREGNANCY CARE CENTER DINNER
HONORING
GOVERNOR MALCOLM WILSON
December 6, 1985

It is indeed an honor to be invited to introduce Malcolm Wilson on any occasion, but particularly to this audience where he is so well known that I could quit right now. However, for those who may have come in this evening from Alaska or Australia, I should note briefly that Malcolm Wilson is a complete product of the Jesuits. He attended Fordham Prep, Fordham College, and Fordham Law School—eleven full years of tuition roughly equal to the cost of one semester at the Law School today. I first heard of Malcolm when I was in college, because Father Ignatius Wiley Cox, s.j., was even then predicting a bright political future for his former student. Malcolm, in fact, was elected to the New York State Assembly just two years after he graduated from the Law School. He served twenty years in the Assembly, fifteen years as lieutenant governor, and one year as governor of the State of New York. He served in all capacities with great distinction. I say without hesitation that he knows more about the operation of this State than anybody else. He is currently Chairman of the Board and Chief Executive Officer of the Manhattan Savings Bank, one of the few in New York making a profit. I am indebted to the Bank by way of a mortgage, which, of course, is the principal reason for my presence here this evening.

All these facts are matters of public record, including my mortgage. What is more important than his outstanding success, both public and in the private practice of the law, are the reasons for it. I do not claim any particular training or expertise in this field, but after having been around several tracks several times, I would suggest the following: His late wife, Katherine, whose deep devotion to him was matched by his own to her, as well as the support and affection of two daughters, Kathy and Anne, and now six grandsons; and a keen and logical mind which was innate but carefully honed and nourished by the Jesuits and even the laymen at Fordham Law School. He is a tireless worker who has the ability to articulate his thoughts with clarity, conviction, and persuasion.

Malcolm Wilson is also a man of courage, not simply the physical order demonstrated by his combat service as a Navy gunnery officer in World War II, but particularly the moral courage he demonstrated in his political career. His firm adherence to the moral views of his Church strongly influenced his political decisions. He did not waiver in his faith; his religious convictions were never compromised for political profit. In today's climate that aspect of his character is particularly appealing and refreshing. He has been a generous, albeit usually anonymous, benefactor of many good and worthy causes, including that which brings us together this evening. I have been honored to work with him in state government and in alumni, religious, and fraternal activities, and I am constantly renewed and inspired by his wisdom, his dedication, his devotion to the concerns of others.

I could go into greater detail even to the extent of discussing his golf game, but he has understandably ordered me to be brief.

ANNUAL LUNCHEON, FORDHAM LAW SCHOOL ALUMNI ASSOCIATION
March 1, 1986

I was indeed flattered to be invited once again to address the Fordham Law Alumni Association luncheon to which I am no stranger. Some of you. including my beloved wife, are wondering "Why Mulligan?" I asked President Paul Curran this question, and he frankly stated that a well-known political figure had backed out at the last minute and he therefore appealed to my loyalty to the Law School to fill in on short notice. In addition, he said my speech could be quite brief and therefore I need not take too much time to prepare it. While I think his logic on this issue is questionable in view of the galaxy of talent he named as other speakers, I realized that mine would have to be either a short speech or a non-speech if we expected to get home for dinner. Although Paul did not identify his first choice, the timing and circumstances of his call could only convince me I was replacing the Borough President of Queens whose decision not to speak at this time was quite understandable.

Some months ago I was the master of ceremonies at the dedication of the new wing of the Fordham Law School. At that time Governor Cuomo in his remarks made reference to the fact that Irish Americans enjoyed a monopoly position in the offices of presidency of Fordham University and the deanship of its Law School. He cited names like Gannon, McGinley, Finlay, O'Keefe, and O'Hare, and Finn, Mulligan, McLaughlin, and Feerick. Although he was our guest, I was sorely tempted but refrained from suggesting that Italians had enjoyed a similar and even more powerful monopoly over the papacy. I thought of this recently, when the governor indicated that some bigots might dismiss the possibility of an Italian American becoming President of the United States, presumably a more prestigious and certainly a better-paying job than Fordham. The obvious rejoinder I thought would have been "But who but an Italo-American would have a better chance of becoming the first American pope?"

If Governor Cuomo were with us today, he might have even greater cause for concern. Alumni President Curran is stepping down to be followed by Jim Tolan; the Medal of Achievement goes to former President Vaughan; the chairman today is Jim Gill; and the speakers include O'Hare, Feerick, and Mulligan. What the governor and even some of you perhaps fail to understand is that this is not at all xenophobic or parochial, a multitude of counties are involved here today—Cork, Limerick, Kerry, Wexford, and Monaghan, to name a few. We therefore represent a wide variety of backgrounds and reject out of hand any claim of monopoly, duopoly, or even oligopoly.

Today, of course, we honor the twenty-fifth and fiftieth graduating classes. Despite appearances, I did not teach the fiftieth, but I did the twenty-fifth. The class of '61 was the last to graduate from 302 Broadway before our trek to the land of Goshen or Beulahland, also known as Lincoln Center. In fact, just thirty years ago, in 1956, at the tender age of 38, I was named Dean of the Law School. Thirty years have passed, and I am now approaching my late fifties with all my faculties intact, except perhaps for mathematics. My appointment as Dean was greeted at the time with great elation by my wife, parents, and children. A disgruntled student was reported to have said that it was the worst appointment since the Emperor Caligula had named his horse proconsul of the Roman Empire. I attribute my success in bringing Fordham into the twentieth—or was it the nineteenth?—century to some of the rules which I put into effect at Lincoln Center and which may be fondly recalled by the older alumni. The three most effective were: (1) No student may eat, drink, or smoke in the classroom while the professor is lecturing. (2) No student can ride on the elevators; that is why we built staircases. (3) Jackets and ties must be worn at all times. The pernicious view that students had constitutional rights was beginning to emerge, but I preferred the older and more sensible doctrine—the Divine Right of Deans. Obviously, Deans McLaughlin and Feerick continued to enforce these regulations. I can attest that every male Fordham student who comes to Skadden, Arps for an interview wears a collar and tie, does not eat in the office, and, I assume, has climbed the forty-seven floors to reach my office.

When I was on the bench, I was shocked one day when a lawyer, while sitting in the courtroom waiting for his appeal to be heard, opened up a brown bag and proceeded to drink from a container of buttermilk while munching on zwieback. I immediately passed a note to the Presiding Judge suggesting that he be admonished or suspended. He paid no attention—he was a Democrat, I suspect. After we left the bench, in defense he said, but he did have on a collar and a tie. *O tempora, O mores!*

My rule on eating in the classroom has had a great impact upon the dietary habits of the law students, not only at Fordham but at all major law schools. Those of you who have summer associate programs may have noticed that unless you have regular luncheon and dinner excursions to such places as Lutèce, Le Côte Basque, or Windows on the World, you may offend your law student guests who will give you a bad review in the *American Lawyer*. Believe me, I had no intention of making law students epicures and gourmets, but it's still better than eating in class in front of law professors who are lunching at McDonald's or Burger King. Except for Professor Fogelman, who prefers Wendy's. I remember when I was working for John Finn as a young lawyer, he took me to Childs on two occasions and suggested griddle cakes, light on the syrup. Had he not been a trustee of Childs I doubt I ever would have gotten the two lunches.

One of the lessons I learned at the Law School still has not been absorbed by the federal bench. As soon as a new chief judge is appointed in the Southern District, his first objective is not to clear the calendar but to improve the elevator service in the courthouse. All efforts have failed miserably, as those of you who visit or work there can attest. My suggestion that all lawyers admitted less than fifteen years be required to use the staircases was not well received by any P.J., and without bold action the problem will never be solved. Not only would my solution prevent congestion on the elevator, but it would substantially improve the leg muscles, lung capacity, and cardiac efficiency of our profession and render unnecessary the health club services now provided by many large firms for a generation of elevator-riding litigators.

Having referred to the governor earlier on, I think it is fair to briefly mention the mayor of the City of New York, Ed Koch, who has now discovered what evil lurks in the minds of some politicians. Many steps are being taken to improve the ethical atmosphere of the city. Yesterday the Mayor made a major appointment which, oddly enough, has escaped the attention of the press, including *Catholic New York*. He swore me in as a member of the Board of Ethics of the City of New York. I don't know how many turned down this job before me, maybe even our intended speaker, but I thought it was a magnificent display of political courage or perhaps naïveté to name a New York City lawyer to sit on a Board of Ethics. The mayor as a fellow lawyer does not realize the low opinion in which we are held.

Newsday, this summer, carried an interview with Stephen Vicinzey, an Hungarian author whose recent novel was reviewed quite favorably. Its title escapes me. He said in the interview, "My father was killed by a Nazi; I was once in danger of arrest and torture by Communists. But I never personally knew evil men until I got involved with New York attorneys."

In any event, in my new job I will come up with some simple rules like those we had at the Law School which will solve all problems. While I have not tried this out on the Board yet, I am thinking of compulsory retreats for all district leaders, surrender of passports or green cards by all elected officials, and body searches of the Board of Estimate. While more severe methods might be more effective, I will continue the liberal programs I instituted at the Law School so successfully.

My serious message is to congratulate all of you alumni on what is unquestionably the best law school in the country—if that is not correct, it certainly has the best dean.

Slainte.

ANNUAL DINNER OF
THE SOCIETY OF THE FRIENDLY
SONS OF SAINT PATRICK
OF WESTCHESTER COUNTY
March 15, 1986

Mr. Toastmaster, Your Eminence Cardinal O'Connor, Governor Wilson, Congressmen Biaggi and DioGuardi, County Executive O'Rourke, Father O'Hare, Brother Driscoll, Distinguished Guests on the Dais, and Fellow Members and Friends of the Friendly Sons:

It is indeed an honor to be invited to address the Friendly Sons of Westchester once again. Isn't it a wonderful privilege to be Irish particularly at this time of year? Except for the ugly ones, we are the most handsome people in the world; except when unduly provoked, we are the most law-abiding; except for impure thoughts, we are the freest of sin; and except for booze, we are the most abstemious.

As the late Frank Hague, the Irish American mayor of Jersey City, once said under circumstances similar to these, "I want to thank you sincerely for the privilege of listening to me." I first spoke here in 1968 when I was the Dean of Fordham Law School. I addressed the late cardinal as "Your Grace, Archbishop-Designate Cooke." My second appearance was in 1976. I was then a judge of the Second Circuit Court of Appeals, and I addressed Terence Cooke, as His Eminence the Cardinal. Now it is 1986, and I am last working for a living at Skadden, Arps, and the archbishop is John Cardinal O'Connor. If the laws of arithmetic progression are accurate, I will next be invited to speak in the year 1998. I will accept and speak, but I wonder who the archbishop will be then. By that time I will be a partner at Skadden, Arps unless something better turns up in the meantime.

When I was on the bench, we seldom if ever had an Irish defendant, and if we did, he was undoubtedly framed. A couple of years ago, however, two Irishmen were indicted and tried for gun running. They were tried before Joe McLaughlin in the Eastern District of New York. Federal agents had recorded several phone conversations between them. The first one went like this: "Paddy, you can never tell when our phone might be tapped, so we should have a code. Now, the merchandise will be called vegetables—a machine gun is an apple, a bazooka is a banana, and a tank is a head of cabbage." "Okay, Mike," says Paddy; "I got it all down." A couple of weeks later, another message was intercepted: "Paddy, this is Mike. I went shopping the other day and I bought some vegetables." "Great," said Paddy; "what did you buy?" "Well," he said, "I got two apples and a head of cabbage." "My God," said Paddy, "where did you put the head of cabbage?" "I got it in my garage." said Mike. "How could you fit a tank in your garage?" said Paddy. "It's only a bazooka," said Mike. "You dope," said Paddy, "a bazooka is a banana; a head of cabbage is a tank." Not only was the recording made, but it was played to the jury—which promptly acquitted Pat and Mike, probably on the theory that people so inept could hardly be seriously engaged in gun running. Incidentally, the story is true, except that I changed the code words since they are probably still using the same ones that got them in trouble.

Another story was told by an Irish solicitor at the A.B.A. meeting in Dublin last summer. When he was a young lawyer he represented Duffy, who was allegedly injured in a lorry accident. His story was that he was hired to ride on a lorry carrying Christmas trees; his job was to ride on the back stretched out full length to hold down the trees so they wouldn't fall off. I suppose a rope or chains would be too much trouble. The lorry driver took a sudden sharp turn, and Duffy allegedly was thrown off to the sidewalk where he suffered severe contusions, abrasions, and a severe affront to his natural dignity. The case could not be settled. It went to trial, and a variety of contradictions appeared in the plaintiff's case. On cross examination, the jaunty Duffy was perspiring freely and was obviously annoyed. The attorney for the insurance company, bearing down hard, said: "Mr. Duffy, you told us that at eleven o'clock that morning you were thrown from the lorry. Yet there is evidence that at the same time you were having your tooth pulled, and there is also some evidence that on that morning you applied for the dole. Now, Mr. Duffy, why don't you tell us what you were really doing that morning?" Duffy screwed up his face and responded, "And why don't you mind your own damned business?"

Irish wit is always quick. On a trip, with Jack Mulcahy, our bus broke down near a peat bog. One of my companions, not a great conversationalist, noticed a big jet airliner in the sky and said to the man in the bog, "How would you like to be up there in that plane?" The man looked up and said to my friend, "I certainly would rather be up there with it than without it."

When I was in Ireland this summer I heard a few stories which may or may not be true. Harrington went to the doctor. When he got inside, the doctor said, "Go into the other room and take off all your clothes." Harrington obeyed and then noticed another fellow totally naked sitting in another chair. Said Harrington, "I don't know what kind of a doctor he is; I only came in because I have a sore throat." Said the other fellow, "And how do you think I feel—I only came to tune the piano." Another doctor story you may have heard is about Sean, the turf accountant, who was not feeling well at all. He went to his doctor, who examined him carefully and said, "Sean, my boy, you are in very bad shape. In fact, you won't last until the morning." Sean was devastated and called his best friend, Flynn, explained his plight, and suggested they spend the evening pub crawling in Dublin. They visited all of Sean's favorite spots and by one A.M. both were feeling no pain at all. Sean said, "Flynn, my friend, let's hit one more spot." Said Flynn, "Well, that's easy for you to say, Sean, but I have to get up in the morning."

Hopkins was driving on a country road in Ireland and could not pass the car ahead, which was stopped in the middle of the road. He kept tooting his horn to no avail. Finally a woman stretched her head out of the car and yelled "Pig, pig, pig!" This was too much for Hopkins. He pulled up even on the shoulder of the road and yelled at her, "Cow, cow, cow." "What happened then?" I said. "Well," said Hopkins, "I drove by her and right into a herd of pigs."

I should confess that preparing this speech has been quite a difficult chore. My dear wife has to listen to them all in draft and she told me last weekend that my material was stale and I should think of something original. I was grievously offended and said, "Well, the Al Smith speech was pretty good, wasn't it?" She said, "No. "That's why I made the remark." I paid no attention to that until the early departure of the cardinal; he looked perfectly healthy to me.

Last week I reached the age of reason, 68, and have to accept the fact that I am now an elder citizen. I am older than the pope, the cardinal, the governor, and the mayor. Thank God for President Reagan. I have had previous intimations of my mortality: About five years ago I was having trouble with the boiler. I said to the repairman, a young Irishman, "Instead of fixing it, do you think I should buy a new one?" He looked at me and said, "How old are you, sir?" I said 63; he responded, "Well, frankly, at that age I wouldn't invest in a new one."

I went shopping at Bloomingdale's some months ago and was asked by a field interviewer if I would answer some questions about a new product. Since the honorarium was a dollar ticket on the lottery, I agreed. I was asked fifteen minutes of pointless questions. Finally I was asked some personal questions, for example, my age—in my case the question was simply "Are you over 60?"—nobody over 70 is apparently admitted inside Bloomies. I reluctantly admitted that I was over 60. The next question involved employment. The lady looked at me then said, "I assume you are retired." "No," I said, "I work." "Surely, not full-time." she said. I left in a huff. Moreover, the lottery ticket was a loser.

Certainly, life has changed for the great percentage of Irish Catholic boys like me from The Bronx or Bay Ridge or even Philadelphia. Instead of wearing uniforms as bank tellers, Irish Americans have become presidents and CEOs of banking institutions; runners on Wall Street have now become investment bankers; in the law business Irish Catholics, once barred from some firms and permitted only in the managing clerk's office in others, are now senior partners in major law firms. Politics, of course, was never a problem, but I did receive a clipping from a Boston newspaper indicating that a Patricia McDermott who applied for a job at City Hall was allegedly told by the Corporation Counsel, Joe Mulligan, that there were enough Irish names around there. Joe denied this, but a Chinese gentleman did get the job involved.

The American Irish talent for investing was first exemplified by the late Mayor Frank Hague who earned only $7,500 a year and yet died with an estate—that is a *reported*—estate of $10 million. Skeptics should be reminded that he was in a low tax bracket which helped his native ability. Apparently our Mediterranean co-religionists have not fared as well as we. Governor Cuomo recently complained that an Italo-Catholic American from the northeast would have a difficult time getting elected President. No more difficult, I assume, than an Irish American cardinal would have in getting elected to the papacy.

The Irish Catholic has become more acceptable socially, and his economic status has risen substantially. Today the fellow who was looking for two chickens in every pot in 1928 has two cars in every garage and at least two houses with garages. But all is not well, gentlemen. With all the success of the Irish, our educational achievement far outstripping those of our parents and grandparents, what mark have we made on the society in which we live? Anyone who watches television, goes to the movies, or reads the press should be fully aware that we live in a pagan society. Sexual morals are almost nonexistent. Deviant behavior which was specifically criminal when I went to law school and even when I taught criminal law not only is legal but is no longer considered deviant. Thank God, we have a cardinal archbishop who does not shrink from expressing our moral values and has the courage to profess them no matter how unpopular this may make him in the eyes of those moral quislings who believe that collaboration or accommodation is the appropriate approach. Can you imagine the North American Martyrs preaching to the savage Hurons—"Gentlemen, I understand you regularly scalp your enemies—I am personally opposed to the practice and believe it is homicide. However, I understand it is sanctioned by the tribal law and I will not try to impose my views upon you."

The problems we face are exacerbated by the fact that young Irish American Catholic men, who once stormed the seminaries, are looking to greener fields. We are forced to consolidate parishes in Westchester and have only a dozen deacons in Dunwoodie who look forward to ordination this spring. The median age of religious in the United States is 62.

With the serious decline in vocations, the obligation of today's Catholic laymen to shoulder their burden of assisting the clergy is correspondingly more pressing. I suggest as a role model the career of one of your former officers, the late Joe Crowley, my close friend for more than fifty years. He did attend the seminary at Dunwoodie for a short time, and although he left and became a lawyer, in a sense he never lost his vocation. He loved God and loved his neighbor and had a great moral influence on the lives of thousands of law students, no matter what their religious affiliation. He was a good man, self-effacing, and not at all concerned with material gain or personal publicity. While his professional expertise was outstanding, his advice, his example, his code of conduct, had a more lasting effect on students. You can forget all the law you ever learned, but the search for the good, the true, and the beautiful must go on. We see little of it today, but it was Joe's constant quest. But if all of us could forget the life of Reilly and remember the life of Crowley, perhaps we will see better days ahead. God bless Joe and all of us.

INDUCTION CEREMONY OF ANDREW J. MALONEY AS UNITED STATES ATTORNEY FOR THE EASTERN DISTRICT OF NEW YORK

July 21, 1986

It is indeed a signal honor to be invited to participate in the public unveiling of Andrew J. Maloney as United States Attorney for the Eastern District of New York. When he applied for admission to Fordham Law School almost thirty years ago, I was the Dean and I well remember his application. Unlike most of the other young Irish Catholics from Brooklyn, he had not gone to St. John's or St. Francis; he went to West Point where he made a great impression not only for his brains and good looks, which are natural Irish characteristics, but also for his ability to use his fists, which is quite uncommon among our peace-loving people. He claims to have inherited this ability from his father, who, he alleges, beat the British Army Light Heavy Weight Champion when he was in the A.E.F. in World War I. However, I believe it really came from his mother, a Roscommon girl, who is with us today, and who claims many decisions, although no knockouts, over her late husband. In any event, whatever natural talents he had, Andy's pugilistic skills were certainly sharpened in combat with the Sisters of St. Joseph at St. Vincent de Paul Academy and the Christian Brothers at Bishop Loughlin. With this genetic and educational background in the martial arts, it is not at all surprising that Andy eschewed the local Catholic institutions of higher learning and entered the Academy. He did well not only in the classroom but on the playing fields of West Point. He became captain of the boxing team, an intercollegiate boxing champion, and then a ranger paratrooper and mountain troop leader. In my review of his application for law school I noted: "will be a tough litigator, and in view of his Alpine experiences, suggest placement in the Catskills or Adirondacks."

Andy did very well at Fordham Law, and in preparation for this performance today, I asked him whether I had ever taught him in class. He waited for a minute and said, "Will you please rephrase the question?" I pondered for a while and said, "Was I ever designated to conduct a class where you had been assigned a seat?" He pondered for a few minutes and said, "I have no present recollection." I abandoned the colloquy but decided that the tone of this eulogy today would be much more restrained than I had planned.

I have a copy of his application to the Law School—he answered all the questions succinctly—for example, No. 34: "If you did not work to earn your living during your college course but expect to do so while studying law, state the circumstances which have made this change necessary." His answer "Acquiring a spouse." While the accuracy of the response is unquestioned, his answer is hardly indicative that young Maloney had inherited the lyric qualities of the ancient Irish bard and poets. However, such characteristics are normally not requisite for the position he now holds. Suffice it to say, the "acquisition" was the best he ever made; one of the offshoots of the merger is now at Fordham Law School, and I hope some day to be invited to his induction as a United States Attorney—assuming, of course, that I am not competing in a swimming meet.

Another strain in the Irish psyche is strong religious faith, and you all have noted that today is the eve of the feast of St. Mary Magdalene. I checked with Andy about its significance, and he, of course, had anticipated that I would ask the question. He said that when he was prosecuting a Mann Act case as a young Assistant, his principal witness was a young lady who followed the same professional calling as the defendant. When her credibility was questioned on this ground, Andrew Maloney advised the jury that Mary Magdalene was saved and was at the foot of the cross with Mary the Mother of God at the crucifixion. He did not volunteer, and I did not ask, what the jury did, but I am sure that this argument will now become quite popular in these cases, which, I assume, still crowd the criminal calendar in the Court.

Andy's credentials for this appointment are compelling. He served not only as an Assistant in the Southern District but as Regional Director of the Drug Abuse Law Enforcement Agency. The drug problem is, admittedly, the most critical we face in law enforcement, and his experience here will indeed prove valuable. It was not too long ago when the goo-goos were claiming that the drug penalties were too harsh and in any event had failed to curb abuses. Even they seem now to begin to realize that lesser punishment can only exacerbate a dangerous situation.

When I went to the Second Circuit, Andy had already established a reputation as an expert prosecutor—tough but fair. In his private practice he was equally successful, representing only those unjustly accused of violating the law. We all of course believe that an accused has the right to competent counsel; however, I must say that Andrew's return to the fold gives us reason to rejoice.

I think all of us had our faith in this country renewed by the recent Fourth of July Statue of Liberty celebration. For most of us, our forebears come here, whether from Russia or Italy or Ireland or Timbuktu, for the same reason as Andy Maloney gave in answer to question No. 48 on his law school questionnaire, "Why do you seek to study law?" Answer: "To better myself and my family's position in life." Right to the point, and the mission was accomplished. Some of you may have been as appalled as I was when some of the so-called prominent naturalized Americans in the recent celebration, in answer to the question "Why did you come here and what does America mean to you?" in essence responded, "It means 'I can do what I want or I can do my own thing or I have the right to be left alone.' " If that is what it means, they should go back home. That isn't liberty; it is license. Liberty has another dimension—the obligation to respect the rights of your fellow man. If it didn't, we have no use for Andy Maloney and those who serve with him. He is the product of a generation that realized that there is a continuing price to pay for this liberty, and he embodies that obligation in accepting this appointment.

I think I speak, I know I speak, for your family, your friends, and your colleagues who are here today, as well as your former clients most of whom would be here if they had shorter sentences. Andrew J. Maloney, we are proud of your accomplishment, we rejoice in your appointment—we pray, dear God, that all the Maloneys, especially the Mrs. Maloneys, senior and junior, thrive and flourish *ad multos annos*.

FORDHAM LAW SCHOOL
DEAN'S DAY
September 27, 1986

It is indeed an honor to come back to the great Fordham Law School and to recall what it was like to come here in 1961. While Judge McLaughlin and Jim Toland have obviously aged over that period, the Law School looks better than ever. To understand what Lincoln Center meant to all of us, one has to realize what we had before we came here. My class entered the Law School in the fall of 1939, about the same time as Hitler entered Poland. The Woolworth Building was still considered to be a skyscraper and had a magnificent spire and a glorious lobby, but it was never designed to house a law school. To enter or leave the first-year classroom one had to go through the second-year room. There were no lounges, no lockers, no lunchroom. The entire administrative staff consisted of the Dean, the Registrar, the Assistant Registrar, the Dean's Secretary, and one clerk-typist. We had a library of sorts: one librarian with no paid assistants and no catalogue at all. Jim Kennedy, the librarian, had no library science degree. His academic career ended at Bay's High School, and his experience was as a book salesman for the West Publishing Company specializing in Words and Phrases.

If a law student wanted help in research, Jim would get the facts. And if it involved personal injury, a man slipping on a banana peel, for instance, Jim would promptly go to Words and Phrases, look up banana peel, and *voilà* all the cases. Concepts like negligence, breach of contract, meant nothing to Jim, just a word was enough. He antedated Lexis by several decades. At the end of World War II we left the Woolworth Building for 302 Broadway, which presumably would give us more space. After the purchase we learned that a second staircase was necessary from top to bottom and promptly lost a great deal of the space. Len Manning and I had adjoining offices which had they been cells in a prison would be found to be constitutionally defective today in any federal court. The lobby was a far cry from the Woolworth Building. Every time I pass an O.T.B. office today, I am reminded of 302. I became Dean while we were still incarcerated in that building. It was 1956, just thirty years ago this month. I was a boy of 38, but I began to age rapidly.

My first problem was an inspection by the American Law School Association. The question was not whether we complied with the rules but how many did we violate. For example, we did have a library, but it was not catalogued. Jim Kennedy advised me that none was necessary—he said all the Reporters have numbers on the spine, all the textbooks are arranged alphabetically by author. We have to assume that the students here can count and know the alphabet, said Jim. His compromise was to hand-letter signs with arrows which pointed to the various Reporters and textbooks. One in particular said "Words & Phrases." All the one-volume handbooks, incidentally, were locked in Jim's desk to prevent larceny. This he thought should be brought to the attention of the inspectors.

The inspection was personally conducted by John Hervey, the Executive Director of the American Law School Association. The reason for his selection as the inspector was that he had a son at N.Y.U. and he liked to make free trips to New York to visit him. John Hervey was the dean of the Oklahoma City Law School, an all-evening or part-time operation which was not even accredited by Oklahoma City, much less the A.B.A. or the A.L.S.A. This in no way diminished his hauteur, his austere manner, and his obvious disdain for the primitive conditions he observed at 302.

We survived this and a second visit for two reasons. The first was our plans for a newer and greater Law School, which I then envisaged on the Fordham Campus and which I described to him as fifty acres of virgin greenery adjacent to the Botanical Gardens. I did not mention the Bronx Zoo.

The second and perhaps more effective point on appeal was that I discovered that this Southern Baptist Oklahoman and this Bronx Irish Catholic had a common and deep appreciation of a deadly potion known as the extra-dry martini straight up with a lemon twist. At that time I was a member of the Lotos Club, which had an Irish bartender who, I think, was a *summa cum laude* graduate of the Fordham Pharmacy School. His ability to make a perfect martini was legendary, and after two magical potions Dean Hervey was in the land of the Lotos-Eaters where it was always afternoon planning with me the new Fordham Law School. The advantage of taking him the first day was that he never bothered coming back that afternoon and if he did arrive the next day it was rather late. Thanks to the foresight of Father

McGinley and Bob Moses, Lincoln Center became a reality; when we opened, John Hervey made his last visit. He took full credit for the building, viewed it as his own, was extraordinarily warm in his report, and after one hour said—"Bill, this is magnificent, why don't we drop in at the Lotos Club." I wish he were here today, because he deserves a lot of the credit.

Let me emphasize that while we did have serious limitations of space and facilities before we came here which certainly did not enhance our reputation, the quality of the faculty and student body was excellent. We had a limited curriculum, which was mandated by a lack of classroom space, so that students were required to take all the basic courses, which is something to think about. We produced great lawyers in the log cabins we occupied—John Loughran, John F. X. Finn, Irving Kaufman, John Sonnet, Ed Dore, Bill Meagher, Leo Kissam, Larry McKay—just to mention a very few who were leaders of the bar. As Vic Kilkenny once observed, Fordham lawyers were good on their feet because they had no place to sit down in law school.

The planning for the Law School was long and difficult— Father Mulcahy and Brother Kenny were intimately involved. We got air conditioning primarily because the *Law Review* space had no windows but saved interior space otherwise useless. Moreover, we had long litigation from civil libertarians so-called, who thought it was unconstitutional for a Catholic University to even bid on a federal project of this type. Marty Fogelman was then a young lawyer at Saxe, Bacon & O'Shea and worked on the case. Despite this we were ultimately victorious. Periodically, faculty survey teams would visit the new site to observe the progress of the work. George Bacon never believed it would be built and if built that it would never be used by the Law School. Gene Keefe used to come up but only to find a convenient watering hole equal in quality to the Pearl Street Restaurant, our regular haunt.

Eventually, a quarter-century ago, the great move was made. In retrospect it reminds me of the scene in "Lost Horizons" where Ronald Colman and his companions are led by the sherpas through the blizzards and ice of the Himalayas into Shangri-La where all was warm and beautiful and the birds twittered all the day. I realize that the analogy between Ronald Colman and William Mulligan is somewhat limping—I am much taller than he was. I insisted that the building be so structured that additional floors and an atrium could later be added. I assume that will be done.

I was awed by my office with wonderful furniture, paneled walls, bright carpeting, and a private john. I had not felt unworthy at 302, but could I last at Lincoln Center? Father McGinley had shown great courage in appointing me Dean at a tender age and virtually unknown, but if he had any misgivings he kept silent, and Father O'Keefe accepted me as inevitable. I will omit any discussions of the regime which followed—the one which founded a new college, Bensalem, where only one course was required: *Urdu*—an Indian dialect; I thought it was insane until Bhopal.

All went swimmingly until Kent State and Vietnam when the students for reasons unknown to me decided that they were so emotionally drained that they could not take examinations. This beautiful place was picketed but never occupied. It was at about this time that like Joan of Arc I began to hear voices calling to me urging that I go on the Second Circuit, Court of Appeals. I have never mentioned this before because there are those who are skeptics. I left the School in the capable hands of Joe McLaughlin, who assured me that he heard no voices urging him to the bench, and he vowed to stay here for life. I served on the bench for ten years, and again I heard voices—this time trumpets as well; they kept calling, Skadden, Arps, Slate, Meagher & Flom. I looked it up in the phone book and found that it was a law firm and that one of my prize students, John Feerick, was there. He urged me to come and assured me he would be at my side for life. I asked him if he heard any angelic voices calling "Go on the federal bench, go on the federal bench." He said no and he had no interest in going on the bench. Of course, he did not dissemble. I should have asked the proper question—the voices he later admitted were calling— "Go back to school, John."

And so we are all back at the School we love so much— nurtured by a strong bond between lay deans and family and a Jesuit administration. It will be difficult for me to make an appearance here for the fiftieth, at least in any speaking capacity. However, you may hear a horn blowing in the distance.

THE AMERICAN JEWISH COMMITTEE PRESENTATION OF LEARNED HAND HUMAN RELATIONS AWARD TO WILLIAM HUGHES MULLIGAN
November 20, 1986

It is indeed an honor and privilege to receive the Learned Hand Award from the American Jewish Committee. I am particularly pleased to be in the company of such distinguished former recipients, many of whom are friends and colleagues, including a partner in the Mulligan firm, Joe Flom. When Leon Silverman invited me to accept this honor, he said that I would be the first non-Jew to receive it. I was indeed surprised to hear that there was a dearth of worthy Jewish lawyers in New York. I told him that my mother had a first cousin named Sam Scriven who still runs a candy store in Cork so it may be that no precedent at all has been created. In any case, when I was a young boy growing up in that tight little island, The Bronx, in the twenties, I thought that all Americans were either Jewish or Irish, although there were rumors that far to the east near Pelham Bay there were also Italo-Americans; I never believed it.

It is particularly appropriate that the Learned Hand Award be made to a former member of the Second Circuit. Let me tell you about my close relationship with Judge Hand. When I was a young Dean at Fordham Law School, I attended the Annual American Law Institute Meeting in Washington, D.C. Although the airplane could fly that far at that time, the accepted mode of transportation was the Pennsylvania Railroad. At Penn Station I saw the great man boarding the train assisted by his bailiff, an evening student at Fordham. I recognized Hand because he, like me, rode the Third Avenue El and I as a law student used to gaze at him in awe. The bailiff asked me to keep an eye on him and get him off the train.

At lunch time I left my reserved parlor car seat and went back to the dining car. The judge was nowhere in sight, so after a martini and a steak sandwich, I wandered back through the coach cars where the steerage passengers purchased sandwiches swathed in cellophane from white-coated hawkers. Sure enough, there was Learned. I did not interrupt the great man as he gnawed away at his ham on rye, with all the dignity he could muster under the circumstances. I always remember the black homburg jumping up and down in rhythm with his jaw-bone. It taught me a great lesson in humility—the humble shall be exalted and the exalted humbled; the first shall be last and the last first. I was deeply impressed by his self-effacement. However, when I became a member of the bench, I realized the ugly truth: on his judicial expense account Judge Hand was lucky not to be riding in the baggage car, and the ham sandwich, I found, was the normal lunch of most federal judges except for Judge Edelstein, who prefers tuna fish.

When we arrived at the great station in Washington, I waited for him to alight, and I approached him with a carefully pre-pared statement. "Your Honor, is there any way I can help you with your baggage or get you to a hotel?" The great man looked up at me, and said simply "No." At least that message was clearer to me than his opinion in the Alcoa case which I had been trying to interpret for classes for some years. When people ask me now, "Did you ever know Learned Hand?" I look up and say, "Of course, we lunched together, traveled together, and had long conversations."

Rather then give one of the learned lectures on the law which have made me so well known, I thought this evening I might give you some reflections on my career, which had they been known to the committee would have made this evening impos-sible.

One of my earliest recollections was marching up and down the hill that is 194th Street in The Bronx with a small group of boys all armed with wooden swords. I don't recall the date, but the chant to which we marched was "Hip, Hip, Hip—the Kai-ser's got the grippe," which gives you some clue. I repeated this jingle to some of my judicial colleagues at lunch one day, and Judge Timbers explained to me who the Kaiser was and what the grippe was. Judge Meskill said he didn't realize how much history Judge Timbers had mastered, and Judge Van Graafei-land claimed that Judge Timbers not only knew the chant, but had written the music. My first vocation was for the priesthood and not the law, but after four years in the junior seminary, I realized that an Irish Catholic from The Bronx could go only so far in the profession, so I left—a decision much appreciated by Catholic hierarchy here and in Rome.

I then went to Fordham College at the foot of the 194th Street hill and graduated in 1939. I couldn't find a job. The Great Depression was still on. I was too nearsighted to be a policeman and did not have enough political clout to become an usher at Loew's Paradise. Rather than remain idle, I went to Fordham Law School where I found a home—not only as a student but for many years as a member of the faculty and Dean; the major interruption was World War II where I learned some very valuable lessons. Although chiropodists, floor walkers, and undertakers were routinely commissioned as second lieutenants, as an attorney I was assigned as a private to the military police—a natural process since I was a large Irishman. I was assigned to the Staten Island Port of Embarkation and, in the winter of 1942, which was extremely frigid, I paraded up and down the sands at Stapleton armed with a World War I rifle over my shoulder, a knitted face-mask, and thick gloves. I sang to myself as I marched "Hip, Hip, Hip—the Kaiser's got the grippe." I kept the bullets for the rifle in my overcoat lest I trip and shoot myself or some innocent civilian. Presumably I was there to prevent any German invasion of Staten Island—and you will recall there was none, at least not that winter. One day I was called into the office, thawed out, and persuaded to subscribe to a $10,000 G.I. life insurance policy. When the lieutenant asked me who the beneficiary should be—as a freshly minted lawyer who had just been admitted to the bar a few months before, I stated casually, "Make it payable 'to my estate.' " Two days later I was taken off the beach, assigned to a desk job, and given the rank of acting corporal. I did not understand my good fortune until the master sergeant, himself a product of The Bronx, asked me where I had lived and what rent we paid. He then asked me "What about that big estate you have?" It was only then that I realized that the lieutenant, who was a high school Spanish teacher, had figured that anyone with an estate was worth cultivating.

I never got back to the beach, because a few days later I was transferred to the Counter Intelligence Corps. This was a choice assignment much sought after because the agents wore civilian clothes and received cash for quarters, rations, and clothing which came to about $4 a day. I felt that the assignment was merited because of my high grades in law school, but when I reported to the lieutenant, a former New York City detective, he said with a smile, "Give my best to your father." I looked blank. He said, "Isn't your father Inspector Mulligan of the N.Y.P.D.?" I said "No." He responded, "My God, we got the wrong Mulligan." And so in a brief period in the army I learned that the appearance of affluence or influence per se is sufficient to secure preferment. That is Mulligan's Law.

When I left the army I brought with me the colonel's secretary, who became my bride during the War. After all I was making $96 a month, and the first year of our marriage she declared me as a dependent. I have been totally dependent on her ever since. I wanted to teach law and I applied for a full-time job as a professor at Fordham. Ignatius Wilkinson was the dean and asked me what my qualifications were. I told him that I had high marks and made the *Law Review* and had spent three years as an agent in the C.I.C. Wilkinson, who resembled Learned Hand, said to me, "Mulligan, if I were running a detective agency, I would hire you; but this is a law school." I should have told him of course that I had an estate and that my father was an Inspector in the Police Department. In any event a few months later, I was appointed. I guess he learned that it was tough to get professors for $4,000 a year. It was a better-paying job than the army, but I had no quarters or rations allowance and had to buy my own clothes.

I stayed at Fordham for twenty five years but then I heard there were several vacancies in the Second Circuit. I applied to the Attorney General for one of the openings and got it—this is really what happened. Apparently I am the only federal judge ever appointed through this unique process—all the rest were forced into the job by the President, a U.S. Senator, ambitious friends, or possibly the Holy Ghost. My induction ceremony was quite unusual. Only two judges showed up, Henry Friendly and Walter Mansfield. When I left ten years later, every one of them showed up at a dinner for me—and practically every district court judge showed up on the last day I sat on the bench. I can only assume that they all wanted to be sure I left. Of course, when I resigned, the government refunded my contribution to the survivors' benefit program plus 2½ percent interest. This I learned later is called a golden parachute. For the first time in my life I had an estate.

In dealing with Skadden, Arps, my intermediary was a partner, John Feerick, a former student of mine, who told me that it was the greatest firm in the world and that he would never leave. I don't see him around there anymore; I assume he went to

Wachtel, Lipton. I was impressed by the firm, but I had learned some lessons in the army—I told Feerick to tell Arps and Flom and Mullen and Garfinkel that I wanted my salary payable to my estate and that my late father was a police inspector. By golly, it worked—I got an excellent offer. I told my mother I was leaving the bench. Her reaction was just the same as when I told her I was leaving the seminary and leaving Fordham: "Whatever you think is best." I then told her what I would be making, actually reducing the amount somewhat; after all, she was old and not too strong. That was a mistake. She said "Billy, at that rate those people won't be able to stay in business very long." Since I joined the firm has grown and prospered. As I learned from the Jesuits, *post hoc ergo propter hoc*.

Since leaving the bench I have not lost my influence on its decision-making. Let me give you, in the confidence of this room, an example of how my opinions still influence the court. A few weeks ago Jim Oakes told me that he was going to use the expression "Serbonian Bog" in an opinion, and that he remembered it from an opinion I had written—he wanted the cite. After consulting one experienced associate, a summer associate, several paralegals, and some sisters, I found that I had used the expression in three separate opinions—usually in dissenting opinions where you charge the majority of plunging the law into a Serbonian Bog. They don't know what it means but they know it is not good. A primary purpose of a dissent, of course, is to annoy the majority. I told this tale to Milton Pollack who immediately decided that he could use the term in an opinion he was writing and since he did not have to get any tabs he might beat Oakes to the punch. However, Judge Cardamone wrote an opinion a few weeks ago using the term "Serbonian Bog" attributing it in a footnote, not to me or even Judge Cardozo from whom I had lifted it, but to the poet Milton who described the Serbonian Bog as a place where entire armies had disappeared. Judge Pollack sent me the Cardamone opinion, and I told him that even though it was a Second Circuit opinion Cardamone should have cited him as Milton Pollack and not simply Milton. I also told him I would like an autographed copy of *Paradise Lost*. Milton seemed happy.

I must say that this evening has been a very special occasion for me—I am very much indebted to the American Jewish Committee whose work I applaud. I thank them for this honor, which I do not deserve but which I accept with alacrity. I also particularly thank my partner, my manager, and, above all, my friend, Barry Garfinkel, who has worked so hard. I thank all of you for coming—my old colleagues at the Fordham faculty, my colleagues on the federal bench, my former students, my partners and associates at Skadden, Arps, my law school classmate and friend for almost fifty years, Lloyd Isler, and, of course, my wife, daughter, daughter-in-law, and son. You have all made this a memorable evening. God bless!

MEMORIAL SERVICES, LESLIE H. ARPS
July 17, 1987

In the glory that was Greece and the grandeur that was Rome, the neophyte sculptor would cover and fill in his mistakes, his gouges, and his gaps with wax, which, hopefully, would blend in with the stone. The true artist would advertise his works as *sine cera*—without wax. And thus the derivation of the English word sincere. Les Arps was "sincere." Les Arps was "sincere" in the true sense of that term. There was no wax—no flummery, no prancing, no dancing, no fake; what you saw was what you got. What you got is what Jim and John described so eloquently: a lawyer in the best traditions of the bar, totally devoted to his firm, his clients, and his profession; not simply the best representation he could provide his clients but a broad obligation to the community in which he lived; his military service to his country; his service as counsel to public agencies; his activity on bar association committees; his private philanthropies, many of which were related to the profession—all attest to his commitment. He was a man whom we all have been proud to introduce as "my partner." We have all observed and noted his gentility, his absence of side and pretense.

We who have spoken have all reached this common ground to stress; it is in a sense unfortunate because these qualities which once were considered the hallmarks of our profession are becoming less and less common. The general public has never been enamored of attorneys in any recorded history. Pettifoggers, procrastinators, and sophists are some of the more gentle descriptive epithets. Today the popular image of the attorney is, if anything, lower, and it may be near its nadir. The distinction once proudly made between the practice of a profession and practicing a trade has become eroded. The motivating force for many is not service but unadulterated greed. Good manners are becoming as rare as professional literacy. The point is that, regrettably, what Les epitomized is apparently becoming unfashionable; it is in short supply, and we and you recognize it.

I first met Les thirty years ago, but I got to know him well only in the past few years. In a firm of young men it was natural that the two eldest in the New York office spend some time together reflecting upon the human condition. I have been thinking about those meetings. I recall one luncheon conversation when Les discussed an attorney who was prominent in his time, but he could not recall his name. I knew exactly whom he meant but was equally at a loss to remember the name. However, I did recall his partner whom I described but I couldn't remember his name. Les knew exactly whom I meant but said the name will come to him later. We both agreed to exchange the names on the phone that afternoon, but I think we forgot.

I remember reminding Les about our lunches together with Tom Moore thirty years ago. I said, "Les, remember we used to have two martinis before lunch." He retorted, rather vehemently for Les, "No, I never had more than one and a half." I told him that I never remember anybody, even including Les Arps, ordering half a martini, and no self-respecting bartender would ever mix one. It was the most serious disagreement I ever had with Les. Before he died, Les told Ruth that he wanted to have a cocktail party after his funeral. We have utilized the euphemism "reception." You are all cordially invited after this service to 919 Third Avenue, 33rd floor, Skadden, Arps—where anyone who wants to order a half a martini will get it without question. We do it to toast *our* dear and cherished partner Les and *his* dear and cherished partner, Ruth. God bless.

FORDHAM LAW ALUMNI CELEBRATION OF THE SEVENTIETH BIRTHDAY OF WILLIAM HUGHES MULLIGAN

March 5, 1988

It is indeed an honor that the Alumni Association would take such public notice of my seventieth birthday. You can imagine how eagerly and gleefully I have been looking forward to becoming 70. The other day in the intimacy and anonymity of a taxicab, I asked the driver, a Russian, how old he thought I was. He turned around, looked at me, and said, "77, 78?" I said in an offended tone "What!" He said, "You mean you are older?"

A couple of years ago the oil burner in my house was being repaired for the upteenth time. I said to the repairman, "Do you think I should buy a new one?" He said, "How old are you?" I said "67"; he responded frankly, "I don't think It would be a good investment."

A particular reason to rejoice, of course, is that today I outlive the generous term life insurance policy provided by my firm. There was a meltdown of my estate last midnight of serious dimension. Rosie now has, however, my G.I. insurance, and I am conveying to her the plenary indulgences I earned at Fordham and the Second Circuit.

I should point out that the man we honor today is John Keenan and not your old dean. Its just a coincidence that my birthday is today and that it falls on the same date as this luncheon. The next time the two events coincide is in 2015; I will be 97 and I invite all now present to join me then.

In honoring John Keenan I am sure that most of you do not know the inside story as to how he ascended the bench. A couple of years before his appointment, Mayor Koch was faced with an extremely difficult and intricate legal problem involving the Legal Aid Society. He formed a committee, of course, and selected John Keenan as the chairman; the two other members were Jim Gill and me. It was an obviously well-balanced committee since each of our families came from different counties in Ireland and each of us belonged to different parishes in New York. It became known as the Keenan Commission, and, of course, Gill and I did all the work. This committee made Keenan nationally prominent, and when he went before the Judiciary Committee Senators Biden and Kennedy were afraid to ask him any questions especially since Keenan's family had worked in Irish gold mines all day and played football all night. Thus, he got the bench, and the mayor took Gill and me to a Chinese restaurant for lunch.

Seriously, John Keenan in a surprisingly short time has established himself as a highly skilled and respected trial court judge. I admit that I did teach him Criminal Law, but I also taught G. Gordon Liddy.

John and I both have close ties to a large group of people in other institutions who are unable to be here today—unfortunately, the visiting hours at the various state and federal penitentiaries do not permit their attendance.

I am very happy to be here today with my family and friends. Fordham Law School has been a close part of my life for fifty years. I have an unabashed and abiding affection for it—all its works and pomps, its faculty and students, and particularly its dean, whose comments today I will cherish even though they were somewhat noncommittal. Whatever success I have had is attributable to my faculty colleagues, my students, the alumni, the Jesuits—particularly Father McGinley, who appointed me Dean at the tender age of 38—and to the support of Roseanna, who never grumbled about the sacrifices academic and judicial life required. I thank you; my dear wife thanks you; my children thank you; and my grandchildren also thank you.

God bless!

TESTIMONIAL DINNER FOR
JOHN SCOTT
October 22, 1988

We are here to pay tribute to John Scott, who purchased Mountain Valley in 1938. At that time he was 50 years old. I have known John Scott for more than forty years. We served together in World War II in the so-called Counter Intelligence Corps. Our work was so secret and so confidential that I have no idea what John did and John had no idea what I did, although I think it is fair to assume that we were on the same side. We served in separate combat zones—John was stationed in the post office building at Grand Central and I was at 50 Broadway until I married the colonel's secretary and was moved to the RCA building, which was particularly hazardous by reason of the high-rise elevators. John, in my view, is an absolute genius; some indeed may say he is a wizard. Water for all practical purposes is absolutely free. It flows out of every tap and hydrant in New York; it is colorless, odorless, and tasteless. In New York it is chemically pure and indeed it is rated among the very best in the United States. Yet John has succeeded in putting water in bottles and selling it by the case to New York housewives otherwise considered to be thrifty shoppers. John's water isn't even effervescent. It does not bubble; it is just as flat as the water that comes out of your tap, and I am assured by chemists that it isn't any wetter. Thomas Edison had great success, but he had a patent monopoly. John Scott did not invent or even discover water, and the bottle had been invented by the Irish centuries before. Any man who can raise and educate a large family and live in a large, presumably mortgage-free, mansion in Bronxville on the profits of selling water to people who already have it free in their home has to be, in my mind, a marketing genius. It is expected that at least three billion gallons of water will be sold by 1996 and John deserves the credit.

My introduction to Mountain Valley was quite dramatic. We were at a New Year's Eve party in Bronxville thirty years ago when I received a phone call from one of my then small children, advising that a funny noise was coming from the cellar. John was at the same party and drove me home. It developed that a pipe had burst in the cellar due to extreme cold, and we had to turn off the main water pipe. The next morning John came over with a case of Mountain Valley which he said should be used to prime the johns. It worked perfectly. In fact, I thought that this was its main use; it never occurred to me that people would drink the stuff.

Although the claim is made that the water in the green bottle comes from Arkansas, some cynics have noted that at night all the faucets in the Scott house keep running. In fact, some say that even the hydrants near his house run at night. His children used to come out with pails and haul it to the cellar. I also have it from a good source that the gutters and leaders on John's house do not go into the ground but into the cellar, where water is collected in large wash tubs. You may draw whatever conclusions you wish, but it is significant that I have never met anyone who has ever been invited to visit the Scott cellar.

John, of course, supplies Mountain Valley water to St. Joseph's Roman Catholic Church in Bronxville. We have the only parish in the archdiocese that has both Mountain Valley holy water and Easter water. Many of your children and grandchildren have been baptized in Mountain Valley water. It is touching indeed that John calls them "my kids." Why do you think St. Joseph's Church in Bronxville has the largest baptismal font in the Western hemisphere? John made a deal with Monsignor Sheridan to keep it filled with Mountain Valley water with a small, as he said, tasteful plaque: "Gift of the Mountain Valley family." The deal fell through when Monsignor Connolly became pastor. He said that some of the older people who came to Mass daily might trip, fall in, and drown in the church.

John cited the Old Testament in rebuttal—Jeremiah 31:7-9—where the Lord said to the Israelites who lost, "I will console them and guide them; I will lead them to brooks of water on the level road, so that none shall stumble." This actually is the first reading in tomorrow's Mass which, I assume, is why John is having this dinner tonight. It did not deter the Monsignor. He said worse than drowning, the elders of the parish might fear to come to Mass and instead join the Dutch Reformed Church, which has no water hazards. John offered to give free swimming lessons to the senior citizens club or to put a display of bottles in the pool, but the Monsignor was adamant.

John has not only been able to make a substantial living out

of this business but has actually been able to sell it to two gentlemen who are our hosts together with John this evening. Their
names are Ix and Braks, which I assume are pseudonyms. The
Mountain Valley office is in New Jersey. When I asked John why
he worked out of New Jersey he said because it's closer to my
source of supply. That seemed odd to me, but I realized that his
office is actually located in a suburb of Weehawken—an Indian
name which translates into English as "Mountain Valley"; it is,
of course, located on the Hudson River, which again suggests a
water source other than Arkansas. I had lunch with Bob Braks,
and he told me that John has also offered to sell them the
George Washington Bridge. They turned it down since Braks
said they had already bought the Brooklyn Bridge from John
and they thought one bridge was enough for awhile. Incidentally, I asked Bob if he liked Mountain Valley water. He said he
hadn't tried it yet but probably would stick to Dr. Brown's Cel-
ray tonic.

John has always spent a lot of time praying in church. In fact,
he was a lector at St. Joseph's until this summer when during
the drought in the Midwest he refused to lead the congregation
in a prayer for rain. He explained to me that drought is good
for the bottled water business, and while he doesn't actually pray
for droughts, he does pray that there will be no floods. This
summer his prayers were most efficacious—he almost dried up
the Mississippi River, and Yellowstone Park will never be the
same. John says that floods do a lot of property damage and
people drown; nobody ever drowns in a drought, says John. He
said nobody, especially the Irish, has ever died of thirst in a
drought, either.

I have asked John what future business plans he has. I can tell
you in the confidence of this room that John is planning to bottle
Mountain Valley air; he wants to sell me the Westchester County
franchise. As he said, "Bill, if I could get away for fifty years with
the water scam, this one is a cinch." Air is even cheaper than
water and much lighter—transportation costs would be cut in
half. I told him that I thought I could persuade Skadden, Arps
to make a partnership investment. Peter Mullen, who is the
ringmaster of the firm and a friend of John's, is very much interested; he told me that it is probably the best investment the firm
would have in its portfolio. There is no question about that.
When I told John about this interest, he asked if we might also
be interested in the Tappan Zee Bridge. I told him to forget it;

Mullen is negotiating with Trump for the Verrazano. In any event, Peter is here tonight presumably to close the air deal.

Ladies and gentlemen, I must confess that not everything I have said is entirely true; in fact, some might suggest it is misleading. I must add, however, that not only is John a great businessman, he is a great husband, father, and friend of all of us. He is a "gentleman" in the fullest sense of the word, and he and Joanie have enriched in many ways the lives of their neighbors and friends. We all respect him and love him and all his works and pomps. *Ave atque vale,* John, *ad majorem Dei gloriam et ad bonam aquam.*

NEW YORK COUNTY LAWYERS ASSOCIATION, WALDORF-ASTORIA

December 8, 1988

It is indeed an honor to be invited once more to address the members and friends of the New York County Lawyers Association. My last appearance here was on December 9, 1971, shortly after I had been appointed to the United States Court of Appeals for the Second Circuit. If all goes according to schedule, my next appearance here will be in seventeen years, early December, 2005 I assume, of course, that this hotel will still be standing and this organization will still be functioning.

In 1971 I was one of nine active judges, and only two were younger than I; the senior judges were of course all older. The two younger judges were Bill Feinberg and Jim Oakes. They are both here this evening, even though they have listened to me speak for ten years straight; I can only assume they were hungry and perhaps thirsty. In contrast, I am now a partner in a firm which has some 960 lawyers, and I am the second oldest—a rather sobering statistic. If the firm continues to expand and all the lawyers go to my funeral, it will have to be held in the Meadowlands. Actually, very few would attend unless the Giants are playing that day.

Whenever I am asked to give a speech, the press people of the organization sponsoring the talk invariably ask me for an advance copy or a condensed version or at least the title. My usual practice is to deny the request, not because I don't know what I want to say but because I believe that serious messages should be published for leisurely reading in the Federal Reporter, Second Series or a law journal—I have no message but attempt to make wry or whimsical comments on the human condition which in my view is continuously deteriorating. About twenty-five years ago, however, not only was I pressed by the Insurance Section of the A.B.A., which was holding its annual meeting in New York, to give a title to my comments but they wanted one which was provocative and not the usual stilted cant such as "The Rule in Shelley's Case Revisited." Without hesitation, I stated that my title was "Sex and the Single Premium, or, Up from the Serbonian Bog."

That title was printed in the program and *Time* magazine actually cited it characterizing it as the best nonsensical title of the convention. It was the only time I ever made *Time*. A few weeks later, I received a letter from a lawyer in Boston who said he fully understood what the title implied and he congratulated me on my perspicacity and courage in raising the issue. Ever since then I have viewed the Boston bar with some degree of respect mixed with a great degree of apprehension.

This year your association has been asking me for weeks what my topic was. Having reached the age of seventy, the age of reason, I thought it was about time that I talked in a serious vein. The most serious things I can think of are the seven deadly sins—pride, covetousness, lust, gluttony, envy, anger, and sloth. I do not want to cover all seven at once. I thought that the one which might be most topical these days when our profession is under such attack for its alleged avarice was the sin of covetousness. A proper title might be "Covetousness Revisited" or even "In Praise of Covetousness." Perhaps "Greed" is a more current term and certainly one more easily articulated. An examination of conscience surprisingly reveals that greed has played a major role in my professional career.

My first professional encounter with covetousness occurred when I was a second-year student at Fordham Law School, forty-eight years ago. Although I was supposed to be studying full time, a classmate told me that I could get a job as a book-boy at the New York County Lawyers Association at the princely sum of $8.00 a week plus free use of a gray linen jacket. This distinguished me from the attorney members most of whom were in shirt sleeves. The relationship between your association and me is best described as master-servant. I was indentured, not employed. Not only did I shelve the books in the South Reading Room, I also lugged up from the basement heavy records on appeal, operated the elevator, and in addition provided legal research assistance for the members. Legal research is now done by machines at considerable cost, but book shelving, I believe, is still a manual operation—at least until the alphabet and counting, like geography, are eliminated from the grammar school curriculum.

In the South Reading Room members were permitted to

smoke, and in those days cigar smoking was an indicium of professional success, no matter what the price of the stogie—hence, the room was in a constant dense fog. The greenhouse effect was created by your association. When I had a few minutes of free time, I would unlatch a window to gasp a few breaths of fresh air and look down at the graveyard of St. Paul's Cemetery and envy those now covered by decaying headstones, their names barely decipherable on their memorial stones rotted with the fumes of the vehicles of the city exacerbated by the escaping smoke from the South Reading Room.

I think that I may be the only book-boy of that era still alive— the rest have all died of respiratory diseases or spinal disorders. I can't even bring a class action against you despite the lack of proof which tort law has generously created for such causes.

In my third year of law school, I encountered my second occasion of the sin of greed. I was advised that a law firm at 154 Nassau Street was looking for a law clerk. I was interviewed by the senior partner of a three-man firm who grilled me at great length not only about my academic record, but about my family background, my religious and ethnic origins, my sex life, my criminal record, and my physical health as well. If these questions were asked today, he could have gotten at least five years in a maximum security federal pen. Today you can't even ask an applicant what day of the week it is unless you say approximately what day of the week it is or, better yet, what day of the week it is.

There are as far as I know no limitations on what the applicant can ask the interviewer—after all, he or she is making a commitment and intimate knowledge of your business, your commitment, and the future of the firm are entirely relevant. I understand that the senior partner of one New York firm became dissatisfied with the caliber of the new associates—they were all bright but lacked savvy and common sense. He decided to interview them himself. His first candidate was a Harvard Law School senior. He said he was *summa cum laude* from Harvard College, was first in his class at Harvard Law School, and in addition wrote briefs for the full-time faculty which is overburdened with litigation. The senior partner said, "Fine, but look at me; do you notice anything unusual about my appearance?" "Yes," he responded; "you have no ears." The senior partner said, "And you have no tact; we do not need you." The next applicant was from Yale. He was also brilliant and in addition to scholastic honors was a tenor soloist in the Whiffenpoofs.

Again the question, "Do you notice anything unusual about me?"; the response, "You have no ears"; the rejoinder, "You have no tact; good-bye." The third applicant arrived. He had gone to Columbia College where he was in the top 90th percent of his class, he said. He had been a cheerleader there, and was deeply frustrated. He had then gone to Fordham Law School—he said it had taken him four years to get out, his average was now up to C-minus. Impatiently, the question was asked: "Look at me; do you see anything unusual about me?" "Yes," said the student; "you have a cataract in each eye which you have covered up with contact lenses." "Wonderful," said the senior partner; "you are precisely correct—how did you ever reach that conclusion?" "Well," said the student, "if you had any ears, you would be wearing glasses."

Getting back to greed in 1941: the senior partner at 154 Nassau Street asked me how much I was making at the New York County Lawyers Association. I told him I was getting $8.00 a week; I did not think it appropriate to add the free use of the gray linen jacket. After considerable thought, he said, "We can match that!" I told him that I would not leave Vesey Street without an increase in salary. After more musing he grudgingly agreed to pay me $9.00 a week but pointed out that I had no tenure and would be on probation for a year. Incidentally, as an associate or clerk at that firm no mention was made at my interview of moving costs, theater tickets, or moonlight cruises. When I left the firm I was taken to Chinatown for a businessman's lunch. In view of the importance of the occasion, I was told that I could order a bowl of wonton soup rather than a cup. My then employer is still alive and is a practicing psychiatrist in The Bronx, I see him occasionally—socially, of course, not professionally.

I graduated from law school in June 1942, and in July 1942 I left the law firm and became a private in the United States Army at $50.00 a month plus free medical care and four free uniforms. I must admit that this move, although it involved financial gain, was not entirely motivated by greed—I had also received a letter "Greetings" from the President of the United States inviting me to join and pointing out the sanctions which would ensue if I failed to accept. In any event I was going up the financial ladder of success—I was probably the only lawyer in the United States who got an increase in salary by becoming a private in the army. Three and a half years later I had reached the giddy heights of technical sergeant at $112 a month—which was enough of course to marry the colonel's secretary so long as she kept her job. Most of my service was in the Counter Intelligence Corps—I was sent to chemical warfare school as part of my training. The final graduation exercise was for each of us to enter a chamber filled with a deadly gas—once inside you were to put on a gas mask, take several breaths, and exit. Due to my experience in the South Reading Room, I entered that chamber without fear or trepidation—in fact, I had to be forced even to bring in the gas mask. I would like to take this public occasion to thank the County Lawyers Association for preparing me so well for that exercise. Much to my chagrin the war ended—the republic was preserved and the Germans and Japanese condemned forever to financial disaster. Although I could have stayed on in the army, greed again prevailed over patriotism. I joined a New York law firm at the then going rate for small and penurious law firms—$50.00 per week. After I had been there six months, my working wife became pregnant, and I had the temerity to ask for a $10-a-week raise. After several weeks and several partnership meetings, I was asked to compromise at five dollars a week. Again greed prevailed over loyalty to the firm, and I joined the Fordham Law School faculty at $4,000 a year. Again I was one of the few attorneys to join a full-time law faculty at a salary higher than I was making in the practice of law. The gnawing urge for the almighty dollar which had characterized my legal career was too strong to suppress.

After twenty-five years on the faculty, the last fifteen as dean, I decided that it was about time that I renounced the sin of greed, and I accepted an appointment to become a judge of the United States Court of Appeals, Second Circuit. It was the first time I ever took a job which paid less than my previous employment. It was a terrible financial mistake. In the ensuing ten years my judicial salary was almost cut in half by double-digit inflation, incurred, I might add, under the administration of a party which purportedly has a monopoly interest in the poor and the homeless. Incidentally, the job of chief judge in the circuit pays no more than any other judgeship so I naturally had no interest in it. In 1981, I reverted to greed in the grand style. I left the bench and I joined what was then a modestly sized and successful firm, Skadden, Arps, Slate, Meagher & Flom. I didn't even have to be interviewed. Since I joined, the firm has become larger and richer—*post hoc ergo propter hoc*, as I was taught by the Jesuits. Actually, I have brought little if any rain or even a cloud to Skadden, only sunshine.

My conclusion after forty-seven years of life in the law is that greed or covetousness is not as evil as it is cracked up to be. Perhaps pride, lust, gluttony, envy, anger, and sloth have been undersold as well. I contemplated this as the first of a series of seven lectures, each devoted to one of the seven allegedly deadly sins and what part they have played in my career, whatever turns it may take in the years to come. I will save lust until last. That speech will be entitled "Some Aspects of Concupiscence, from a Distant Perspective." I thank you for having me. God bless!

IN MEMORIAM:
WILLIAM HUGHES MULLIGAN

*Joseph M. McLaughlin**

In his lifetime a man plays many roles. I was fortunate—blessed would be a better word—to know Bill Mulligan in his many incarnations: teacher, dean, judge, and, most memorably, friend. Our lives and careers spiraled and intersected for forty-two years.

A superb teacher, a fine administrator, and then a gifted judge, he never lost that sense of humor which gave him the fortitude to serve Fordham for a quarter of a century, under five presidents during times ranging from the halcyon days of the '50s through the Vietnam era. A man without mirth is like a wagon without springs: he is jolted by every pebble in the road. And, indeed, there were many pebbles in the career of William Mulligan from the Bronx to the Bench.

He came to Fordham College in 1935 and achieved success as Editor of *The Ram*, when the school paper was still literate. Young William Mulligan came to Fordham Law School in 1939 as just plain Bill, and later adopted the clerical middle name when he learned that he was a collateral descendant—in those days the clergy did not acknowledge direct descendants—of John Hughes, the first archbishop of New York. He served as an editor of the *Law Review* and upon graduation entered the army. He spent all of World War II chasing spies in New York City, more particularly in Brooklyn, where he protected the Gowanus Canal from German treachery.

Doffing his uniform, he came back to Fordham Law School, first as a part-time teacher, while he practiced law at what would evolve into the Shea, Gould firm, and then on a full-time basis. Professor Mulligan taught me Criminal Law in my first year at the Law School. He subsequently taught me three other courses. At the end of my first year, he became dean of the Law School.

*United States Circuit Judge, United States Court of Appeals for the Second Circuit, 1990 to present. Formerly, United States District Judge (E.D.N.Y.) 1981–1990.

His accomplishments as dean require no Boswell, for it is universally known that Dean Mulligan brought Fordham Law School to Lincoln Square. For fifteen years his constancy demonstrated to student and faculty alike that DEAN is not just another four-letter word. Aristotle has observed that there are some professions in which a gentleman cannot be virtuous. Bill Mulligan's career as dean sorely tested this dictum, but I think Dean Mulligan bested Aristotle in that arena.

It was the boast of Caesar Augustus that he found Rome of brick and left it of marble. While I know that Dean Mulligan would have shrugged off that comparison, I succeeded him as dean and can attest that the Law School he left had grown to prominence on his watch.

I became dean on July 1, 1971. I remember it well. July, 1971 was a steamy, sultry month, and Dean Mulligan had just been elevated to the Court of Appeals for the Second Circuit. Also ascended with him were his desk, the better office appointments, and his secretary.

Working alone, midst a motley assembly of three-legged chairs and a table—not unlike what I had seen in a M.A.S.H. unit in Korea—I answered the phone to hear a man asking to speak "to Dean Mulligan." "He is not here," I responded, "for he is risen as he said he would" (Matt. 28:6). Risen he had, to make a lasting impression on the Second Circuit and to leave us a trove of hundreds of opinions, sparkling with grace, learning, and, most notably, that lightning wit that was his signature.

He first sat in August of that *annus mirabilis*. The judicial planets were in alignment that month, for his first opinion, a criminal case,[1] had drawn a galaxy of legal stars who would themselves eventually ascend to the Bench: for the Government: Raymond J. Dearie (now an Eastern District Judge) and on the brief David G. Trager (also a District Judge); for the Defendant: Phylis Skloot Bamberger (now an Acting State Supreme Court Justice). Anyone who knew Bill can sense immediately that he struggled to restrain his natural impish streak. He churned out a unanimous opinion of impeccable prose and logic, but lacking the expected flashes of wit.

His self-control lasted three weeks. In his second opinion, also a garden-variety criminal case,[2] Bill Timbers, a New Englander,

---

[1] *United States v. Howell*, 447 F.2d 1114 (2d Cir. 1971).

[2] *United States v. Trudo*, 449 F.2d 649 (2d Cir. 1971), *cert. denied*, 405 U.S. 926 (1972).

first by disposition and then by choice, was on the panel. A bank had been held up by three masked men, and without eye-witness identifications, the evidence was largely circumstantial. Trudo and Tatro were convicted and mounted an appeal on sufficiency of the evidence grounds. Doubtless, with one eye on winning Timbers's concurrence, Mulligan capitalized on Timbers's flinty respect for the virtues of parsimony:

> There was abundant evidence of sudden acquisition of wealth on the part of both Trudo and George Tatro after the robbery. Trudo had a very meager income in the fall of 1969 and lived very modestly. In the weeks following the robbery there was an abrupt change in his spending habits. He purchased a used car for $500 and gave a $100 gift to a girl friend. In January, 1970 he paid $70 to have his road plowed of snow, a most lavish and quixotic gesture for any Vermonter irrespective of means. George Tatro was regularly employed at a modest salary and did cash an insurance refund for $542.44 on December 29th, 1969. However, in January, 1970 George Tatro participated in poker games where the stakes were as high as $1,200 a hand. Although known as an average tipper, on three occasions in January, 1970 he bought drinks for everyone at the bar (8 to 10 people), paid his check with $100 bill and left the waitress a $10 tip, all of which was unprecedented.[3]

Bill Mulligan had gone to Cathedral Prep, which in those days prepared young men to enter the seminary. Though he abandoned his clerical aspirations to enter Fordham College, that early clerical/Jesuit formation surfaced in many of his opinions. Thus, in one of the many IBM appeals that filled the Federal Reporters in the early 1970s, he dissented on jurisdictional grounds from Leonard Moore's opinion reviewing an interlocutory order. Loosing an anathema, Mulligan wrote: "It must languish in Purgatory until the Day of Final Judgment."[4]

A lifelong devotee of Latin and Greek classics, he often laced his opinions with classical allusions. In that same IBM dissent he repeated Judge Edelstein's (another classical scholar) caution against opening "a Pandora's Box," which Mulligan quickly en-

---

[3] *Id.* at 651.
[4] *IBM Corp. v. United States,* 471 F.2d 507, 519 (2d Cir. 1971), *cert. denied,* 416 U.S. 980 (1974).

dorsed as being "not as Delphic a pronouncement as it might first appear."[5]

His favorite allusion—and of this let there be no doubt—was to the fabled "Serbonian Bog." Because even the Colorado Supreme Court was befuddled by this reference ("Whatever kind of bog that is"),[6] a little background may be helpful. In the time of the Pharaohs there was a marshy Lake Serbonis in Egypt. Herodotus, who was notoriously given to exaggeration, reported that entire armies disappeared into the marshes. John Milton, in *Paradise Lost*,[7] carried the story into English; and, then Cardozo, wrestling in insurance law, with the distinction between accidental results and accidental means, characterized the dichotomy as doomed to "plunge this branch of the law into a Serbonian Bog."[8] Teaching the Insurance course at Fordham (I was one of his students), Dean Mulligan had led us through this bog, only to become mired in the indemnity distinction between friendly fires and hostile fires. The Serbonian Bog metaphor is about all I recall of the course on Insurance.

The Bog resurfaced a year after Judge Mulligan joined the Second Circuit. The same dissenting opinion in the IBM case chastised Leonard Moore's majority opinion as destined to "lead us only into the Serbonian Bog."[9] When I upbraided him (ever so mildly) for this conceit he told me that nobody would know what it meant and, besides, said he, "the primary purpose of a dissent is to annoy the majority." His love for the Bog is evident in three[10] other majority opinions that he wrote. (As his faithful acolyte, I threw into one of my opinions[11] a Monet–Manet distinction to the bemusement of two of my colleagues.)

Judge Mulligan served for ten years on the Second Circuit. With the celestial regularity of Haley's Comet, the judicial planets once again fell into alignment for his final opinion. The panel, *mirabile dictu*, included Bill Timbers (again) and District

---

[5] *Id.* at 521.

[6] *Equitable Life Assurance Soc'y v. Hemenover*, 67, P.2d 80, 81 (Colo. 1937).

[7] John Milson, *Paradise Lost*, bk. II, 1.592 (1667) ("that Serbonian bog . . . where armies have sunk").

[8] *Landress v. Phoenix Mut. Life Ins. Co.*, 291 U.S. 491, 499 (1934) (Cardozo, J., dissenting).

[9] 471 F.2d at 519.

[10] *Hunt v. Mobil Oil Corp.*, 550 F.2d 68, 77 (2d Cir.), *cert. denied*, 434 U.S. 984 (1977); *Diematic Mfg. Corp. v. Packaging Indus., Inc.*, 516 F.2d 975, 978 (2d Cir.), *cert. denied*, 423 U.S. 913 (1975); *Agur v. Wilson*, 498 F.2d 961, 968 (2d Cir.), *cert. denied*, 419 U.S. 1072 (1974).

[11] *United States v. Cropper*, 42 F.3d 755, 759 (2d Cir. 1994).

Judge Kevin Thomas Duffy, two other jurists not adverse to a
touch of Celtic wit. Neither, it would seem, were the defendant
(Janet Byrnes) or the trial judge (Neal McCurn, N.D.N.Y.). The
defendant was implicated in smuggling rare birds from Canada
into the United States and then lying to a grand jury about her
involvement.

This landmark case, *United States v. Byrnes*,[12] affirmed her conviction unanimously. Bill Mulligan's opinion opened as follows:

> Who knows what evil lurks in the hearts of men? Although
> the public is generally aware of the sordid trafficking of
> drugs and aliens across our borders, this litigation alerts us
> to a nefarious practice hitherto unsuspected even by this
> rather calloused bench—rare bird smuggling. This appeal
> is therefore accurately designated as *rara avis*. While Cana-
> dian geese have been regularly crossing, exiting, reenter-
> ing and departing our borders with impunity, and
> apparently without documentation, to enjoy more salubri-
> ous climes, those unwilling or unable to make the flight
> either because of inadequate wing spans, lack of fuel or fear
> of buck shot, have become prey to unscrupulous traffickers
> who put them in crates and ship them to American ports of
> entry with fraudulent documentation in violation of a host
> of federal statutes.[13]

Several of the footnotes command attention. Footnote 8, for
example comments upon an observation that Judge McCurn
had made during the trial:

> The trial judge, perhaps to relieve the tension, observed
> that while he had enjoyed goose dinners he had never con-
> sumed swan—some indication of the limited cuisine avail-
> able in the Northern District.[14]

There apparently was a difference of opinion as to whether
swans were birds for purposes of the federal statute. Footnote 9
is illuminating:

> For a liberal construction of the term "birds," by a Cana-
> dian court *see Regina v. Ojibway*, 8 Criminal Law Quarterly
> 137 (1965–66) (Op. Blue, J.), holding that an Indian who
> shot a pony which had broken a leg and was saddled with

---

[12] 644 F2.d 107 (2d Cir. 1981).
[13] *Id*. at 108–109.
[14] *Id*. at 110 n.8.

a downy pillow had violated the Small Birds Act which defined a "bird" as "a two legged animal covered with feathers." The court reasoned that the statutory definition

> "does not imply that only two-legged animals qualify, for the legislative intent is to make two legs merely the minimum requirement. . . . Counsel submits that having regard to the purpose of the statute only small animals 'naturally covered' with feathers could have been contemplated. However, had this been the intention of the legislature, I am certain that the phrase 'naturally covered' would have been expressly inserted just as 'Long' was inserted in the Longshoreman's Act.
>
> "Therefore, a horse with feathers on its back must be deemed for the purpose of this Act to be a bird, *a fortiori*, a pony with feathers on its back is a small bird." *Id.* at 139.[15]

The opinion concludes: "The judgment of conviction is affirmed, justice has triumphed and this is my swan song."[16]

It is not without significance that this last Mulligan opinion was filed on St. Patrick's Day, 1981.

Sean O'Casey once observed that we Irish never hesitate to give a serious thought the benefit and halo of a laugh. In a city of carbon copies, William Hughes Mulligan was an original. He touched all who knew him with his kindness and his unforgettable wit.

In the melancholy words from the refrain of an old Irish ballad:

> The music in my heart I bore,
> Long after it was heard no more.

---

[15] *Id.* at 112 n.9.
[16] *Id.* at 112.

EULOGY FOR WILLIAM HUGHES MULLIGAN ST. JOSEPH'S CHURCH MAY 17, 1996

William Hughes Mulligan, Jr.

Your Eminence Cardinal O'Connor, Father O'Hare, Monsignor Connolly, Dean Feerick, reverend clergy and friends:

On behalf of my father and my entire family, thank you so much for attending this beautiful and fitting funeral Mass for my father.

John Feerick, my father always said, "A Fordham man is a gentle man." You, sir, epitomize the Fordham man. You and so many others, like Dennis McInerney, and Irene, who gave our family so much comfort over the past ten months, will never be forgotten.

How many men can truthfully say at the time of their father's death that he was the greatest man they ever knew? Probably all too few, but count me among them.

Perhaps William Hughes Mulligan was your friend, your professor, your mentor, your dean, your colleague, your partner, your neighbor, or your counselor. He was one or all to untold thousands of men and women.

But only three can boast that he was their father. And only one can claim that he was her husband.

For you see, for all my father's achievements in life, which are well documented (none of which you would hear about from him) and were hard earned, they pale in comparison to his achievements as a husband and a father.

Can you imagine the unparalleled experience of having such a thoroughly decent human being as your father?

I believe, and I'm sure you would agree, that you were fortunate to have known him whether you met him once or knew him for sixty years.

But Anne and Stephen and I had him full time. We were the lucky ones.

You may have been in attendance at one of his many, many triumphs as an after-dinner speaker.

But we were there for the dress rehearsals. He loved to use us as guinea pigs for his next speaking engagement, usually at the dinner table on Sunday. I can hear him as if it were yesterday. "Kids, I think I've got a good one in the hopper!" and he would proceed to deliver his perceived next gem.

Since to us he was only our father—nor did he *ever* pretend to be anything else—we would usually sit there nonplussed.

Just as we knew he was growing closer to the punch line with his expert build-up, peering over his glasses, awaiting the explosion of laughter, one of us would say, "Ma, could I have some more milk?"

He would be crestfallen. "Maybe I have to re-work this, Rose!" The devastation would be only momentary, of course, as we would tell him we were only kidding and the speech was great. His smile would return, he'd take a puff on his pipe and retreat to the den—confident of his next success.

Of course, my father never laid an egg. He delivered every time and I am further happy to report, especially after hearing such nice snippets this morning, that you can expect this fall the publication of a collection of my father's greatest speeches. The book will be published, appropriately, by the Fordham University Press.

My father was noted for his wit and humor, of course, but you always knew that the humor, more often than not, was at his own expense and was never vulgar or cruel.

But he had many other outstanding attributes. Foremost was his treatment of others, no matter their standing in life, with respect and dignity.

His greatest asset was his capacity to love. His family always came first—and not just his wife and children. He loved my wife as if she were his own daughter. He loved his role as Uncle Bill. He loved his grandchildren as all grandparents do—that love which you can only understand when you experience it. He had many titles—Judge, Professor, Dean, etc., but the one that warmed his soul was "Grandpa."

He had other loves. He loved his God. He loved the Holy Roman Catholic Church and the Jesuits. It was never just the Catholic Church to my father—it was the *Holy Roman* Catholic Church. He had a million friends, of all colors and persuasions.

If he thought highly of a man, he was a "prince." If he thought highly of a woman, she was "a real peach."

My father loved his schools. Particularly, he loved that *premier* Jesuit institution in the country, Fordham University in The Bronx. A *cum laude* graduate of the college and the Law School, he was a sportswriter for the school newspaper, *The Ram,* and he sang in the glee club.

If you were a family friend, and you happened to be in our house on a weekend afternoon *and* you were lucky, my father would regale you with tales of the Seven Blocks of Granite, the three scoreless ties with Pitt in his Freshman through Junior years; the trips to the Cotton Bowl and the Sugar Bowl; Wojcie-chowicz—the 13-letter man.

My father's love for Fordham is legendary and Fordham's love for him has always been returned. Be assured, Father O'Hare, when those trumpets were blaring today upon my father's entry into heaven, there was only one song that was playing:

"With a Ram, Dad—With a Ram."

My father loved his country. He was an unabashed patriot. He served proudly in World War II. As my father tells it:

> In 1942 when I was shipped out of Fort Dix as an Army private and arrived by train at an Army pier on 58th Street in Brooklyn, I had a total of six days of Army service and the rest of my colleagues were equally untrained and un-skilled. After lining up on the pier with our barracks bags, we were given the command "Prepare for embarkation." This was a rather unnerving experience. We were loaded on a seagoing tug which we thought would take us out to a troop transport but instead took us to Fort Hamilton. I took basic training at Fort Hamilton and the Brooklyn Army Base and became a military policeman, patrolling the tav-erns on 58th Street armed with a nightstick and a Colt 45— the perfect assignment for an Irishman with a law degree. After several months in the Peace Corps in Brooklyn, I was shipped overseas—to Staten Island.

You see what I mean about self-deprecating humor.

It was the war experience as well that created the greatest opportunity of my father's lifetime, for it was in 1944 that he met Rosie Connelly, the colonel's secretary.

A classic love affair that would last fifty years. Complete love and affection, loyalty and fidelity—in sickness and in health. My father habitually called my mother from one to three times a day from work just to tell her he loved her.

This loving relationship produced three children and six grandchildren who adore their parents and grandparents. Their love was evident to all who knew them. Certainly it was clear in the good times and there were so many—and so many of you were a part of them. I can't begin to describe them because we don't have the rest of the month and there aren't enough tissues in Bronxville.

Many words have been used the last few days to describe my father. They have all been heartfelt and they have all been accurate.

A prince among men, a giant, a mighty oak. He *was* a giant. Physically, intellectually, spiritually, and emotionally.

As a child, I viewed him as a human jungle gym. You could hang from his arms and dangle from his knees and legs as he sat and read his books or watched T.V., smoking his pipe.

His hands were strong. He had a vise-like grip. Of course, he never much talked about or was impressed by his physical strength because he was taught, believed and passed on the simple truths that you were born to know, love, and serve God in this world to be happy with Him in the next.

Some people may snicker, of course, but my father was steadfast. He was not impressed with material things. He always had the proper perspective. He was just a little better focused than most. How many times did we hear him say, after having listened to the usually exaggerated tales of someone else's financial killing or latest conspicuous consumption: "But what has he done to save his immortal soul?"

The yuppie maxim "He who dies with the most toys wins" is simply antithetical to everything in which my father believed.

My father did not have toys. He had values. He didn't know a Mercedes from a Volkswagen and he could not have cared less. He never even had a driver's license.

The values which he held he imparted to everyone with whom he ever came into contact. Witness the outpouring of respect for my father over the last few days. Tell me again, who wins?

My father had the comedic writing ability of Neil Simon. He had the timing of Bob Hope and the delivery of Jack Benny.

Neither Broadway nor Hollywood was his destiny, of course. Perhaps they could have been. He did serve on the Board of Directors of 20th Century Fox under Darryl Zanuck. They became friends. This provided great fodder for the after-dinner circuit. Did you know that my father directed "Tora Tora Tora"?

My father would have been the ideal Commissioner of Baseball. He had the knowledge of the game, the stature, and the experience. Had he held the position in 1994, I can't believe that what happened to our national pastime would have occurred.

My father loved New York. He loved The Bronx of his youth. He loved the Dominican nuns who taught him in grammar school and he loved his experience at Cathedral Prep. Fortunately, certainly for me, my father, as well as his lifelong friend, the brother he never had, Joe Crowley, realized before it was too late that they didn't really have a calling for the priesthood and they left to continue their education at Fordham.

He worshipped his father, Steve, and his mother, Jane, our daughter Jenny's namesake. Many of you knew Mom Mulligan, who was legendary around here. She doted on her son. I wish you knew his father. A large, devout, quite simple man who, my mother says, was the sweetest man she ever knew. He loved his sister Jane, twelve years his junior. Beautiful, effervescent, and a great aunt. I pray they are reunited today in paradise.

My father loved his years as Dean of the Law School. He loved his faculty. He also loved the martini lunches at Des Artistes, 100 to 1 straight up with a twist, and Lord help the waiter who botched that order! Keefe, O'Keefe, Calamari and Perillo, Fogelman, Kessler, Phillips, Manning, McLaughlin, McGonagle, McAniff, Sweeney, Byrne, Crowley, and his beloved Gus Katsoris and so many more—they each left their mark on generations of Fordham lawyers.

My father loved his home at Sturgis Road into which we moved in February 1956 when we moved from North Pelham. The Bronxville experience began. The happiest days of our life. St. Joseph's School, the Men's Club, the Mother's Club. The good times. As Bobby Linder said the other night, "the happy house." All friends were welcome. The parties were legendary. It broke my heart to miss my parent's twenty-fifth wedding anniversary. I was serving diligently in the National Guard at the time. I did not miss my father's fiftieth birthday party in March 1968. It is a fact that this party is still talked about. It was impromptu—less than twenty-four hours' notice. *No one* declined. *Everyone* was overserved. It was the Irish Mafia at its best. Singing and laughter well into the night—what a group.

You had to know this group. This World War II generation. They worked hard and they played hard. They were faithful mates and loyal friends. They took trips together; they stood by each other in good times and bad. The legacy continues through today. You could take an invitation list to a cocktail party at my parents' house in 1962 and match it thirty-four years later against the names on the floral arrangements at McGrath's this week. That says it all about continuity and loyalty.

My father loved to teach and he loved being Dean. But I believed he most cherished his career on the United States Court of Appeals for the Second Circuit from 1971 to 1981. This was a court, as my father once pronounced to the New York County Lawyers Association, which was known, up *until* the time of his abrupt elevation to it, for the "the wisdom, scholarship, probity, and dignity of its membership." Any self-doubt or doubts of others about my father's qualifications to serve on the bench quickly dissipated.

His scholarship, temperament, collegiality, knowledge, and pursuit of excellence, always tinged with the right amount of humor, served him well and gained him the respect and devotion of his colleagues, as witnessed by the presence of so many federal jurists both at his wake on Wednesday and Thursday and in attendance today. This experience was shared by my father with a special group. As Jesus Christ had His apostles, my father had his clerks. He loved each one of you as if you were his own.

My father resigned from the bench in 1981. Why retire from such a prestigious bench with a lifetime salary guarantee? Why leave a job you so thoroughly enjoyed? My father's response was simple, but his decision was not easily made: "I love the federal bench but I love my family more. I can live on the salary but I can't die on it."

My father enjoyed an all-too-short career at Skadden, Arps, the most successful law firm in the history of this country. He loved the firm, was able to put all of his talents to use, and contributed to the continuing success of the firm. I want to thank that firm for the consideration and concern which they extended to my father and family, especially in those critical months following my father's first illness in 1989, and which continues today. It will never be forgotten.

So, as you can see, my father had a long and rewarding life. His children never lacked for love, attention, guidance, or advice.

I have talked about my parents' love and affection for each other. In health, it glowed. But, in sickness, it took on dimensions that most people can only dream about. I thought my father and mother had reason to be bitter, to complain. How could such a mighty man be robbed of his vitality? How could such a loving couple be denied the peace and tranquility of their golden years? But there was never a complaint, not a whimper. For they still had each other—which is all that ever counted.

God bless you, Dad. Heaven is a bit brighter today and the laughter a little louder. May you rest in peace.

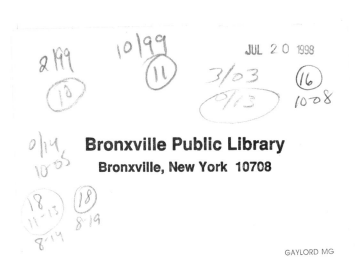